Microsoft Excel 2010
Explained

Books Written by the Same Authors

BP719	Microsoft Office 2010 Explained
BP718	Windows 7 Explained
BP714	An Introduction to Google for the Older Generation
BP710	An Introduction to Windows Live Essentials
BP706	An Introduction to Windows 7
BP703	An Introduction to Windows Vista
BP595	Google Explored
BP590	Microsoft Access 2007 explained
BP585	Microsoft Excel 2007 explained
BP584	Microsoft Word 2007 explained
BP583	Microsoft Office 2007 explained
BP581	Windows Vista explained
BP580	Windows Vista for Beginners
BP569	Microsoft Works 8.0 & Works Suite 2006 explained
BP563	Using Windows XP's Accessories
BP557	How Did I Do That ... in Windows XP
BP555	Using PDF Files
BP550	Advanced Guide to Windows XP
BP545	Paint Shop Pro 8 explained
BP538	Windows XP for Beginners
BP525	Controlling Windows XP the easy way
BP514	Windows XP explained
BP509	Microsoft Office XP explained
BP498	Using Visual Basic
BP341	MS-DOS explained
BP284	Programming in QuickBASIC
BP258	Learning to Program in C

Microsoft Excel 2010 Explained

by

N. Kantaris
and
P.R.M. Oliver

**Bernard Babani (publishing) Ltd
The Grampians
Shepherds Bush Road
London W6 7NF
England**

www.babanibooks.com

Please Note

Although every care has been taken with the production of this book to ensure that all information is correct at the time of writing and that any projects, designs, modifications and/or programs, etc., contained herewith, operate in a correct and safe manner and also that any components specified are normally available in Great Britain, the Publishers and Author(s) do not accept responsibility in any way for the failure (including fault in design) of any project, design, modification or program to work correctly or to cause damage to any equipment that it may be connected to or used in conjunction with, or in respect of any other damage or injury that may be so caused, nor do the Publishers accept responsibility in any way for the failure to obtain specified components.

Notice is also given that if equipment that is still under warranty is modified in any way or used or connected with home-built equipment then that warranty may be void.

First Published - August 2011

British Library Cataloguing in Publication Data:

A catalogue record for this book is available from the British Library

ISBN 978 0 85934 726 6

Cover Design by Gregor Arthur

Printed and bound in Great Britain for Bernard Babani (publishing) Ltd

About this Book

Microsoft Excel 2010 explained was written to help users to get to grips with the new Excel spreadsheet application which is a component part of the *Microsoft Office 2010.*

Excel 2010 builds on the previous version's user interface (the Ribbon) which replaced the old menus, toolbars and most of the task panes and dialogue boxes with a ribbon of buttons organised into theme tabs, a Quick Access toolbar that you can customise with commands you use the most, and just one menu.

The program also incorporates several new features, as well as improvements on Excel 2007's capabilities. These features include:

A **File** button which opens the Backstage full-screen interface for accessing all of the options relating to the application and the current Workbook document.

A powerful charting engine.

Tiny charts that fit in a cell, called sparklines, which helps you to visualise trends alongside data.

Worksheets which support over 1 million rows and over 16 thousand columns.

An unlimited number of types of formatting in the same workbook, and support for 16 million colours.

The ability to format Excel tables, charts, PivotTables, shapes and diagrams using styles with themes of predefined colours, fonts, lines and fill effects. Also the use of conditional formatting to allow visual annotation of data to make it easier to spot trends in your data.

A formula bar that automatically re-sizes to accommodate long, complex formulae, which prevents them from covering other data in the worksheet.

Support for structured references which allow the use of named ranges and named tables in a formula.

The provision of a Page Layout View which allows you to see how your work will look in printed format before applying the changes to your data.

Excel 2010 can either be used by itself or made to share information with other Office 2010 applications. This book first introduces Excel by itself, with sufficient detail to get you working, then discusses how to share information with Word 2010 and other Office 2010 applications.

The material in this book is presented using simple language, avoiding technical jargon as much as possible. The book was written with the non technical, non computer literate person in mind, and is structured on the 'what you need to know first, appears first' basis.

No prior knowledge of Excel is assumed, although more experienced users don't have to start at the beginning and go right through to the end, as the chapters have been designed to be fairly self-contained.

It is hoped that with the help of this book, you will be able to come to terms with Excel 2010 and do it in the shortest, most effective, and enjoyable way. Have fun!

About the Authors

Noel Kantaris graduated in Electrical Engineering at Bristol University and after spending three years in the Electronics Industry in London, took up a Tutorship in Physics at the University of Queensland. Research interests in Ionospheric Physics, led to the degrees of M.E. in Electronics and Ph.D. in Physics. On return to the UK, he took up a Post-Doctoral Research Fellowship in Radio Physics at the University of Leicester, and then a lecturing position in Engineering at the Camborne School of Mines, Cornwall, (part of Exeter University), where he was also the CSM Computing Manager. At present he is IT Director of FFC Ltd.

Phil Oliver graduated in Mining Engineering at Camborne School of Mines and has specialised in most aspects of surface mining technology, with a particular emphasis on computer related techniques. He has worked in Guyana, Canada, several Middle Eastern and Central Asian countries, South Africa and the United Kingdom, on such diverse projects as: the planning and management of bauxite, iron, gold and coal mines; rock excavation contracting in the UK; international mining equipment sales and international mine consulting. He later took up a lecturing position at Camborne School of Mines (part of Exeter University) in Surface Mining and Management. He has now retired, to spend more time writing (www.philoliver.com).

Acknowledgements

We would like to thank friends and colleagues, for their helpful tips and suggestions which assisted us in the writing of this book.

Trademarks

HP and **LaserJet** are registered trademarks of Hewlett Packard Corporation.

Microsoft, **Windows**, **Windows XP**, **Windows Vista**, **Windows 7**, **Excel**, **Word**, **Access**, **PowerPoint** and **Microsoft Office 2010** are either registered trademarks or trademarks of Microsoft Corporation.
PostScript is a registered trademark of Adobe Systems Incorporated.

All other brand and product names used in the book are recognised as trademarks, or registered trademarks, of their respective companies.

Contents

1

Package Overview

Microsoft Excel 2010 is part of the Office 2010 suite and is fully integrated with all the other Office 2010 applications. Excel is a powerful and versatile program which has proved its usefulness over the years, not only in the business world, but with scientific and engineering users as well.

The program's power lies in its ability to emulate everything that can be done with a pencil, paper and a calculator. Thus, it is an 'electronic spreadsheet' or simply a 'spreadsheet', a name which is also used to describe it and other similar products. The program is extremely flexible and can deal with the solution of the various applications it is programmed to manage very accurately and very fast. These can vary from budgeting and forecasting to the solution of complex scientific and engineering problems.

Excel 2010 has been designed to use a similar interface to that found in the other Office 2010 applications, and includes several improvements over the pre-2007 versions of the program. These are:

Worksheets which support 1,048,576 rows by 16,384 columns, which is 1,500% more rows and 6,300% more columns than Excel 2003!

An unlimited number of types of formatting in the same workbook, instead of the 4 thousand available in the pre-2007 versions.

The number of cell references per cell is now only limited by available memory.

Memory management has been increased to 2 GB. Both Excel 2010 and its predecessor (Excel 2007) now supports dual-processors and multithreaded chip sets as well as up to 16 million colours.

The formula bar automatically re-sizes to accommodate long, complex formulae, which prevents them from covering other data in the worksheet.

The provision of a Page Layout View which you can use to create a worksheet while keeping an eye on how it will look in printed format. You can base a new workbook on a variety of templates that are installed with Excel, or you can quickly access and download templates from the Microsoft Office Online Web site.

The **File** button which opens the Backstage full-screen interface for accessing all of the options relating to the application and the current Workbook document.

A powerful charting engine.

Tiny charts that fit in a cell, called sparklines, which helps you to visualise trends alongside data.

In addition, Excel 2010 allows the creation of 3D super-spreadsheets by using multi-page workbooks which support 3D *drill-through* formulae, and includes a long list of 'goal-seeking', 'what-if?' analysis tools and an excellent set of database capabilities.

Hardware and Software Requirements

If Microsoft Office 2010 is already installed on your computer, you can safely skip this and the next section of this chapter, otherwise you'll need to install Office 2010.

The **minimum** requirements for Office 2010 are:

- An IBM-compatible PC with a processor of at least 500 MHz, (1 GHz processor or higher for Outlook with Business Contact Manager), 256 MB of RAM (512 MB of RAM or higher is recommended for graphics features and certain Outlook advanced functionality).

- 3 GB (gigabytes) of available hard disc space.

- Microsoft Windows 7, Vista with SP1 or XP with SP3.

- A CD-ROM or DVD drive.

- 1024x768 or higher resolution monitor.

- Connectivity to Microsoft Exchange Server is required for certain advanced functionality in Outlook 2010 and connectivity to Microsoft Windows Server running Microsoft Windows SharePoint Services is required for certain advanced collaboration functionality.

- To share data among multiple computers, the host computer must be running Windows Server 2003 R2 with MSXML 6.0, Windows Server 2008 or later.

- Microsoft Internet Explorer 8.0 or later, and Internet functionality requires access to the Internet.

Additional requirements: Product functionality can vary based on the system configuration and operating system. Best results are obtained, according to our experience and if you want to run a few programs at the same time, with a PC running Windows 7 with at least 2 GB of RAM.

Installing Microsoft Excel 2010

To Install Excel, you'll have to install Office 2010 on your computer's hard disc, a process that is now fairly painless. Simply place the distribution DVD in your CD/DVD drive and close it. The auto-start program on the disc should start the SETUP program automatically. If it doesn't, click the **Start** button, and in the **Search programs and Files** text box type **run** and select the **Run** option from the displayed list. This opens the Run dialogue box, as shown in Fig. 1.1 on the next page.

Next, type in the opened Run box:

```
E:setup
```

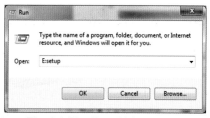

Fig. 1.1 The Run Dialogue Box

In our case the CD/DVD was the E: drive; yours could be different. Clicking the **OK** button, starts the installation of Microsoft Office 2010.

With both methods, SETUP opens the Enter your Product Key window, shown in Fig. 1.2.

Fig. 1.2 Entering the Product Key

From now on you just follow the instructions given on screen, having made sure you enter the Product Key code correctly. Clicking the **Continue** button opens the next window for you to read and accept Microsoft's licence terms.

In the next window, you are asked whether you want to **Upgrade** or **Customise**. Selecting the first option, opens the Upgrade window with the Upgrade tab opened which allows you to select options between removing all previous versions of Office, keep all previous versions or remove only the core applications of a previous version, as shown in Fig. 1.3 on the next page.

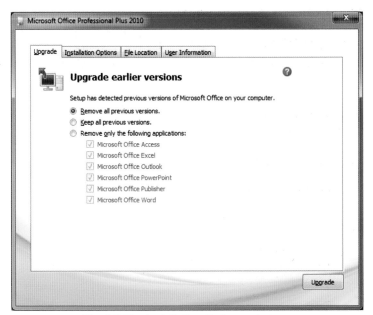

Fig. 1.3 The Installation Options window

The Installation Options tab, lists the Office 2010 applications to be installed and how they will run. This window is the same as the one you would have been presented with had you selected **Customise** in the previous screen.

The File Location tab lets you set where on your hard disc(s) Office will be installed. The User Information tab lets you enter or change your name, initials and company.

We chose to **Remove all previous versions** and clicked the **Upgrade** button. You have to let SETUP do its own thing and not be impatient. At times the only indication that something is happening is the flicking light of the hard disc. In the next half hour or so, SETUP copies files to your computer's hard disc, sets up the applications and hopefully displays the Successful Installation window. A reboot is necessary to complete installation.

The Excel 2010 Interface

Excel 2010 continues with the built-in consistency with all the other Office applications, first introduced in Office 2007, which makes it easier to use. Pre-2007 releases of Microsoft Office applications used a system of menus, toolbars, task panes and dialogue boxes to access commands and get things done.

Because Office 2010 and Office 2007 applications do so much more, these menus, toolbars, task panes and dialogue boxes have been replaced with the **Ribbon** user interface which makes it easier to find and use the full range of features these programs provide. If you have not used Office 2007 then you might find this somewhat daunting at first, but once you start using the new interface you will very rapidly get used to it. We will be discussing these features in Excel in some detail in the next chapter.

In the meantime, however, let us have a quick look at Excel. To start the program use the **Start**, **All Programs** command, click the **Microsoft Office** entry, then click the **Microsoft Excel 2010** option on the drop-down sub-menu, pointed to in Fig. 1.4.

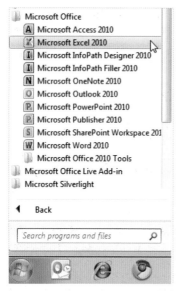

Fig. 1.4 The Microsoft Office Menu

The opening Excel screen is displayed as shown in Fig. 1.5 on the next page. Note how different this is from pre-2007 versions of the program. The most striking difference being the presence of the **Ribbon**, which appears at the top of the worksheet replacing the previous versions' Menu bar, Formatting bar, and Toolbar.

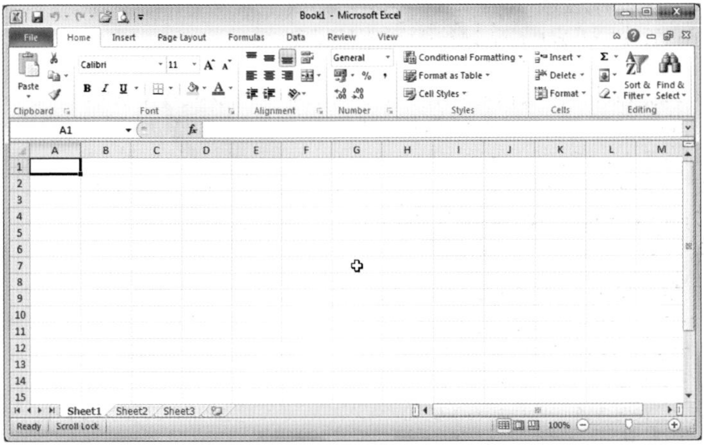

Fig. 1.5 The Excel Opening Screen

Note: As the width of the Excel window is made smaller the Ribbon buttons shrink to accommodate as many of them as possible on the available space.

At this point we will only have a look at the **Help** system included with Excel 2010. The rest of the opening screen will be discussed in Chapter 2.

Getting Help in Excel 2010

No matter how experienced you are, there will always be times when you need help to find out how to do something in Excel. There are several ways to get help, but don't look for the Office Assistant, as it has now been switched off for good.

The Built-in Microsoft Help System

To illustrate the built-in Help System, click the **Help** button shown here, or press the **F1** function key. The Help window will open as shown in Fig. 1.6 on the next page. The screen shown here, displays the Office Help System available to you when Online as discussed on the next and subsequent pages.

Fig. 1.6 The Microsoft Excel Help Window

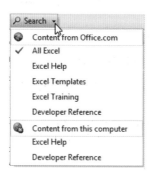

The program expects you to be 'Online'. You can control where Help searches for its content in two ways. If you click the down arrow to the right of the Search button, pointed to in Fig. 1.6 above, a drop-down menu opens as shown here in Fig. 1.7.

Fig. 1.7 The Help Options

The Help Options drop-down menu has several online and PC based options. If you click the **Excel Help** option under **Content from this computer** the Help system will only look on your computer for its help data.

Whether you are looking at Help online or offline is shown in the lower-right corner of the Help window, as shown in Fig. 1.6 on the previous page.

Clicking this area with the mouse opens the **Connection Status** menu shown in Fig. 1.8. As can be seen, this offers an easier way to tell Help where to look for its content. This setting is retained after you close the Help window, so if you don't want to search online you only have to set this once whatever Office application you are working with.

Fig. 1.8 The Help Options

The Help Toolbar

At the top of the Help window (see Fig. 1.6) there are icons to help you with navigation, printing a Help topic or displaying the Table of Contents list, to mention but a few. You can control the Help window with these buttons, as follows:

Back – Opens the last Help page viewed in the current session list.

Forward – Opens the previous Help page viewed in the current session list.

Stop – Stops loading a document.

Refresh – Reloads the current Help page.

Home – Opens the first (or Home) Help page for the open application.

Print – Opens the Print dialogue box to let you print all, or a selection, of the current Help topic.

Change Font Size – Opens a sub-menu to let you control the size of text in the Help window.

 Hide/Show Table of Contents – A toggle key which closes or reopens the left pane of the Help window, giving more room for the Help text.

 Keep On Top / Not On Top – A toggle key you can click to keep the Help window displaying on top of, or below, any open Office 2010 application.

Clicking the **Show Table of Contents** icon, displays an enlarged window, as shown in Fig. 1.9.

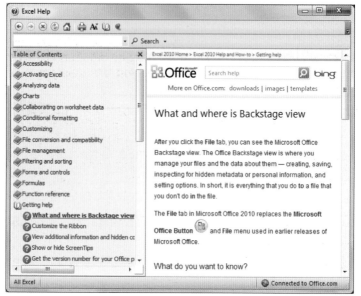

Fig. 1.9 Using Excel Help with Table of Contents Open

In the Help window the **Table of Contents** list displays all available topics in the form of closed books. Left-clicking one of these books opens it and displays a further list of topics with an icon, as shown in Fig. 1.9.

Clicking any of these opens the relevant Help page in the right-hand pane as shown in Fig 1.9.

If you want to know more about the options in a dialogue box, click the **Help** button ⓦ in the top right corner of the box. This will open the Help window usually with relevant help showing in the right-hand pane.

Searching Help

Fig. 1.10 Searching for a Topic

A quick way to find what you want in the Help system is to enter the text you want to search for in the **search text** box, as shown here in Fig. 1.10. Typing 'What is new' and clicking the **Search** button ⌕, displays the appropriate Help page, as shown in Fig. 1.11.

Fig. 1.11 Searching Excel Help for a Specific Topic

A search using 2 to 7 words returns the most accurate results. If you want to repeat a search, you click the down-arrow pointed to in Fig. 1.12 below (to the right of the **search text** box), and then click the search term that you want in the drop-down list.

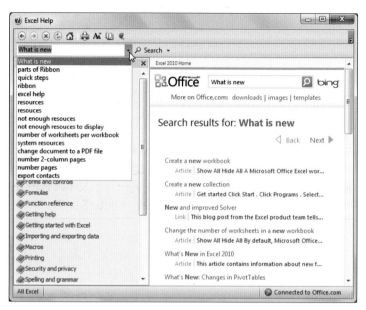

Fig. 1.12 Typing Words to Search for

The Excel 2010 **Help** system is quite comprehensive and it is usually easy to find the information you are looking for. We strongly recommend you spend some time working your way through the Help system to find out how it works. Time spent now will be time saved later!

Screen Tips

If you want to know what a particular button or feature does in Excel 2010, hover the mouse pointer over the button or feature to get **Screen Tips** help. A floating box will appear as shown in Fig. 1.13 on the next page.

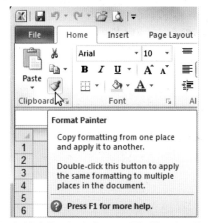

Fig. 1.13 A Typical Screen Tip Floating Box

Here we hovered the mouse pointer over the **Format Painter** button and a quite detailed description was given, as can be seen above.

2

The Excel 2010 Environment

Built-in Consistency

All Office 2010 applications have a built-in consistency which makes them easier to use. For example, all applications now use a simplified Ribbon which makes it easier to find and use the full range of features that they provide. If you have not used the previous version of Office (2007) then you might find this somewhat daunting at first, but once you start using the new interface you will very rapidly get used to it.

The Ribbon

Traditional menus and toolbars in Excel 2010 have been replaced by the Ribbon – a device that presents commands organised into a set of tabs, as shown in Fig. 2.1. The Ribbon was first adopted in the previous version of Office (2007).

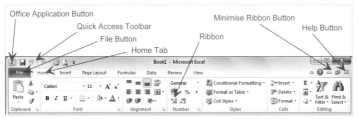

Fig. 2.1 The Home Tab of the Excel 2010 Ribbon

The tabs on the Ribbon display the commands that are most relevant for each of the task areas in Excel (in this case).

Note the **Minimise the Ribbon** button which you click to gain more space on your screen. It then changes to the **Expand the Ribbon** button, which you click to display the Ribbon again.

Note: To see all the groups available on the Ribbon you must maximise the Excel window. If you reduce the width of the window the Ribbon shrinks, group icons reduce in size and eventually disappear from view. To see these differences, compare the display in Fig. 2.2 shown below and that of Fig. 2.3 which is maximised and shown on the next page.

There are four basic components to the Ribbon, as shown in Fig. 2.2. These are:

Tabs   There are several basic tabs across the top, each representing an activity area.

Groups   Each tab has several groups that show related items together.

Commands   A command is a button, a box to enter information, or a menu.

Dialogue Box   Many groups have an icon shown in lower-
Launcher   right corner (shown here and pointed to below) to open an 'old style' dialogue box.

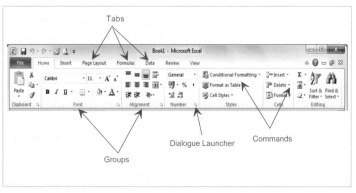

Fig. 2.2 The Components of a Ribbon

For each activity in all Office applications the Home tab contains all the things you use most often, such as creating **Copy**, **Cut** and **Paste** commands shown above for Excel. Clicking a new tab opens a new series of groups, each with its relevant command buttons. This really works very well.

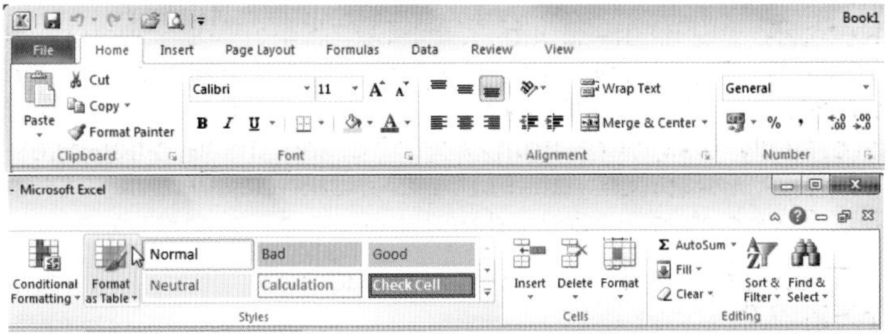

Fig. 2.3 The Maximised Ribbon Displayed in two Tiers for Ease of Viewing

The Ribbon Tabs

As we have seen, the Excel Ribbon has seven tabs, each one with the most used controls grouped on it for the main program actions.

A quick look at the Home tab, shows that it contains groups for the more common worksheet activities. The Clipboard cut and paste commands, Font, Alignment, Number Styles and Cells groups for manipulating cells and their contents, and Editing for other worksheet tasks.

Clicking a new tab opens a new series of groups, each with its relevant command buttons. The content of the other tabs allow you to do the following:

- The Insert tab, enables you to immediately insert Tables, Illustrations, Charts, Links, and Text based features, as shown in Fig. 2.4.

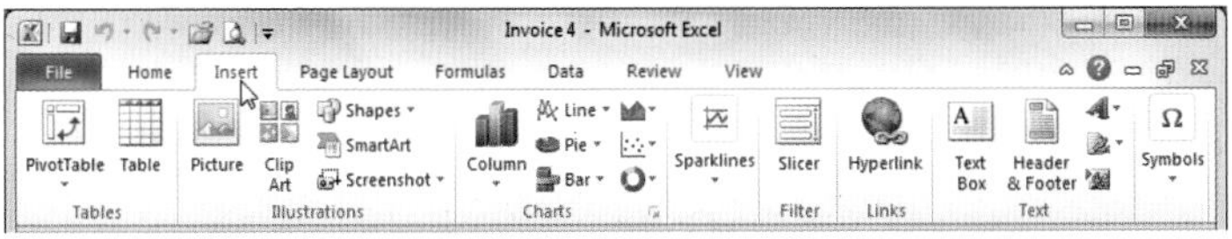

Fig. 2.4 The Insert Tab of the Excel 2010 Ribbon

- The Page Layout tab allows you to set your Themes, Page Setup, Scale to Fit, Sheet Options and to Arrange and group sheets, as shown in Fig. 2.5 on the next page.

Fig. 2.5 The Page Layout Tab of the Excel 2010 Ribbon

- The Formula tab allows you to add and control formulas, consisting of a Function Library, Defined Names, Formula Auditing and sheet Calculation options, as shown in Fig. 2.6.

Fig. 2.6 The Formula Tab of the Excel 2010 Ribbon

- The Data tab groups the actions used for handling and analysing your data. These include Get External Data from various sources, Connections for handling external links, Sort & Filter selected data, Data Tools and working with an Outline so that joined cells can be collapsed and expanded, as shown in Fig. 2.7.

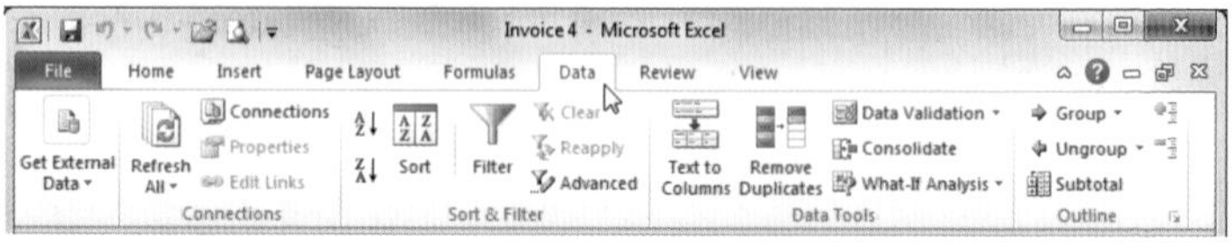

Fig. 2.7 The Data Tab of the Excel 2010 Ribbon

- The Review tab groups controls for Proofing your worksheets and to initiate and track document review and approval processes. It lets you deal with Comments, and control how Changes made to a worksheet will be handled, as shown in Fig. 2.8.

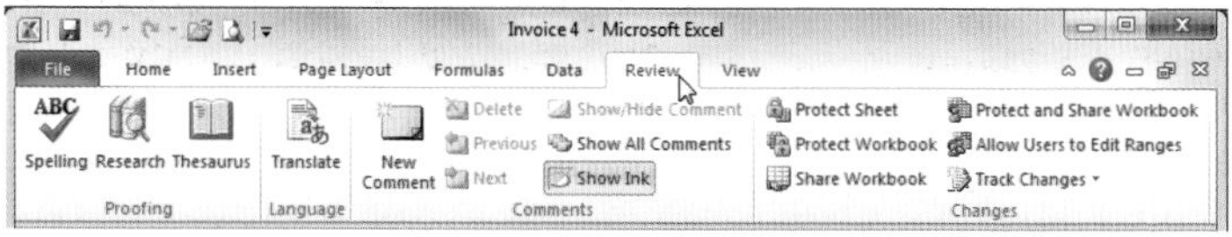

Fig. 2.8 The Review Tab of the Excel 2010 Ribbon

- The View tab allows you to set what you see on the screen. You can choose between Worksheet Views, Show or Hide screen features, Zoom to different magnifications, control Windows and run and record Macros, as shown in Fig. 2.9.

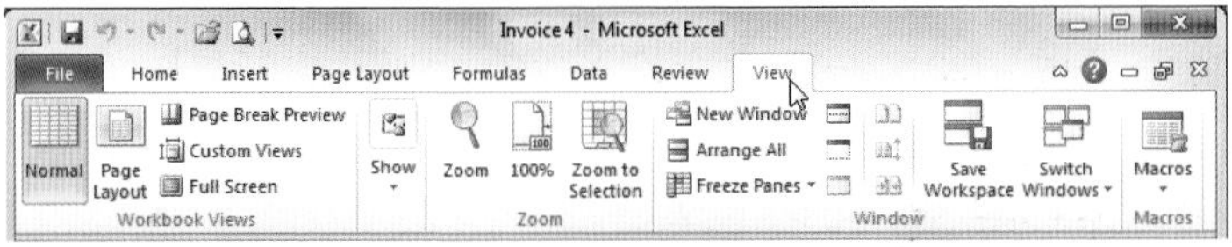

Fig. 2.9 The View Tab of the Excel 2010 Ribbon

Contextual tabs (to be discussed shortly) also appear when they are needed so that you can very easily find and use the commands needed for the current operation.

The Ribbon is scalable, and adapts to different sized screens. It displays smaller versions of tabs and groups as screen resolution decreases. When you make the Ribbon smaller, the groups on the open tab begin to shrink horizontally. The most commonly used commands or features are left open as the program window shrinks. Excel 2010 is probably best used with large high resolution screens, but there again, so is almost everything else in computing!

Contextual Tabs

Not all of the available tabs are visible. Some only appear when they are needed.

As an example, in Excel 2010, clicking on a picture inserted previously in a document, opens a contextual tab on the Ribbon with commands used for editing and formatting a picture, as shown in Fig. 2.10 on the next page. Once you leave the shape, by clicking outside it, this **Picture Tools** tab disappears. Very clever.

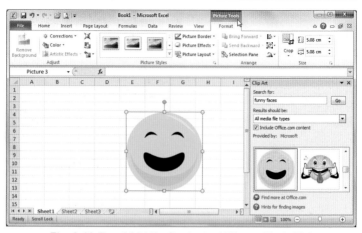

Fig. 2.10 Excel 2010's Contextual Picture Tools Tab

Dialogue Box Launcher

As we have mentioned, the Ribbon holds the most commonly used command buttons for Excel 2010, but by no means all of the available commands. Some groups have a small diagonal arrow, shown here, in the lower-right corner.

This is the **Dialogue Box Launcher**. You click it to see more options related to that group. They often appear as a Dialogue box similar to those of pre-2007 versions of Excel, as shown in Fig. 2.11 on the next page.

The display in Fig. 2.11 was opened by clicking the **Dialogue Box Launcher** located on the **Font** group of the **Home** tab of the Excel 2010 Ribbon.

However, to confuse matters slightly, some Dialogue Box Launchers actually open task panes, not dialogue boxes. Try clicking the Launcher on Excel's **Home**, **Clipboard** group to see what happens. What is displayed is Fig. 2.12, also shown on the next page.

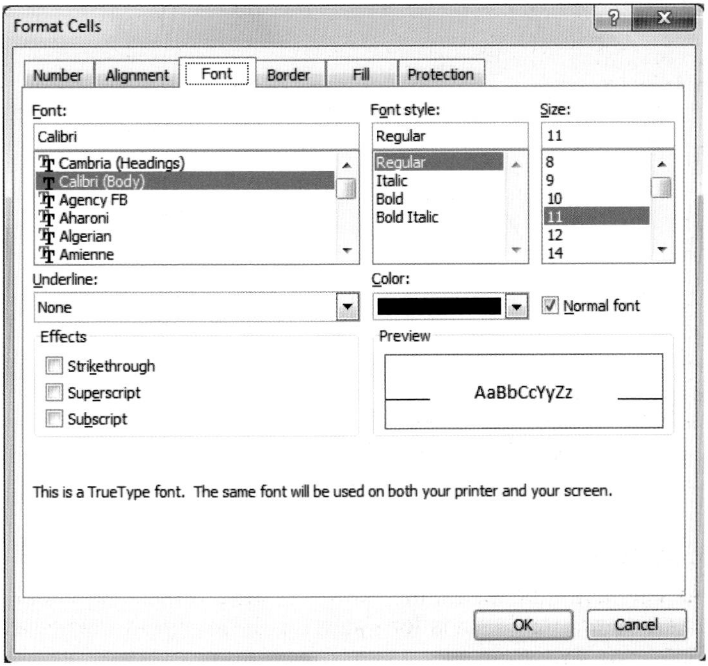

Fig. 2.11 The Font Tab Screen of the Format Cells Dialogue Box

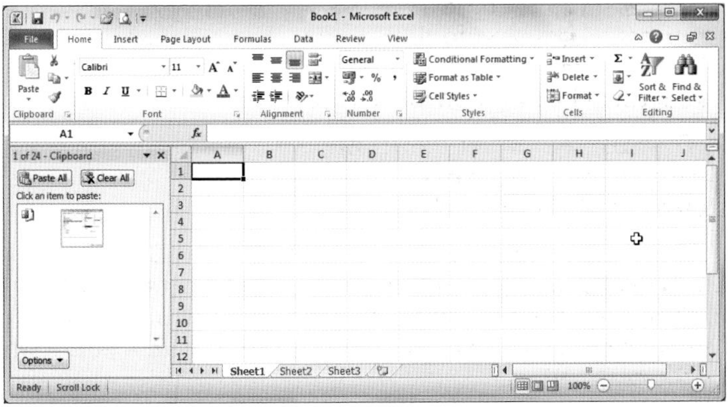

Fig. 2.12 The Home Tab Screen of the Clipboard Dialogue Box

Hiding the Ribbon

The Ribbon makes everything in Excel 2010 centralised and easy to find, but if you just want to work on your document, then you can maximise your working area by hiding it.

To hide the Ribbon just double-click the active tab. All the groups disappear. Go on, try it. When you want to see the Ribbon commands again, double-click the active tab to bring back the groups.

If you find you hate the Ribbon in Excel 2010, you have a problem as there is no easy way to delete or replace it with the toolbars and menus from the earlier versions.

Ribbon Keyboard Shortcuts

Those of you who have trouble using a mouse will be glad to hear that all the Ribbon features are available from the keyboard using what are now called **Key Tips**.

Pressing the **Alt** key makes **Key Tip** badges appear for all Ribbon tabs, the **Quick Access** toolbar commands, and the new **Office File** button, as shown in Fig. 2.13.

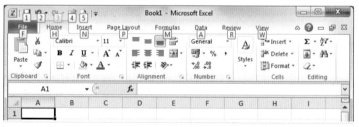

Fig. 2.13 Excel 2010 Ribbon Showing Key Tips

Then you can press the **Key Tip** for the tab you want to display. If that tab is the active one, all the Key Tips for the tab's commands appear, as we show in Fig. 2.14 on the next page, where we pressed the 'H' keyboard key. Then you can press the **Key Tip** for the command you want.

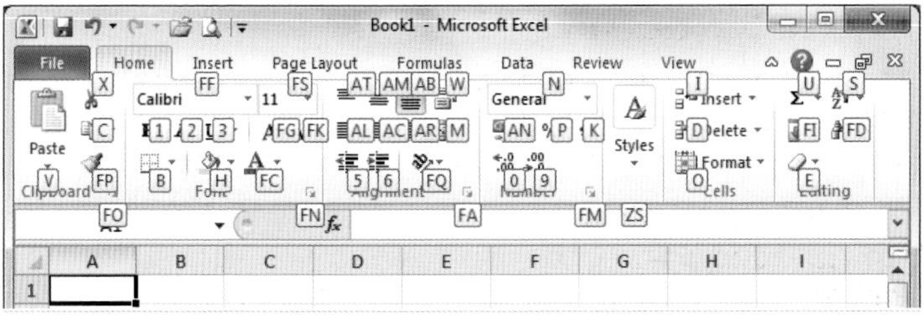

Fig. 2.14 Excel 2010's Home Tab Key Tips

When you press a **Key Tip** for a non-active tab, the tab is opened and all the **Key Tips** for the tab's commands appear. Access keys let you quickly use commands by pressing a few keystrokes, no matter where you are in the program. Press the **Alt** key again to close them.

The Mouse Pointers

In Microsoft Office applications, as with all other graphical based programs, using a mouse makes many operations both easier and more fun to carry out.

Excel 2010 makes use of the mouse pointers available in Windows, some of the most common of which are illustrated below. When an Office or other application program running under Windows 7 is initially started up the first you will see is the rotating timer, which turns into an upward pointing hollow arrow once the individual application screen appears on your display. Other shapes depend on the type of work you are doing at the time.

 The rotating timer which displays when you are waiting while performing a function.

 The arrow which appears when the pointer is placed over menus, scrolling bars, and buttons.

I   The I-beam which appears in normal text areas of the screen.

✥   The 4-headed arrow which appears when you choose to move a table, a chart area, or a frame.

↔   The double arrows which appear when over the border of a window, used to drag the side and alter the size of the window.

🖑   The Help hand which appears in the Help windows, and is used to access 'hypertext' type links.

Office 2010 applications, like other Windows packages, have additional mouse pointers which facilitate the execution of selected commands. Some of these are:

↓   The vertical pointer which appears when pointing over a column in a table or worksheet and used to select the column.

→   The horizontal pointer which appears when pointing at a row in a table or worksheet and used to select the row.

⇗   The slanted arrow which appears when the pointer is placed in the selection bar area of text or a table.

↔|↔   The vertical split arrow which appears when pointing over the area separating two columns and used to size a column.

±   The horizontal split arrow which appears when pointing over the area separating two rows and used to size a row.

+   The cross which you drag to extend or fill a series.

𝒷   The draw pointer which appears when you are drawing freehand.

The New File View

To see the new Office Backstage view, start Excel 2010, open a file, and click the 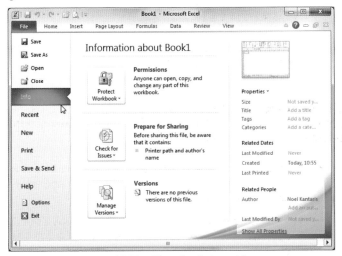 button. This replaces the old **File** menu across all the Office 2010 applications with a new full-screen interface for accessing all of the options relating to the application and the current document, as shown in Fig. 2.15.

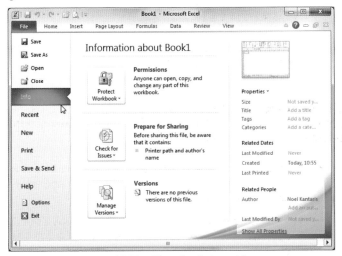

Fig. 2.15 The New Backstage View

As you can see, many Excel settings that are not directly related to creating or managing Excel documents, such as the **Save**, **Open**, **Print** and **Save & Send** commands, are now in the Microsoft Office Backstage view. From here you can manage your documents, protect your documents, prepare documents for sharing, and find other behind-the-scenes options such as user interface options and personalising your copy of Microsoft Office. These latter options can be accessed by clicking the **Options** button on the Backstage screen.

We leave it to you to explore the facilities available to you on the Backstage screen. It is worth spending some time here investigating the available options.

The Quick Access Toolbar

The Quick Access Toolbar is the small area to the upper left

of the Ribbon, as shown in Fig. 2.15, and enlarged here. This is one of the most useful features of Excel 2010. It contains buttons for the things that you use over and over every day, such as **Save**, **Undo** and **Repeat**, by default. The bar is always available, whatever you are doing in a program, and it is very easy to add buttons for other commands, as shown above.

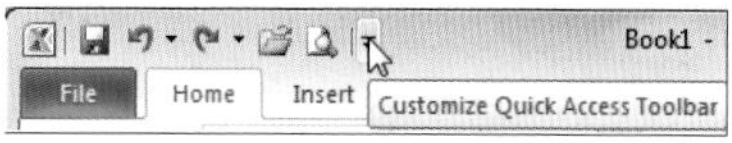

Clicking the **Customize Quick Access Toolbar** button ▾ pointed to above shows a menu of suggested items for the toolbar (Fig. 2.16). Select the **More Commands** option from the drop-down menu to open the Excel Options window shown in Fig. 2.17.

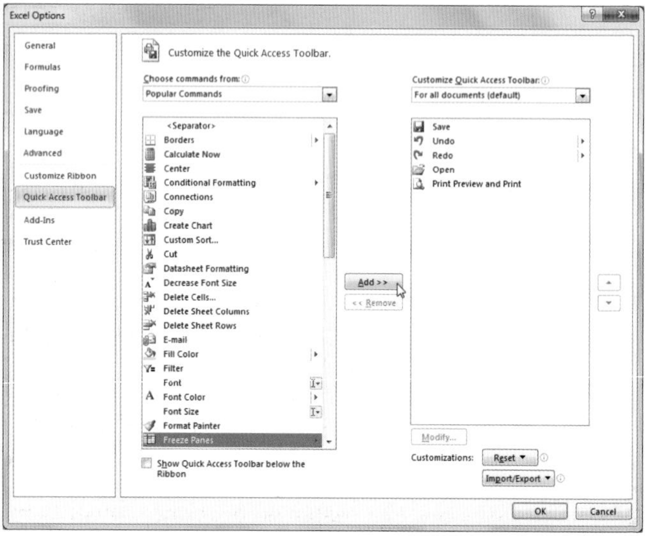

Fig. 2.16 Quick Access Options

Fig. 2.17 Customising the Quick Access Toolbar

To add a command to the **Quick Access** toolbar, select it in the left pane and click the **Add** button. To remove it just do the opposite. You can change the position of a new button by selecting it in the right pane and clicking the up and down arrows . To finish, click the **OK** button.

The Mini Toolbar

Some text formatting commands are so useful that you want

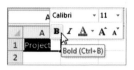

to have them immediately available without having to go to any of the tabs on the Ribbon. For these, Excel 2010 shows a 'hovering' **Mini** toolbar over your work as shown here.

In this example, we typed some text in an Excel cell, then selected it by dragging the mouse pointer over the text and pointed at the selection. A faded **Mini** toolbar appeared, which when pointed to became solid, as shown above. A **Mini** toolbar will stay active for a selection until you click outside the selection.

The Right-click Menu

Fig. 2.18 The Right-click Menu

The **Mini** toolbar displays a rather limited formatting choice. A much larger choice of formatting and other commands is available to you by right-clicking a cell, as shown in Fig. 2.18. These menu options, however, are applicable to the entire content of a cell, so highlighting part of the text is not necessary. If you do, right-clicking a highlighted selection displays only the rather limited **Mini** toolbar.

Galleries

Galleries are at the heart of the redesigned 'Pick and Click' Excel 2010, as they are also with the other Office applications. Galleries provide you with a set of clear visual results to choose from when you are working in a workbook. By presenting a simple set of potential results, rather than a complex dialogue box with numerous options, Galleries simplify the process of producing good looking work. As we have seen, dialogue boxes are still available if you want more control over an operation, but a simple Gallery choice will very often be enough.

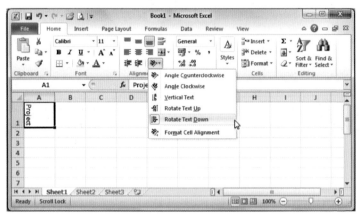

Fig. 2.19 A Style Gallery in Excel 2010

As we show above, you can apply pre-set orientation of text in a cell from the appropriate gallery in the Ribbon. In Fig. 2.19 we show the result of clicking the **Rotate Text Down** option in the Gallery.

Live Preview

Live Preview is a new feature to Excel and other Office 2010 applications. It previews the results of applying an editing or formatting change as you move the pointer over the options in a Gallery.

In our example in Fig. 2.20 below, as we moved the pointer over the font style options in the gallery, the cell text automatically changed to show how it would look if that style were chosen.

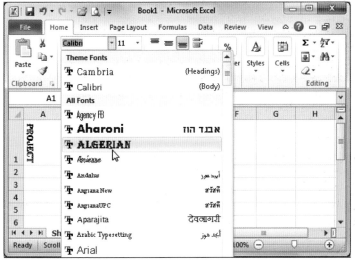

Fig. 2.20 A Live Preview of a Gallery Style in Excel 2010

Excel 2010 File Formats

Excel 2010, like other Office 2010 and Office 2007 applications, uses the Microsoft Office Open XML file formats, based on Extensible Markup Language (XML). File extensions change from **.xls** to **.xlsx**. If you are saving a file with macros, the extension changes again to **.xlsxm**, so you know if the file contains macros or not.

The full range of Excel's file extensions is as follows:

XML file type Extension Workbook   .xlsx

Macro-enabled workbook   .xlsm

Template   .xltx

Macro-enabled template	.xltm
Non-XML binary workbook	.xlsb
Macro-enabled add-in	.xlam

XML files have practical advantages. Each file is actually a zip file of individual elements. If your file gets corrupted, it's easier to recover more of the data. They are compressed to around half the size of standard files.

If you need to, you can still save your files in the older Excel formats with the **Save As** command, but all the .XML advantages will be lost.

Excel 2010 can open files created in all pre-2007 versions of Excel in 'compatibility' mode. You know this because at the top of the document "(Compatibility Mode)" appears next to the name of the file. You can then convert the older document to the new file format by clicking the **File** button, and selecting the **Convert** command on the drop-down menu.

The new file format also gives you the ability to use features that are available only in Excel 2010 and Excel 2007. One example of such a feature is the new SmartArt Graphics. The new file format supports plenty of other new features, such as math equations, themes, and content controls.

3

The Excel 2010 Spreadsheet

Starting the Excel Program

To start Excel 2010, use the **Start**, **All Programs** command, select the **Microsoft Office** entry from the displayed menu, and click **Microsoft Excel 2010**, as shown in Fig. 3.1.

Fig. 3.1 Using the Start Menu

You can also double-click on an Excel worksheet file in a Windows folder, in which case the worksheet will be loaded into Excel at the same time.

The Excel Screen

When Excel is loaded, a 'blank' spreadsheet screen displays with a similar Title bar and Ribbon to those of Word, but with some differences, as shown below.

The layout, as shown in Fig. 3.2 on the next page, is in a window, but if you click on the application Restore button, you can make Excel take up the full screen area available. Working in a smaller window can be useful when you are running several applications at the same time.

The Excel window, which in this case displays an empty and untitled book (Book1), has some areas which have identical functions to those of other Office 2010 applications, and other areas which have different functions. Below, we describe the areas that are exclusive to Excel.

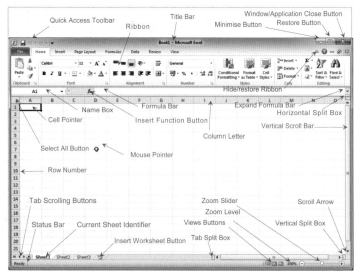

Fig. 3.2 The Excel Screen

Area	Function
Name box	Identifies the selected cell (by name or by cell co-ordinates), chart item, or drawing object.
Formula Bar	Can display a number, a label, or the formula behind a result.
Expand Formula Bar	Click to expand the Formula Bar.
Insert Function	Click to open the Insert Function dialogue box.
Select All Button	Click to select the whole worksheet.
Cell pointer	Marks the current cell.

Column letter	The letter that identifies each column.
Row number	The number that identifies each row.
Tab Scrolling Buttons	Clicking on these buttons, scrolls sheet tabs right or left, when there are more tabs than can be displayed at once.
Insert Worksheet	Click to insert another worksheet.
Tab split box	The split box which you drag left to see more of the scroll bar, or right to see more tabs.
Current sheet	Shows the current sheet amongst a number of sheets in a file. These are named Sheet1, Sheet2, Sheet3, and so on, by default, but can be changed to, say, North, South, East, and West. To move to a particular sheet, click its tab.

Finally, note the location of the horizontal and vertical split boxes. The first is located at the extreme right of the screen above the 'top vertical scroll arrow' button. The second is located at the extreme bottom-right corner of the screen, to the left of the 'right horizontal scroll arrow' button.

Workbook Navigation

When you first enter Excel, it sets up a series of worksheets, in your computer's memory, many times larger than the small part shown on the screen. Individual cells are identified by column and row location (in that order), with present size extending to 16,384 columns and 1,048,576 rows. The columns are labelled from A to Z, followed by AA to AZ, BA to BZ, and so on, to XFD, while the rows are numbered from 1 to 1048576.

The point where a row and column intersect is called a cell, and the reference points of a cell are known as the cell address. The active cell (A1 at first) is boxed.

With the large increase in the possible size of Excel 2010's worksheets, finding your way around them is even more important than it used to be. There are four main ways of moving around a worksheet, key combinations, the **Go To** box, scrolling with the mouse, or using the scroll bars.

Key Combinations

To Scroll	*Press*
To the start and end of ranges	**Ctrl+→**, **←**, **↓** or **↑** to scroll to the start and end of each range in a column or row before stopping at the end of the worksheet.
One row up or down	**Scroll Lock**, then ↑ or ↓.
One column left or right	**Scroll Lock**, then ← or →.
One window up or down	**PgUp** or **PgDn**.
One window left or right	**Scroll Lock**, then **Ctrl←** or **Ctrl→**.
A large distance	**Scroll Lock+Ctrl+→**, **←**, **↓** or **↑**.

Please note:

- Pressing the arrow keys while **Scroll Lock** is on will scroll one row up or down or one column left or right.

- To use the arrow keys to move between cells, you must turn **Scroll Lock** off.

The Go To Box

Pressing the **F5** function key will display the **Go To** dialogue box shown in Fig. 3.3.

Fig. 3.3 The Go To Box

In the **Go to** box a list of named ranges in the active worksheet (to be discussed shortly) is displayed, or one of the last four references from which you chose the **Go To** command.

In the **Reference** text box you type the cell reference or a named range you want to move to.

Mouse Scrolling

If you have a mouse with a wheel, such as a Microsoft IntelliMouse, you will be able to move easily around Excel 2010's enormous worksheets, as follows:

- To scroll up or down: Rotate the wheel forward or back.

- To pan through a worksheet: Hold down the wheel button, and drag the pointer away from the origin mark ✛ in any direction that you want to scroll.

- To zoom in or out: Hold down **Ctrl** while you rotate the mouse wheel forward or back. The percentage of the zoomed worksheet is displayed on the Status bar.

Using the Scroll Bars

- To scroll one row up or down: Click the ▲ or ▼ scroll arrows on the vertical scroll bar.

- To scroll one column left or right: Click the ◀ or ▶ scroll arrows on the horizontal scroll bar.

- To scroll one window up or down: Click above or below the scroll box on the vertical scroll bar.

- To scroll one window left or right: Click to the left or right of the scroll box on the horizontal scroll bar.

When you have finished navigating around the worksheet, press the **Ctrl+Home** key combination which will move the active cell to the A1 position (provided you have not fixed titles in any rows or columns or have no hidden rows or columns – more about these later).

The area within which you can move the active cell is referred to as the working area of the worksheet, while the letters and numbers in the border at the top and left of the working area give the 'co-ordinates' of the cells in a worksheet. The location of the active cell is constantly monitored by the 'selection indicator' in the Name Box. As the active cell is moved, this indicator displays its address, as shown in Fig. 3.4.

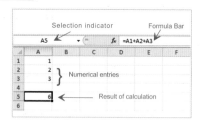

Fig. 3.4 The Selection Indicator and Formula Bar

The contents of a cell are displayed above the column letters within the 'Formula Bar'. If you type text in the active cell, it appears in both the Formula Bar and the cell itself.

Typing a formula which is preceded by the equals sign (=) to, say, add the contents of three cells, causes the actual formula to appear in the Formula Bar, while the result of the actual calculation appears in the active cell when the **Enter** key is pressed.

Moving Between Sheets

You can scroll between worksheets by clicking one of the 'Tab scrolling buttons' situated to the left of Sheet1, as shown below. The inner arrows scroll sheets one at a time in the direction of the arrow, while the outer arrows scroll to the end, or beginning, of the group of available worksheets. A worksheet is then made current by clicking its tab.

Fig. 3.5 Tab Scrolling Buttons and the Active Sheet

To display more sheet tabs at a time, drag the Tab split box to the right, or to the left to display less sheet tabs. To rename sheets, double-click on their tab, then type the new name to replace the highlighted name.

To insert a sheet, click the **Insert Worksheet** button and drag the new tab to where you want it in the stack (see the next section on the next page).

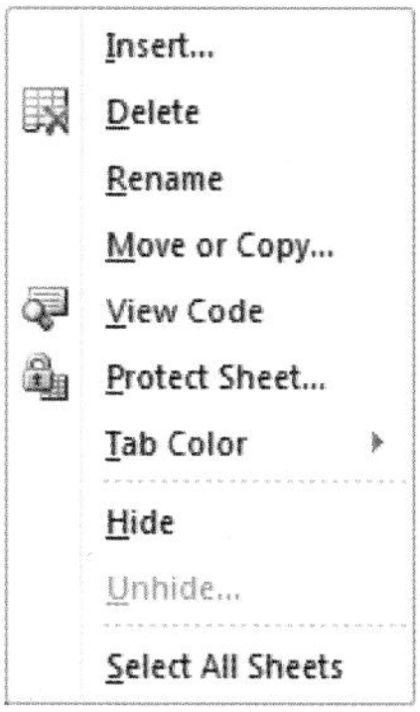

To delete a sheet, right-click on its tab and select **Delete** from the context menu shown in Fig. 3.6. As you can see, you can also **Insert**, **Rename** and **Move or Copy** sheets this way.

Insert...
Delete
Rename
Move or Copy...
View Code
Protect Sheet...
Tab Color   ▶
Hide
Unhide...
Select All Sheets

Fig. 3.6 Right-click Context Menu

Rearranging Sheet Order

To rearrange the order in which sheets are being held in a workbook, drag the particular sheet (point to it and with the left mouse button depressed move the mouse pointer) in the required direction, as shown in Fig. 3.7 on the next page.

Fig. 3.7 Moving an Active Sheet

While you are dragging the tab of the sheet you want to move, the mouse pointer changes to an arrow pointing to an image of a sheet. The small solid arrowhead to the left of the mouse pointer indicates the place where the sheet you are moving will be placed.

Grouping Worksheets

You can select several sheets to group them together so that data entry, editing or formatting can be made easier and more consistent.

To select adjacent sheets, click the first sheet tab, hold down the **Shift** key and then click the last sheet tab in the group. To select non-adjacent sheets, click the first sheet tab, hold down the **Ctrl** key and then click the other sheet tabs you want to group together.

Selecting sheets in the above manner, causes the word '[Group]' to appear in the Title bar of the active window, and the tabs of the selected sheets to be shown in white. To cancel the selection, right-click a group tab and select **Ungroup Sheets**, or click the tab of any sheet which is not part of the selected group.

Selecting a Range of Cells

To select a range of cells, say, A3:C3, point to cell A3, press the left mouse button, and while holding it pressed, drag the mouse to the right.

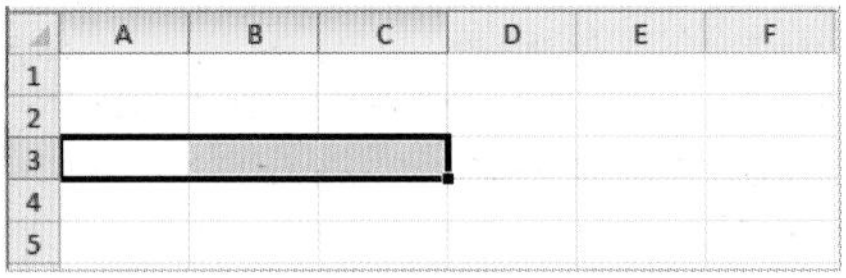

⊿	A	B	C	D	E	F
1						
2						
3						
4						
5						

Fig. 3.8 Selecting a Range of Cells

To select a range from the keyboard, first make active the first cell in the range, then:

• Hold down the **Shift** key and use the right arrow key (→) to highlight the required range.

To select a 3D range across several sheets, select the range in the first sheet, then release the mouse button, hold down the **Shift** key, and click the Tab of the last sheet in the range.

Remember that while a range of cells in a sheet is selected, or a group of sheets is active, pressing the right mouse button displays a shortcut menu with the most common commands relevant to what you are doing at the time, as described in Chapter 2, page 27.

Viewing Multiple Workbook Sheets

To see more clearly what you are doing when working with multiple workbook sheets, click the **Insert Worksheet** button to add a fourth sheet to your Workbook. This, by default, will be named Sheet4, unless you have added more sheets in your current session, as shown below.

Fig. 3.9 Moving an Active Sheet

Then click the **View** tab on the Ribbon and click the **Window**, **New Window** command button three times to add three extra windows to your worksheet. To see them, use the **View**, **Window**, **Arrange All**, **Tiled** command to display the four sheets as shown in Fig. 3.10 on the next page. Finally, type the text '1st' in location A1 of Sheet1 of window 1, the text '2nd' in location A1 of Sheet2 of window 2, and so on. What we have done here is to make active Sheet1 in Book1:1, Sheet2 in Book1:2, and so on, to demonstrate that each window contains all four sheets.

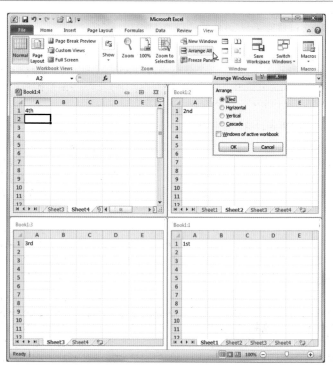

Fig. 3.10 Multiple Workbook Sheets in Tile View

The top left window is the active one above. To move from one window to another, simply point with the mouse to the cell of the window you want to go to and click the left mouse button. To display a different sheet in each window, go to a window and click the sheet's tab.

To return to single-window view from a tiled or cascade mode, click the maximise button of the active window.

You can then use the **View**, **Window**, **Switch Windows** button, shown in Fig. 3.11, to see what windows are open and to move between them. To close an active window, click its **Close** button ☒.

Fig. 3.11 Switching Windows

Entering Information

We will now investigate how information can be entered into a worksheet. But first, make sure you are in Sheet1, then return to the Home (A1) position, by pressing the **Ctrl+Home** key combination, then type the words:

`Project Analysis`

As you type, the characters appear in both the 'Formula Bar' and the active cell. If you make a mistake, press the **BkSp** key to erase the previous letter or the **Esc** key to start again. When you have finished, press **Enter** to move to the cell below, or the **Tab** key to move to the next cell to the right.

Note that what you have just typed in has been entered in cell A1, even though the whole of the word 'Analysis' appears to be in cell B1. If you use the right arrow key to move the active cell to B1 you will see that the cell is indeed empty.

Typing any letter at the beginning of an entry into a cell results in a 'text' entry being formed automatically, otherwise known as a 'label'. If the length of the text is longer than the width of a cell, it will continue into the next cell to the right of the current active cell, provided that cell is empty, otherwise the displayed information will be truncated.

To edit information already in a cell, either

* double-click the cell in question, or

* make that cell the active cell and press the **F2** function key.

The cursor keys, the **Home** and **End** keys, as well as the **Ins** and **Del** keys can be used to move the cursor and/or edit information as required. You can also 'undo' the last 16 actions carried out since the program was last in the **Ready** mode, using the **Undo** button 🔄 ▾ on the Quick Access toolbar (see page 26), or the **Ctrl+Z** keyboard shortcut.

Before you proceed, delete any information that might be in Sheet1 of your workbook by selecting it and pressing **Del**.

Next, move the active cell to B3 and type

`Jan`

Pressing the right arrow key (→) will automatically enter the typed information into the cell and also move the active cell one cell to the right, in this case to C3. Now type

`Feb`

and press **Enter**.

The looks of a worksheet can be enhanced somewhat by using different types of borders around specific cells. To do this, first select the range of cells, then click the down arrow of the **Home**, **Font**, **Borders** button which, as shown here, opens an extensive list of border types. In our example, we have selected the cell range A3:C3, then we chose the **Top and Double Bottom** Border option from the displayed table.

Fig. 3.12 The Border Button

Next, move to cell A4 and type the label **Income**, then enter the numbers **14000** and **15000** in cells B4 and C4, respectively, as shown below. Do note that by default, the labels **Jan** and **Feb** are left justified, while the numbers are right justified.

Fig. 3.13 Default Justification of Labels and Numbers

Changing Text Alignment and Fonts

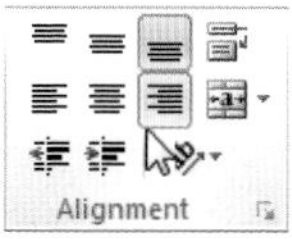

Fig. 3.14 The
Alignment
Group

One way of improving the looks of this worksheet is to also right justify the text **Jan** and **Feb** within their respective cells. To do this, move the active cell to B3 and select the range B3 to C3, then click the **Home**, **Alignment**, **Align Text Right** command button, pointed to here.

For more control you can use the Format Cells dialogue box shown in Fig. 3.15 below. This is opened by clicking the **Alignment** Dialogue Box Launcher 🖾. In its Alignment tab sheet select **Right (Indent)** in the **Horizontal** drop-down list and press the **OK** button.

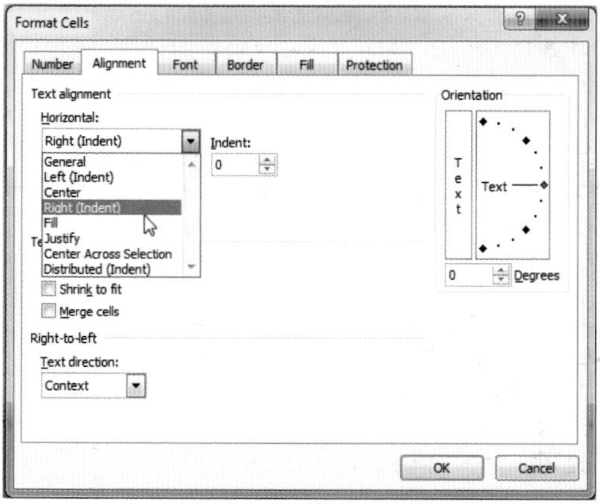

Fig. 3.15 Formatting Cells using the Alignment Tab Sheet

No matter which method you choose, the text entries should now appear right justified within their cells. The second method provides greater flexibility in displaying text, both in terms of position and orientation.

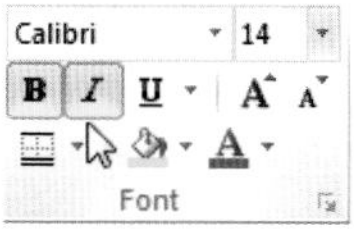

Fig. 3.16 The
Font Group

To improve the looks of our work, select cell A1, then click on the down arrow against the **Home**, **Font**, **Font Size** button on the Ribbon, and choose point size 14 from the displayed list, then click both the **Bold** and **Italic** buttons, shown in Fig. 3.16.

Fig. 3.17 Setting
Currency Format

Finally, since the numbers in cells B4 to C4 represent money, it would be better if these were prefixed with the £ sign. To do this, select the cell range B4:C4, and click the **Home**, **Number**, **Accounting Number Format** button, shown here in Fig. 3.17, and select **£ English (U.K.)**.

The numbers within the chosen range will now be displayed in currency form, and the width of the cells will automatically adjust to accommodate them, if they are too long.

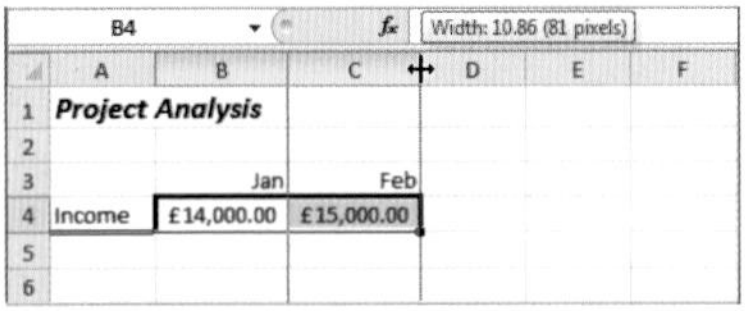

Fig. 3.18 Finding the Width of a Cell

To see the actual new width of, say column C, place the mouse pointer to the right of the column letter on the dividing line. When the mouse pointer changes to the shape shown above, press the left mouse button without moving the mouse. The cell width will then display within a pop-up text box as 81 pixels, increased from the default column width of 64 pixels. To widen a column, place the mouse pointer in between the column letters, and drag the pointer to the right, until the width of the column displays as 82 pixels, which happens to be 11 characters wide.

Saving a Workbook

Now, let's assume we want to stop at this point, but would like to save the work entered so far before leaving the program. First, it's a good idea to return to the Home position by pressing **Ctrl+Home**. This is good practice because the position of the cell pointer at the time of saving the file is preserved.

The quickest way to save a document to disc is to click the **Save** button on the **Quick Access** toolbar. If this is the first time you use this facility, you will be asked to provide a filename and a location.

The usual way, however, is to click the **File** [File] button and select the **Save As** command from the displayed Backstage screen, which gives you more control on the saving operation.

In Fig. 3.19 below, we show the action (giving our workbook the filename **Project 1**), and the result of that action.   .

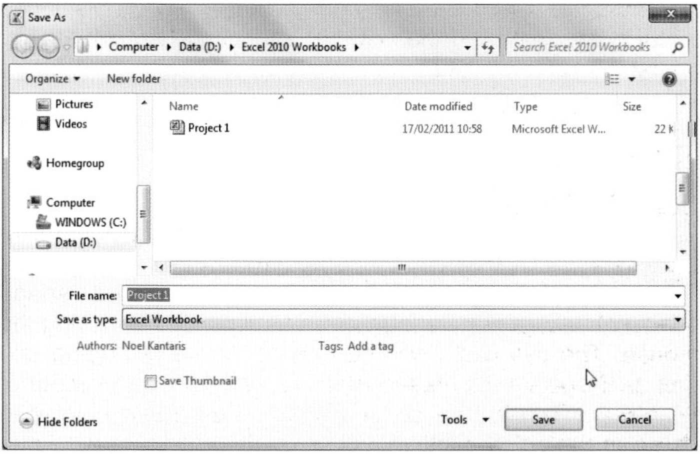

Fig. 3.19 Saving a Workbook

We have selected to save our work in the folder **Excel 2010 Workbooks** we created in our D: drive. You could choose to create this folder within your **Documents** folder on your C: drive by navigating there, then using the **New Folder** command.

To save our work, we selected the newly created folder in the **Address Bar** of the Save As dialogue box, then moved the cursor into the **File name** box, and typed **Project 1**. We suggest you do the same.

The file will be saved in the default file type *Excel Workbook*, as displayed in the **Save as type** box. Excel adds the file extension **.xlsx** automatically and uses this to identify it.

By clicking the down arrow at the right-hand side of the **Save as type** box, you can save your work in a variety of other formats, including Web Page (html), Template (xltx), and earlier versions of Excel, as shown in Fig. 3.20.

Save as type:	Excel Workbook ▼
	Excel Workbook
	Excel Macro-Enabled Workbook
	Excel Binary Workbook
	Excel 97-2003 Workbook
	XML Data
	Single File Web Page
	Web Page
	Excel Template
	Excel Macro-Enabled Template
	Excel 97-2003 Template
	Text (Tab delimited)
	Unicode Text
	XML Spreadsheet 2003
	Microsoft Excel 5.0/95 Workbook
	CSV (Comma delimited)
	Formatted Text (Space delimited)
	Text (Macintosh)
	Text (MS-DOS)
	CSV (Macintosh)
	CSV (MS-DOS)
	DIF (Data Interchange Format)
	SYLK (Symbolic Link)
	Excel Add-In
	Excel 97-2003 Add-In
	PDF
	XPS Document
	OpenDocument Spreadsheet

Fig. 3.20 Saving Options from the File Button

If you want to create backup files or provide password protection to your file, click the down-arrow against the **Tools** button at the bottom of the Save As dialogue box, and select **General Options** from the displayed drop-down menu. This opens the General Options box, shown in the composite Fig. 3.21. Fill in this dialogue box appropriately, press the **OK** button, then click the **Save** button.

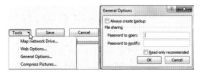

Fig. 3.21 The Tools Menu and the General Options Box

The Excel 2010 Spreadsheet   3

Opening a Workbook

Fig. 3.22
Part of the File Menu

To open a previously saved worksheet in Excel you click the **Open** button on the **File** button menu, shown here in Fig. 3.22, or use the **Ctrl+O** keyboard shortcut. Both launch the Open dialogue box, shown in Fig. 3.23 below. Excel asks for a filename to open, with the default *All Excel Files* being displayed.

If you work mainly with the mouse, you could include the **Open** button on the Quick Access toolbar, as we have.

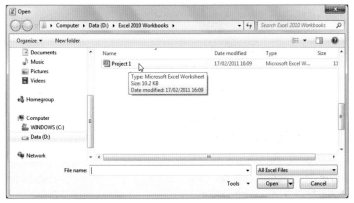

Fig. 3.23 The Open Dialogue Box

To open our previously saved example file **Project 1**, double-click the **Excel 2010 Workbooks** folder and select it by clicking its name in the list box, then click the **Open** button.

If you want to change the logged drive, select a new drive from the left pane shown above, then select the file you want to open, in this case, **Project 1**. If you haven't saved it, don't worry as you could just as easily start afresh and create it.

Exiting Excel

To exit Excel, close any displayed dialogue boxes by clicking the **Cancel** button, and make sure that the word **Ready** is displayed on the Status bar (press the **Esc** key until it does), and use one of the following methods:

* Use the **Alt+F4** keyboard shortcut.

* Click the **Close** button at the top right of the Excel window.

* Click **Exit** on the **File** button menu.

No matter which command you choose, if you have changed any opened worksheet, Excel will warn you and will ask for confirmation before exiting the program, as follows.

Fig. 3.24 An Excel Warning Box

If you do not want to save the changes, then click the **Don't Save** button, otherwise click **Save**. If you click **Cancel**, the **Exit** command is aborted.

4

Filling in a Worksheet

As an example of how a worksheet can be built up, we will use the few entries we created in the previous chapter. As we have seen, to open a previously saved worksheet in Excel you first click the **File** ▄▄▄ button, then you select it from the **Recent Documents** list. If it isn't there, click the **Open** button and in the displayed dialogue box navigate to the folder in which you saved **Project 1** in the first place. If you haven't saved it, don't worry as you could start afresh.

Our aim is to build the worksheet shown in Fig. 4.1. For how to do this and formatting details see next page.

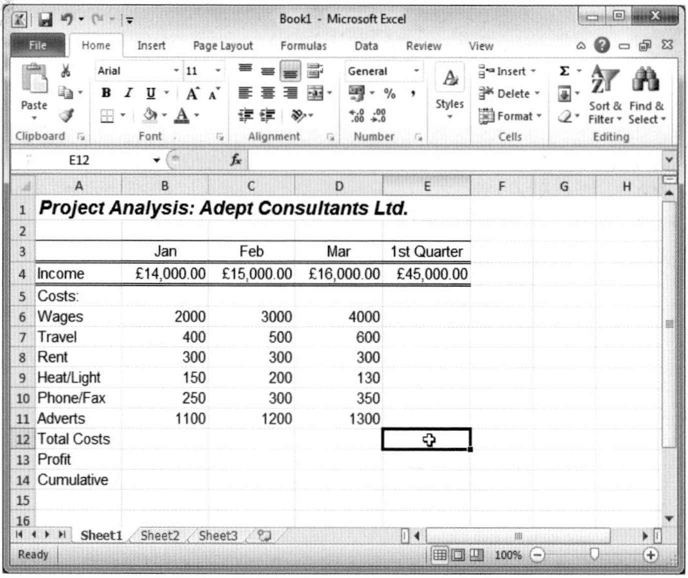

Fig. 4.1 Entering Data in Project 1 Worksheet

To edit existing entries in a worksheet, either double-click on the contents of a cell then change them, or simply retype the contents of cells to replace them, so that your worksheet looks as similar as possible to the one in Fig. 4.1, on the previous page.

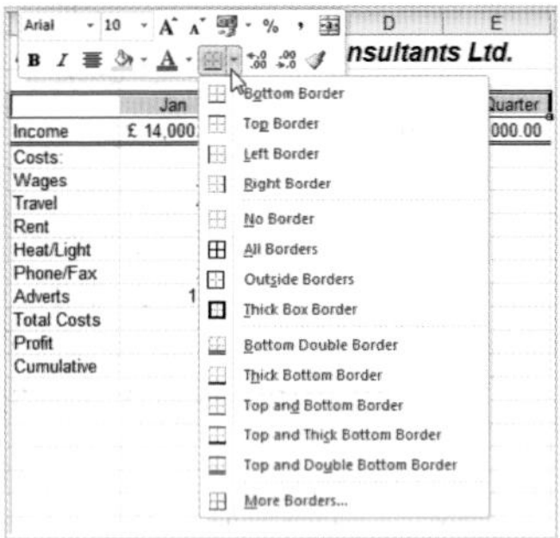

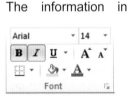

The lines, like the double line at the bottom of the A3 to E3 and A4 to E4 ranges were entered by first selecting each range, then right-clicking it and using the **Borders** button on the Mini Toolbar that hovers over the selection, as shown in Fig. 4.2. A super feature, this!

Fig. 4.2 The Mini Toolbar

You can also use the Ribbon by clicking the down-arrow of the **Home**, **Font**, **Borders** button, and selecting the appropriate border from the same drop-down list options.

Formatting Entries

The information in cell A1 (Project Analysis: Adept Consultants Ltd.) was entered left-justified and formatted from the **Home**, **Font** group in Arial from the drop-down **Font** list, 14 from the drop-down **Font Size** list, and then clicking in succession the **Bold** and **Italic** buttons, all as shown in Fig. 4.3.

Fig. 4.3 Home, Font Group

The text in the cell block B3:E3 was formatted by first selecting the range and then clicking the **Home**, **Alignment**, **Center** command button, shown here, to display the text in the range centre-justified.

The numbers within the cell block B4:E4 were formatted by first selecting the range, then clicking the **Home**, **Number**,

 Accounting Number Format button, shown here, and selecting **£ English (U.K.)** from the drop-down list. By default, this sets the numbers to appear with two digits after the decimal point and prefixed with the £ sign.

Fig. 4.4 The Format Button

All the text appearing in column A (apart from that in cell A1) was just typed in (left justified). The width of all the columns A to E was adjusted to 12 characters; a quick way of doing this is to select one row of these columns, then click the **Home**, **Cells**, **Format** button, select **Column Width** from the menu shown in Fig. 4.4, type 12 in the displayed box, as shown in Fig. 4.5, and click **OK**.

Fig. 4.5 The Column Width Box

Filling a Range by Example

To fill a range by example, select the first cell of a range, point at the bottom right corner of the cell and when the mouse pointer changes to a small cross, as in Fig. 4.6, drag the mouse in the required direction to fill the range.

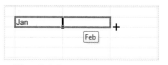

Fig. 4.6 Dragging a Range

In this case, we started with a cell containing the abbreviation 'Jan'. The next cell to the right will automatically fill with the text

'Feb' (Excel anticipates that you want to fill cells by example with the abbreviations for months, and does it for you). Not only that, but it also copies the format of the selected range forward.

The Auto Fill Smart Tag

When you release the mouse button, Excel places a Smart Tag next to the end of the filled-in range. Clicking the down-arrow of this Smart Tag displays a drop-down menu of options, as shown in Fig. 4.7.

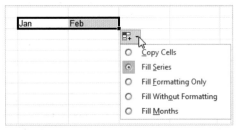

Fig. 4.7 The Auto Fill Smart Tag Options

Entering Text, Numbers and Formulae

Excel 2010 allows you to format both text (labels) and numbers in any way you choose. For example, you can have numbers centre justified in their cells.

When text, a number, a formula, or an Excel function is entered into a cell, or reference is made to the contents of a cell by the cell address, then the content of the status bar changes from **Ready** to **Enter**. This status can be changed back to **Ready** by either completing an entry and pressing **Enter**, **Tab**, one of the arrow keys, or pressing **Esc**.

We can find the 1st quarter total income from consultancy, by activating cell E4, typing

    =b4+c4+d4

and pressing **Enter**. The total first quarter income is added, using the above formula, and the result (£45,000) is placed in cell E4.

When you have entered everything in Fig. 4.1 click the **Save As** button on the **File** ▭File▭ button to save the resultant worksheet under the filename **Project 2**, before going on any further. Remember that saving your work on disc often is a good thing to get used to, as even the shortest power cut can cause the loss of hours of hard work!

Using Functions

In our example, writing a formula that adds the contents of three columns is not too difficult or lengthy a task. But imagine having to add 20 columns! For this reason Excel has an inbuilt summation function which can be used to add any number of columns (or rows).

To illustrate how this and other functions can be used, activate cell E4 and first press **Del** to clear the cell of its formula, then click the **Insert Function** button in the **Function Library** group of the **Formulas** tab, shown here.

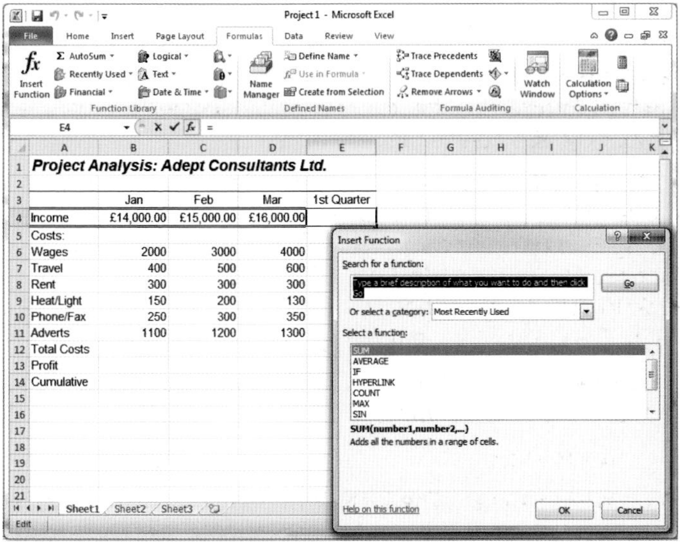

Fig. 4.8 Selecting a Function

If the function you require appears on the displayed dialogue box under **Select a function**, choose it, otherwise type a brief description of what you want to do in the **Search for a function** text box and press **Go**, or select the appropriate class from the list under **Or select a category**.

Choosing the **SUM** function, inserts the entry SUM(B4:D4) in the Formula bar, as shown in Fig. 4.9. Clicking the **OK** button, places the result of the calculation of the function in the selected worksheet cell (E4 in our case).

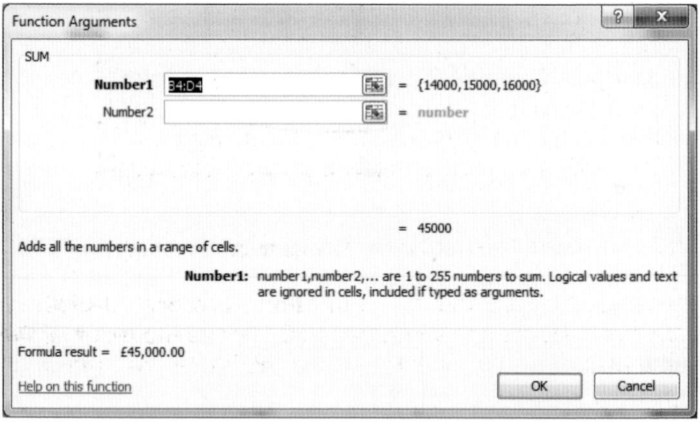

Fig. 4.9 The Function Arguments Dialogue Box

Note that the arguments in the above case are given as B4:D4 in the **Number1** box and the actual result of the calculation is displayed underneath. Pressing the **OK** button, causes the function to be pasted into cell E4, but only the formula result is displayed in the cell. If you click in the **Number2** box you can select another cell range to be summed. The overall result appears at the bottom of the box.

The AutoSum Button

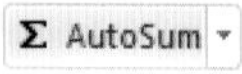

With addition, there is a better and quicker way of letting Excel work out the desired result. To illustrate this, select the cell range B6:E12, which contains the 'Costs' we would like to add up.

To add these in both the horizontal and vertical direction, we include in the selected range an empty column to the right of the numbers and an empty row below the numbers, as shown in Fig. 4.10.

	A	B	C	D	E	F
1	**Project Analysis: Adept Consultants Ltd.**					
2						
3		Jan	Feb	Mar	1st Quarter	
4	Income	£14,000.00	£15,000.00	£16,000.00	£45,000.00	
5	Costs:					
6	Wages	2000	3000	4000		
7	Travel	400	500	600		
8	Rent	300	300	300		
9	Heat/Light	150	200	130		
10	Phone/Fax	250	300	350		
11	Adverts	1100	1200	1300		
12	Total Costs				✛	
13	Profit					
14	Cumulative					

Fig. 4.10 Selecting the Range to be Summed

Pressing the **Formulas**, **Function Library**, **AutoSum** command button, shown on page 59, inserts the result of the summations in the empty column and row, as shown in Fig. 4.11.

	A	B	C	D	E	F
1	**Project Analysis: Adept Consultants Ltd.**					
2						
3		Jan	Feb	Mar	1st Quarter	
4	Income	£14,000.00	£15,000.00	£16,000.00	£45,000.00	
5	Costs:					
6	Wages	2000	3000	4000	9000	
7	Travel	400	500	600	1500	
8	Rent	300	300	300	900	
9	Heat/Light	150	200	130	480	
10	Phone/Fax	250	300	350	900	
11	Adverts	1100	1200	1300	3600	
12	Total Costs	4200	5500	6680	16380	
13	Profit					
14	Cumulative					
15						

Fig. 4.11 The Result of the AutoSum Action

The selected range remains selected so that any other formatting can be applied by simply pressing the appropriate Ribbon buttons.

Note that the **AutoSum** button now has a down-arrow to the right of it. Clicking this arrow, displays a list of alternative options, as shown in Fig. 4.12. From this list you can choose to calculate the **Average**, **Count Numbers** in the entries, find the **Max** or **Min** values in a row or column, or open the Insert Function dialogue box discussed earlier by selecting the **More Functions** option.

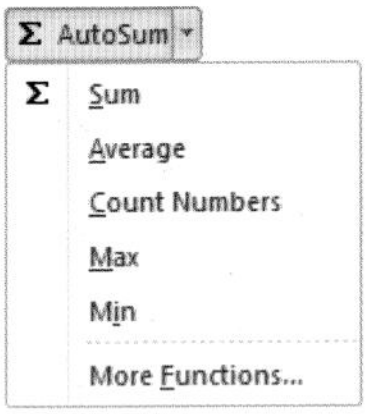

Fig. 4.12
AutoSum Menu

Now complete the insertion of formulae in the rest of the worksheet, noting that 'Profit', in B13, is the difference between 'Income' and 'Total Cost', calculated by the formula **=b4-b12**. To complete the entry, this formula should be copied using the 'fill by example' method we discussed earlier, into the three cells to its right.

The 'Cumulative' entry in cell B14 should be a simple reference to cell B13, that is **=b13**, while in cell C14 it should be **=b14+c13**. Similarly, the latter formula is copied into cell D14 using the 'fill by example' method.

Next, format the entire range B6:E12 by selecting the range and clicking the **Home**, **Number**, **Accounting Number Format** button, shown here, and selecting **£ English (U.K.)**

If you make any mistakes and copy formats or information into cells you did not mean to, use the **Undo** button on the **Quick Access** toolbar, or the **Ctrl+Z** keyboard shortcut. To blank the contents of a range of cells, select the range, then press the **Del** key.

The data in your worksheet, up to this point, should look like that in Fig. 4.13 on the next page. Finally, use the **Save As** button on the Backstage screen to save the resultant worksheet with the filename **Project 2**.

	A	B	C	D	E	F
1	Project Analysis: Adept Consultants Ltd.					
2						
3		Jan	Feb	Mar	1st Quarter	
4	Income	£14,000.00	£15,000.00	£16,000.00	£45,000.00	
5	Costs:					
6	Wages	£ 2,000.00	£ 3,000.00	£ 4,000.00	£ 9,000.00	
7	Travel	£ 400.00	£ 500.00	£ 600.00	£ 1,500.00	
8	Rent	£ 300.00	£ 300.00	£ 300.00	£ 900.00	
9	Heat/Light	£ 150.00	£ 200.00	£ 130.00	£ 480.00	
10	Phone/Fax	£ 250.00	£ 300.00	£ 350.00	£ 900.00	
11	Adverts	£ 1,100.00	£ 1,200.00	£ 1,300.00	£ 3,600.00	
12	Total Costs	£ 4,200.00	£ 5,500.00	£ 6,680.00	£16,380.00	
13	Profit	£ 9,800.00	£ 9,500.00	£ 9,320.00	£28,620.00	
14	Cumulative	£ 9,800.00	£19,300.00	£28,620.00		
15						

Fig. 4.13 The Completed 1st Quarter Worksheet

Formulae and Functions

As we have seen, **Formulas** in Excel (or formulae to the rest of us!) are equations that perform calculations on values in your worksheet. A formula starts with an equal sign (=) and can contain any of the following:

- **Function**s – Built in Excel formulas that take a value or values, perform an operation, and return a value or values. You use functions to simplify and shorten worksheet formulas.

- **References** – Addresses of cells in the worksheet.

- **Operators** – Signs or symbols that specify the type of calculation to perform in an expression. Operators can be mathematical, comparison, logical, or reference.

- **Constants** – Values that are not calculated and, therefore, do not change.

Excel Functions

Excel's functions are built-in formulae that perform specialised calculations. Their general format is:

NAME(arg1, arg2, ...)

where **NAME** is the function name, and **arg1**, **arg2**, etc., are the arguments required for the evaluation of the function. Arguments must appear in a parenthesised list as shown above and their exact number depends on the function being used. However, some functions, such as **PI**, do not require arguments and are used without parentheses.

There are four types of arguments used with functions: numeric values, range values, string values and conditions, the type used being dependent on the type of function. Numeric value arguments can be entered either directly as numbers, as a cell address, a cell range name or as a formula. Range value arguments can be entered either as a range address or a range name, while string value arguments can be entered as an actual value (a string in double quotes), as a cell address, a cell name, or a formula. Condition arguments normally use logical operators or refer to an address containing a logic formula.

Excel has many types of functions, including financial, logical, text, date and time, lookup and reference, mathematical and trigonometric, statistical, database, engineering and information. Each type requires its own number and type of arguments.

To find out in detail about all of Excel 2010's functions go to the **Function reference** section in Excel Help. This gives working examples of everything, but you must be online to receive them.

In Excel 2010 you can use the **Formulas** tab to place and work with formulae and functions. As shown in Fig. 4.14 on the next page, the main function types have their own Ribbon buttons (to see these as they are displayed, maximise the Excel window). Just clicking these and pointing to a function on one of their lists, gives a good overview of what the function does and what parameters it needs.

Fig. 4.14 The Formulas, Function Library

That's enough theory, if you want to go deeper you can study the Help system.

Building a Formula

You can enter formulae straight into a selected cell, or into the Formula bar, which is now re-sizeable. In Fig. 4.15 we will step through the procedure of building a simple formula in cell D3, to average the contents of cells B2 to B4, normally referred to as the range (B2:B4).

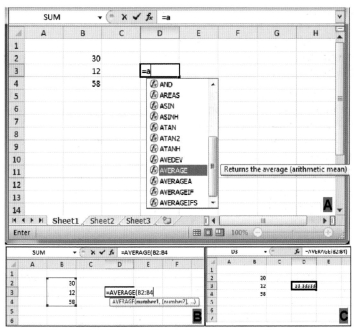

Fig. 4.15 Building a Simple Formula with a Function

In **A** (see previous page), we typed '=a' into cell D3. Excel, expecting a formula, opened the drop-down list for you to select one. This is the new Formula AutoComplete feature which helps you write the proper formula syntax.

We double-clicked on **AVERAGE** and selected the range B2:B4 with the pointer, which as you can see in **B** on the previous page, entered the function and the selected range into the formula, with a syntax pop-up below to help. Pressing the **Enter** key completed the operation.

The result is shown in the cell and the completed formula in the Formula bar when the cell is selected, as shown in **C** of Fig. 4.15 on the previous page. Microsoft have made function use in Excel as intuitive as possible.

Printing a Worksheet

Before we tell you any more about worksheets, you might like to print **Project 2** to see how it looks on paper.

The quickest way of printing your work is to load the worksheet you want to print into Excel, click the **File** button, then click the **Print** button to display the screen shown in Fig. 4.16 below.

Fig. 4.16 Print Menu Options

Note the **Preview** pane on the right of the displayed screen. What you see here is dependent on the selected printer. You can also change the number of copies to be printed, the settings, the orientation and paper size.

Use the **Zoom to page** button, to be found at the bottom right corner of the Print screen, to get the best view of your work and, if you are happy with it, click the **Print** button to send your spreadsheet to the selected printer, provided your printer is connected and switched on.

The idea of the **Preview** pane is to make it easy for you to see your work on screen before committing it to paper, thus saving a few trees and a lot of ink!

Next, we discuss in much more detail how to Print large spreadsheets, how to use **Page Setup** to transform your printout to your liking, and how to use headers and footers.

Printing a Large Worksheet

Fig. 4.17 The
Page Setup Group

Before you print from a large worksheet you should check and if necessary change the print settings. Most of the commands for this are in the **Page Layout**, **Page Setup** group shown in Fig. 4.17.

Setting a Print Area

To choose a smaller print area than the current worksheet, select the required area by highlighting the starting cell of the area and dragging the mouse to highlight the block, click the **Print Area** command button selected above, and choose the **Set Print Area** option on the drop-down menu.

As an example, open the **Project 2** file, if not already opened, and set the print range as A1:E14. Next, click the View tab and click the **Page Layout** button shown here. This opens the screen shown in Fig. 4.18 on the next page, with the View tab open.

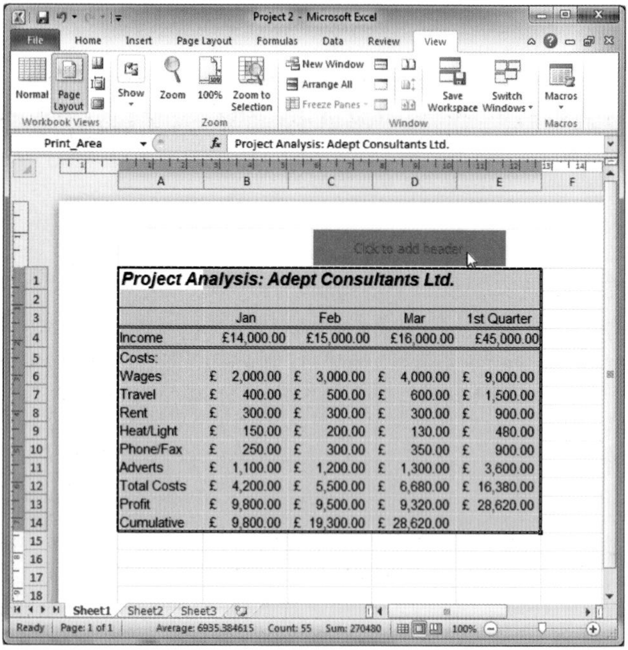

Fig. 4.18 Adjusting Page Settings

Clicking the area pointed to in Fig. 4.18, allows you to add a header. Doing so, Excel displays a contextual tab, shown in Fig. 4.19 below.

Fig. 4.19 The Contextual Header and Footer Tab

From here, you can navigate to the Header or Footer, add page numbers, current date, etc., very quickly. It is worth spending some time examining the facilities offered within this tab, but we leave it to you to explore by yourself.

Nevertheless, in the next chapter we shall be discussing an alternative method of adding Header and Footer information into a spreadsheet. As always, there is more than one way of achieving the same goal!

5

Enhancing Excel Worksheets

Opening an Excel File

To open a previously saved file in Excel, select it from the **Recent** list, or click the **File** button, then click the **Open** button on the Backstage screen, or use the **Ctrl+O** keyboard shortcut. All of these launch the Open dialogue box, shown in Fig. 5.1 below. Excel asks for a filename to open, with the default *All Excel Files* being displayed in the **Files of type** box.

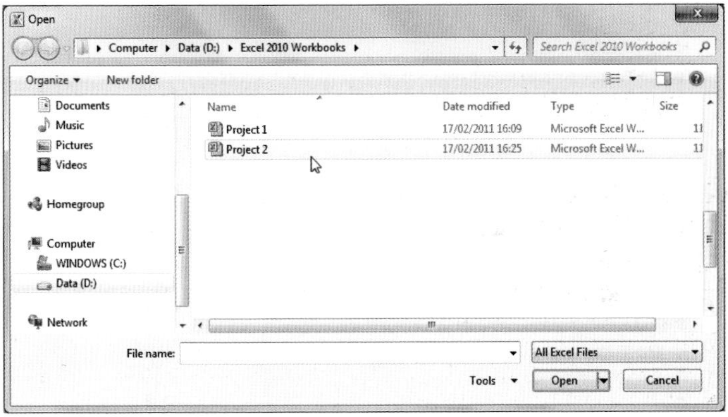

Fig. 5.1 The Open Box

To open our previously saved example, **Project 2**, navigate to where you saved it (in our example in drive D:, in the **Excel 2010 Workbooks** folder), select it by clicking its name in the list box, then click the **Open** button.

In what follows, we will use the contents to **Project 2** to show you how to apply enhancements to it, and eventually how to create 3-D worksheets and how to create professional looking charts from your data.

Applying Enhancements to a Worksheet

You can make your work look more professional by adopting various enhancements, such as single and double line cell borders, shading certain cells and adding meaningful headers and footers.

Formatting Cells

With Excel 2010 it is easy to enhance cells by colouring them appropriately. To do this, select the range you want to format, say A5:A14, then click the **Format** button on the **Home**, **Cells** group, and select **Format Cells** from the displayed menu, as shown in Fig. 5.2.

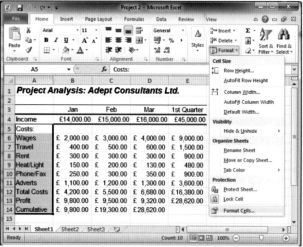

Fig. 5.2 Selecting and Formatting Cells

This opens the Format Cells dialogue box with a number of tabs which can be used to apply different types of formatting to cells. Using the Fill tab and clicking the **Fill Effects** button, opens a similarly named dialogue box in which you can select one or two colours, the shading styles and variants of your preference. We selected a pinkish colour for all the **Costs** labels (A5:A14), and repeated the process, but this time gave the **Income** labels (A3:E4) a bluish tint.

Below we show the Format Cells and Fill Effects screens in a composite display in Fig. 5.3.

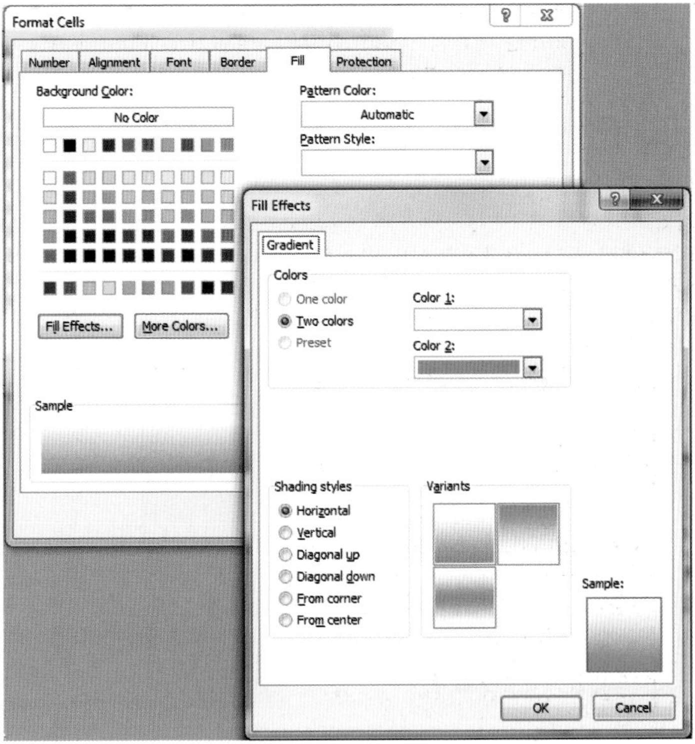

Fig. 5.3 Selecting Fill Effects

Next, reduce the title of the worksheet to 'Project Analysis', then centre it within the range A1:E1, by first selecting the range, then clicking the **Home**, **Alignment**, **Merge** button and selecting **Merge and Centre**, as shown in Fig. 5.4. This centres the title within the selected range. Finally, save the worksheet as **Project 3**, before going on.

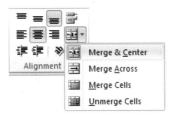

Fig. 5.4 Selecting the Merge & Center Alignment option

Next, highlight the cell range A1:E14 and select the width as **1 page** from the **Scale to Fit** group of the **Page Layout** tab on the Ribbon. Finally, with the same cell selection, click the down-arrow against **Accounting** in the **Home**, **Number** group and select **Currency** from the drop-down menu, as shown in Fig. 5.5 below.

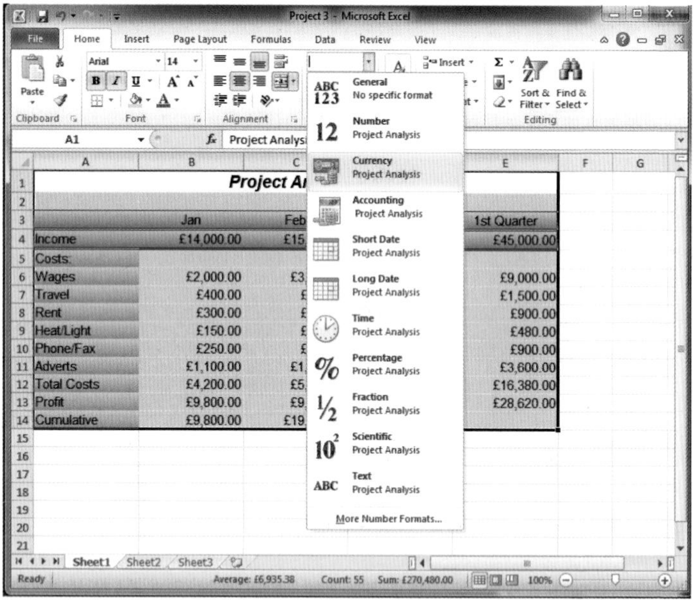

Fig. 5.5 Selecting to Display Numbers in the Currency Format

Above you also see what the result of your selection would be, as you hover the mouse pointer over the menu entries.

When you are satisfied that all is as it should be, click the **Save** button on the Quick Access Toolbar to save your work under the current filename. However, if you are not sure, and want to check later, then you could always use the **Save As** button and give your work a temporary filename (such as **Project 3a**) until you verify that your worksheet is identical to ours. When that is done, use the **File**, **Info** option, examine the contents of the displayed screen, then click the **Open File Location** button, which will allow you to rename your temporary file from a right-click menu. Try it!

Page Setup

Before printing a worksheet you should check and, if necessary, change the print settings. Most of the commands for this are in the **Page Layout**, **Page Setup** group shown here in Fig. 5.6.

Fig. 5.6 The Page Setup Group

Next, open **Project 3**, unless already opened, and click the Dialogue Box Launcher 🔽 to display the Page Setup screen shown in Fig. 5.7, with the Page tab open.

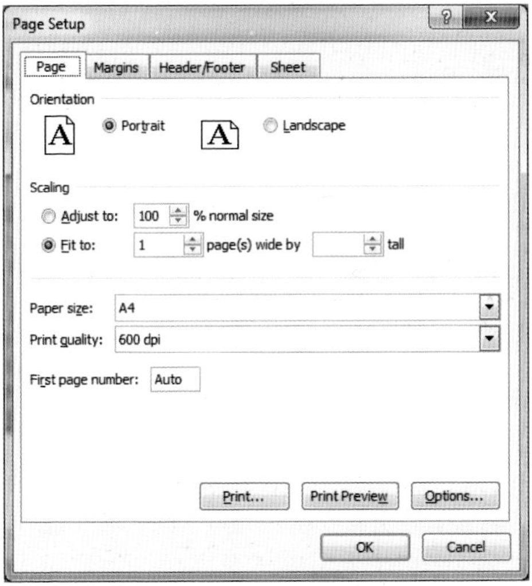

Fig. 5.7 Adjusting Page Settings

A very useful feature of Excel is the **Scaling** facility shown in the above dialogue box. You can print actual size or a percentage of it, or you can choose to fit your worksheet on to one page which allows Excel to scale your work automatically. We set the **Adjust to % normal size** to 130.

In the **Margins** tab we set the **Center on page** setting to **Horizontally** and clicked the Header/Footer tab to display Fig. 5.8.

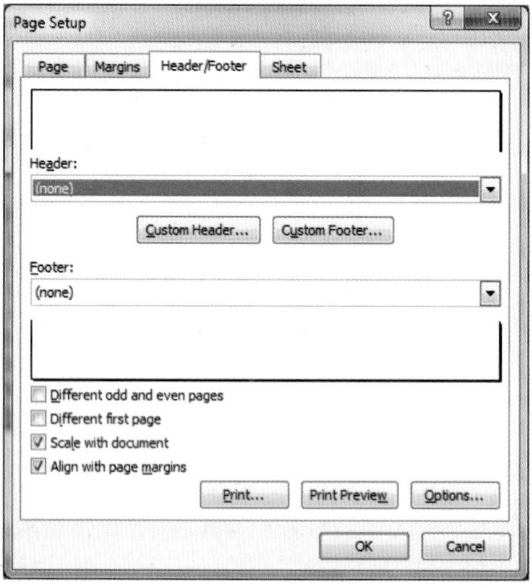

Fig. 5.8 The Header/Footer Tab Settings

Header and Footer Icons and Codes

Clicking the **Custom Header** button opens the Header box shown in Fig. 5.9 on the next page.

You can type text into any of the three boxes, or click on one of the buttons. **Sheet Name**, for example, inserts the **&[Tab]** code which has the effect of inserting the sheet name of the current active sheet at the time of printing. The first icon button displays the Font dialogue box, while the others display the following codes:

Code	*Action*
&[Page]	Inserts a page number.
&[Pages]	Inserts the total number of pages.
&[Date]	Inserts the current date.
&[Time]	Inserts the current time.
&[File]	Inserts the filename of the current workbook.

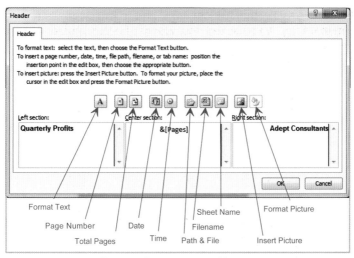

Fig. 5.9 Customising a Header

On the **Left** and **Right** sections we clicked the **Format Text** button and typed the displayed text in Arial 10 bold, while on the **Center section** we clicked the **Insert Page Number** button. Clicking **OK** returns you to the Page Setup screen, and clicking the **Print Preview** button, displays Fig. 5.10.

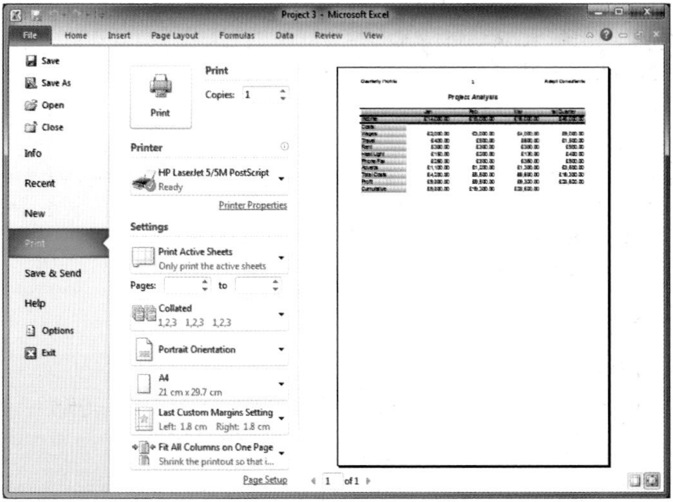

Fig. 5.10 The Print Preview Screen

Before pressing the **Print** button, check your work using the **View**, **Page Layout** command in the **Workbook Views** group, to display the screen in Fig. 5.11 below.

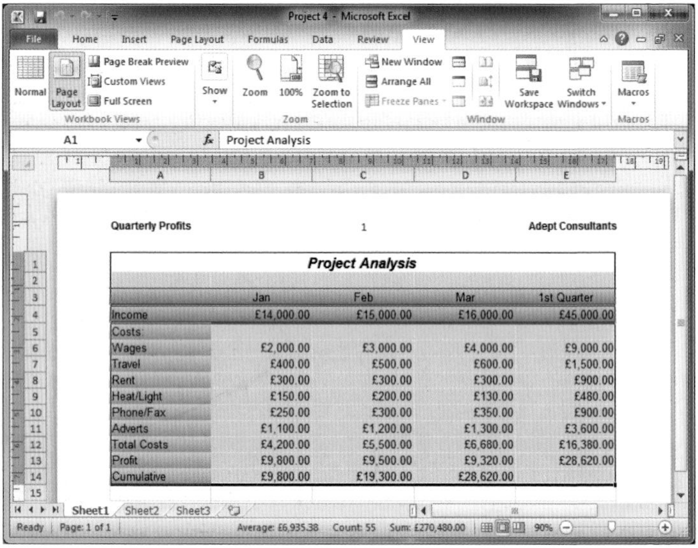

Fig. 5.11 The Page Layout View

When all is set, save your work as **Project 4**, then click the **File**, **Print** button to return to the screen in Fig. 5.10.

From this screen, you can choose your printer and its properties. Under **Settings** click the down-arrow against

Print Active Sheets to display Fig. 5.12. As you can see, you can choose to print the **Active Sheets**, the **Entire Workbook**, or a **Selection**. If you have included headers and footers, these will be printed out irrespective of whether you choose to print a selected range or a selected worksheet. Clicking the **Print** button will start the printing operation.

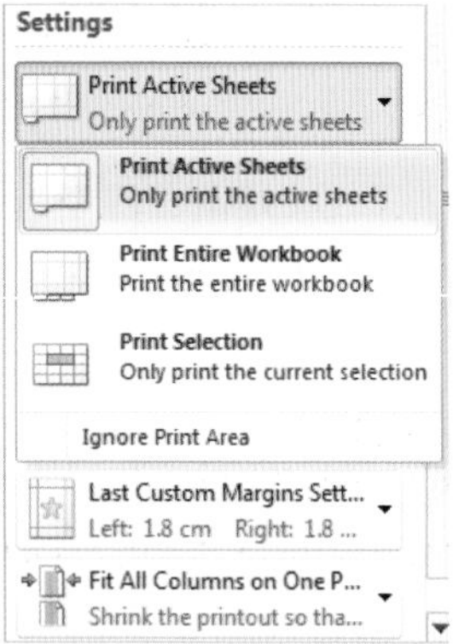

Fig. 5.12 The Settings Options

3-Dimensional Worksheets

In Excel, a Workbook is a 3-dimensional file made up of a series of flat 2-dimensional sheets stacked 'on top of each other'. As mentioned previously, each separate sheet in a file has its own Tab identifier at the bottom of the screen. Ranges can be set to span several different sheets to build up 3-dimensional blocks of data. These blocks can then be manipulated, copied or moved to other locations in the file. A cell can reference any other cell in the file, no matter what sheet it is on, and an extended range of functions can be used to process these 3-dimensional ranges.

The best way to demonstrate a new idea is to work through an example – we will use the worksheet saved under **Project 4**. But first use the **View**, **Normal** command buttons before proceeding with the copying.

Copying Sheets in a Workbook

We will now fill another three sheets behind the present one, in order to include information about ADEPT Consultants' trading during the other three quarters of the year. The easiest way of doing this is by copying the information in Sheet1, including the formatting and the entered formulae, onto the other three sheets, then edit the numerical information in these appropriately.

To simplify this operation, Excel has a facility which allows you to copy a sheet into a workbook. There are two ways of doing this: (a) with the mouse, or (b) from the Ribbon. With the mouse (being the easiest method), make the sheet you want to copy the current sheet, then press the **Ctrl** key, and while keeping it pressed, point with the mouse on the Tab of Sheet1 and drag it to the right, as shown in Fig. 5.13.

Fig. 5.13 Drag Copying a Sheet into a Workbook

A small black triangle indicates the place where the copy will be inserted, as shown above.

If you insert a copy, say before Sheet2, when you release the mouse button the inserted sheet will be given the name Sheet1(2), while inserting a second copy before Sheet2 will be given the name Sheet1(3). To delete a worksheet, right-click its tab and select **Delete** from the pop-up menu.

With the above method you retain not only the formatting, but also the width of the columns. If you try copying a worksheet to the clipboard, then pasting in onto another sheet, you will lose the column widths, but retain other formatting.

When you have three copies placed on your workbook, double-click the Tabs of Sheet1 and the three new sheets and change their names to 'Quarter 1', 'Quarter 2', etc., then change the formatting of cells E5:E14, as well as those of B12:D14, of all the worksheets, so they stand out from the rest, as shown in Fig. 5.14. We use the **Home**, **Format Cells** commands, then the **Border** & **Fill** tabs of the Format Cells dialogue box. We leave it to you to experiment with this.

	A	B	C	D	E
1			*Project Analysis - 2nd Quarter*		
2					
3		Jan	Feb	Mar	2nd Quarter
4	Income	£15,500.00	£16,000.00	£16,500.00	£48,000.00
5	Costs:				
6	Wages	£3,500.00	£4,000.00	£4,500.00	£12,000.00
7	Travel	£500.00	£550.00	£580.00	£1,630.00
8	Rent	£300.00	£300.00	£300.00	£900.00
9	Heat/Light	£150.00	£120.00	£100.00	£370.00
10	Phone/Fax	£300.00	£350.00	£400.00	£1,050.00
11	Adverts	£1,250.00	£1,300.00	£1,350.00	£3,900.00
12	Total Costs	£6,000.00	£6,620.00	£7,230.00	£19,850.00
13	Profit	£9,500.00	£9,380.00	£9,270.00	£28,150.00
14	Cumulative	£9,500.00	£18,880.00	£28,150.00	
15					

⊞ ◀ ▶ ▶│ Quarter 1 │ **Quarter 2** ╱ Quarter 3 ╱ Quarter 4 ╱ She◀ ▶
Ready   ⊞▢⊞ 100% ⊖ —⬤— ⊕

Fig. 5.14 The Data for the Second Quarter

The correct contents of the second sheet should be as shown above. Be extra careful, from now on, to check the identification Tab at the bottom of the window, so as not to get the sheets mixed up. You don't want to spend time editing the wrong worksheet!

Next, build two additional sheets for the last two quarters of the year (see below for details on the 3rd and 4th quarters).

	Jul	Aug	Sep	Oct	Nov	Dec
Income	17,000	17,500	18,000	18,500	19,000	19,500
Costs:						
Wages	4,000	4,500	5,000	4,500	5,000	5,500
Travel	600	650	680	630	670	700
Rent	300	300	300	300	300	300
Heat/Light	50	80	120	160	200	250
Phone/Fax	350	380	420	400	420	450
Adverts	1,400	1,450	1,500	1,480	1,500	1,530

After building up the four worksheets (one for each quarter), save the file as **Project 5**.

Linking Sheets

Use the **Home**, **Cells**, **Insert** command and click **Insert Sheet** to place a worksheet in front of the 'stack' of data sheets to show a full year's results. Next, make a copy of the 1st Quarter sheet (using the **Home**, **Copy** button), and place it in the new front sheet (using the **Home**, **Paste** button). Note that column widths are not retained with this method, therefore you'll have to adjust these. Next, highlight cells B3 to E14, and press the **Delete** keyboard key and finally, rename the worksheet's Tab to 'Summary'.

We will now link the summary sheet to the other quarterly

Fig. 5.15
Pasting
Linked Cells

data sheets so that the information contained on them is automatically summarised and updated on it. The quarter totals in each Quarter's worksheet (cells E3 to E14) are selected and copied in turn using the **Home**, **Clipboard**, **Copy** button, and then pasted to the appropriate column of the summary sheet by selecting the destination range, and clicking the **Paste** button down-arrow and clicking the **Paste Link** icon pointed to in Fig. 5.15.

Do note that empty cells linked with this method, like those in cell E5 of each quarter, appear as 0 (zero) in the Summary sheet. These can be removed with the **Delete** key.

Next, insert appropriate formulae in row 14 to correctly calculate the cumulative values in the Summary sheet. The result should be as shown in Fig. 5.16 with the **Totals** shown in column F. Save the resultant workbook as **Project 6**.

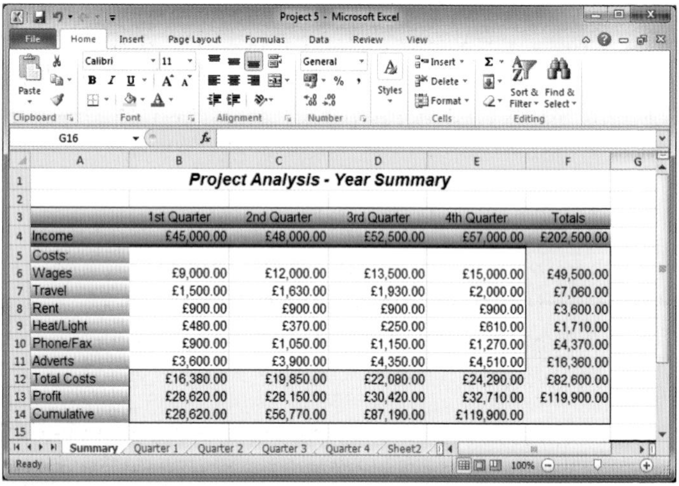

Fig. 5.16 Linked Data in the Summary Sheet

Relative and Absolute Cell Addresses

Entering a mathematical expression into Excel, such as the formula in cell C14 which was

=B14+C13

causes Excel to interpret it as 'add the contents of cell one column to the left of the current position, to the contents of cell one row above the current position'. In this way, when the formula was later copied into cell address D14, the contents of the cell relative to the left position of D14 (i.e. C14) and the contents of the cell one row above it (i.e. D13) were used, instead of the original cell addresses entered in C14. This is relative addressing.

To see the effect of relative versus absolute addressing, copy the formula in cell C14 into C16 using the **Copy** and **Paste** buttons, as shown in Fig. 5.17.

	C16		f_x	=B16+C15			
	A	B	C	D	E	F	G
12	Total Costs	£16,380.00	£19,850.00	£22,080.00	£24,290.00	£82,600.00	
13	Profit	£28,620.00	£28,150.00	£30,420.00	£32,710.00	£119,900.00	
14	Cumulative	£28,620.00	£56,770.00	£87,190.00	£119,900.00		
15							
16			£0.00 (Ctrl) ▾				

K ◀ ▶ ▶I Summary ╱ Quarter 1 ╱ Quarter 2 ╱ Quarter 3 ╱ Quarter 4 ╱ Sheet2 ╱ ▮ ◀ ▯ ▶ ▯
Select destination and press ENTER or choose Paste   100% ⊖ ○ ⊕

Fig. 5.17 Demonstrating Relative and Absolute Cell Addressing

Note that in cell C14 the formula was =B14+C13. However, when copied into cell C16 the formula appears as

=B16+C15

This is because it has been interpreted as relative addressing. In this case, no value appears in cell C16 because we are attempting to add two blank cells.

Now change the formula in cell C14 by editing it to

=$B$14+$C$13

which is interpreted as absolute addressing. Copying this formula into cell C16 calculates the correct result. Highlight cell C16 and observe the cell references in its formula; they have not changed from those of cell C14.

When creating a financial model in a spreadsheet it is common practice to put all the control parameters on a sheet of their own. These might be the $/£ exchange rate, or the % rate of inflation for example. Whenever these parameters are needed in a cell formula in the model they should not just be entered straight into the formula, but absolute references should be made to them in the parameter sheet. In this way you can change a parameter in one place on the parameter sheet and see the overall effects when the model is recalculated. The $ sign must prefix both the column reference and the row reference.

Mixed cell addressing is permitted; as for example when a column address reference is needed to be taken as absolute, while a row address reference is not.

Freezing Panes on Screen

With large sheets when you are working in the data area you may not be able to see the label cells associated with that data and it is easy to get very confused.

To get over this you can freeze column (or row) labels of a worksheet on screen so that they are always visible. To do this, move the cell pointer to the right (or below) the column (or row) which you want to freeze, and click the **View**, **Window**, **Freeze Panes** command button shown in Fig. 5.18.

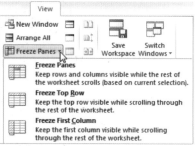

Fig. 5.18 The Freeze Panes Button

Selecting **Freeze Panes** from the drop-down menu will place black lines in the sheet to show what is frozen. Then everything to the left of, or above the cell pointer will freeze on the screen when you scroll through the worksheet.

To unfreeze panes, click the **View**, **Window**, **Freeze Panes** button again and select the **Unfreeze Panes** option. This is only available if you have rows or columns frozen.

In Excel 2010 you cannot use Page Layout view with frozen panes in your sheet. The warning message shown below opens. If you click the **OK** button, the sheet will be unfrozen.

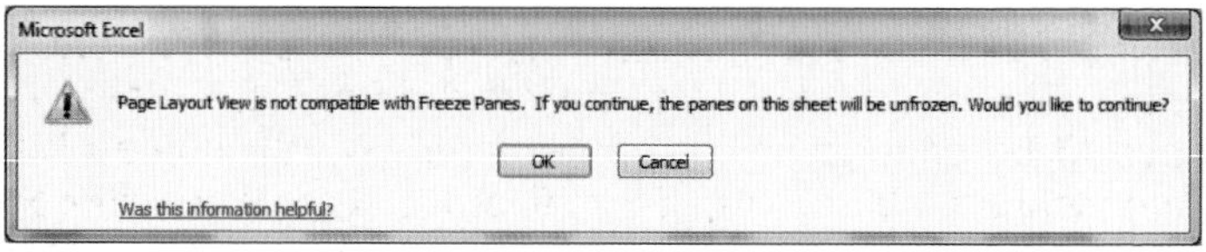

Microsoft Excel

Page Layout View is not compatible with Freeze Panes. If you continue, the panes on this sheet will be unfrozen. Would you like to continue?

OK   Cancel

Was this information helpful?

Fig. 5.19 Another Excel Warning Message

6

Spreadsheet Charts

Excel 2010 makes it very easy to create professional looking charts or graphs from your data – they allow you to graphically display data trends and patterns.

As we shall see, the package can almost instantly create many different chart and graph types, including area, bar, column, line, doughnut, radar, XY, pie, combination and several 3-D options of these charts. These are made available to you once you have selected the data you want to chart from the **Charts** group on the **Insert** tab.

Charts (you can have several per worksheet) can be displayed on screen at the same time as the worksheet from which they were derived, since they are created in their own chart frame and can be embedded anywhere on a worksheet. They can be sent to an appropriate output device, such as a printer, or copied to other Office 2010 applications.

A Simple Column Chart

To illustrate some of the graphing capabilities of Excel, we will plot the income of the consulting company we discussed in **Project 6**. If you haven't already done so, you will need to complete the exercise described earlier on pages 71 & 73 and have to hand the linked workbook on page 74.

Now we need to select the range of the data we want to graph. The range of data to be graphed in Excel does not have to be contiguous for each graph, as with some other spreadsheets. With Excel, you select your data from different parts of a sheet with the **Ctrl** key pressed down. This method has the advantage of automatic recalculation should any changes be made to the original data. You could also collect data from different sheets to one 'graphing' sheet by linking them as we did with the summary sheet.

If you don't want the chart to be recalculated when you do this, then you must use the **Home**, **Clipboard**, **Copy** and **Paste**, **Paste Special** command buttons and choose the **Values** option from the displayed dialogue box. This copies a selected range to a specified target area of the worksheet and converts formulae to values. This is necessary, as cells containing formulae cannot be pasted directly since it would cause the relative cell addresses to adjust to the new locations; each formula would then recalculate a new value for each cell and give wrong results.

Creating a Chart

To obtain a chart of 'Income' versus 'Quarters', select the data in cell range A3..E4, then click the **Insert**, **Charts**, **Column** button, shown below in Fig. 6.1.

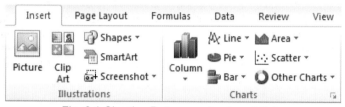

Fig. 6.1 Charting Buttons on the Insert Tab

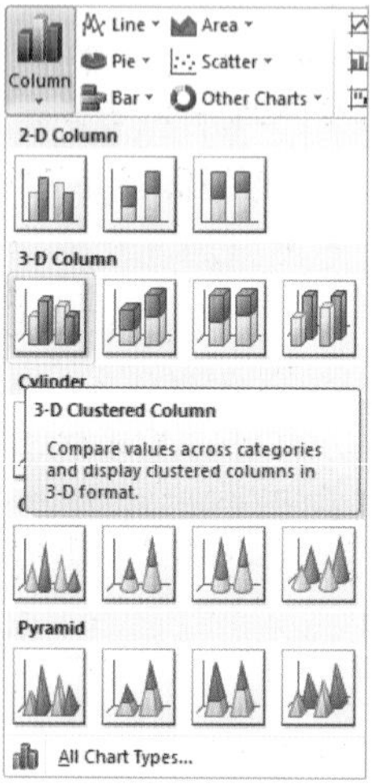

This opens the drop-down gallery of chart options shown in Fig. 6.2. Now select the **3-D Clustered Column** type and just click it to create the chart shown in Fig. 6.3 on the next page. That's all there is to it, just a few clicks!

Fig. 6.2 The Column Charts Gallery

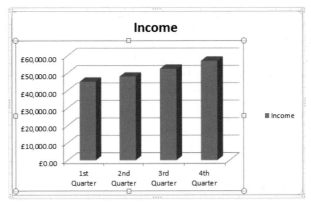

Fig. 6.3 A 3-D Clustered Column Chart

While the frame containing a chart is selected (you can tell from the presence of the handles around it), you can change its size by dragging the small two-headed arrow pointer (which appears when the mouse pointer is placed on the handles at the corners or middle of the frame). You can also move the frame and its contents to another position on the worksheet by dragging it to a new position.

The Chart Tools

When you select a chart in Excel by clicking it, the **Chart Tools** add the **Design**, **Layout**, and **Format** tabs, as below.

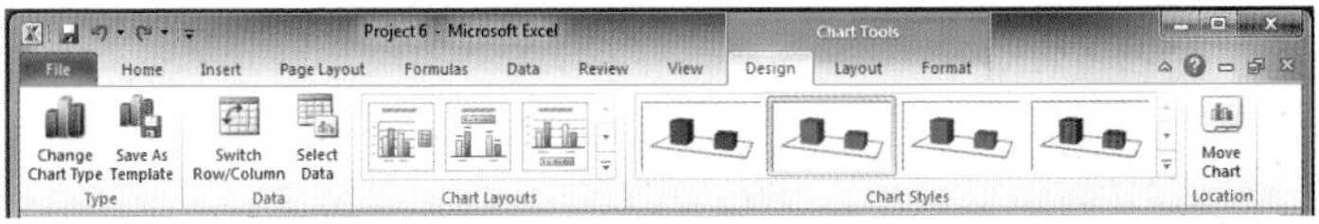

Fig. 6.4 The Design Tab of the Charting Ribbon

The Design tab groups controls for you to change the chart Type, Data, Chart Layouts, Chart Styles and Location.

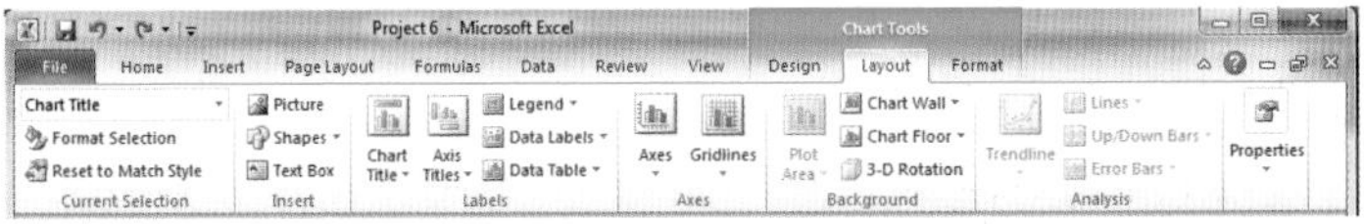

Fig. 6.5 The Layout Tab of the Charting Ribbon

With this tab you control the layout of the Current Selection, Labels, and Axes, Insert a layout, and Background, Analysis and Properties.

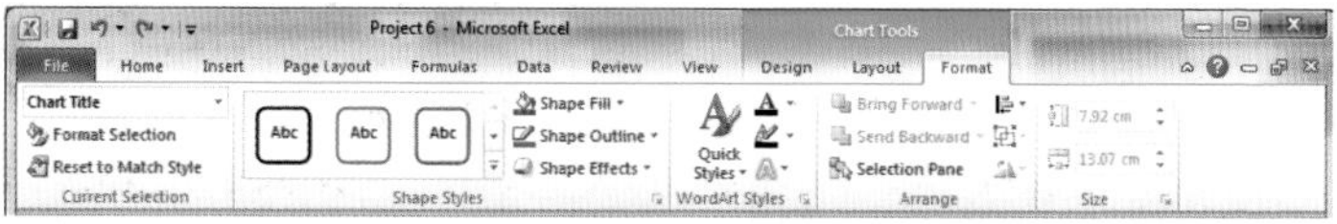

Fig. 6.6 The Format Tab of the Charting Ribbon

From the Format tab you format the Current Selection, set Shape Styles and WordArt Styles, Arrange objects and Size.

Customising a Chart

Now it is time for you to 'play'. The only way to find out what all the charting controls do is to try them all out. Remember that some options are applied to the chart element that is currently selected, others to the whole chart.

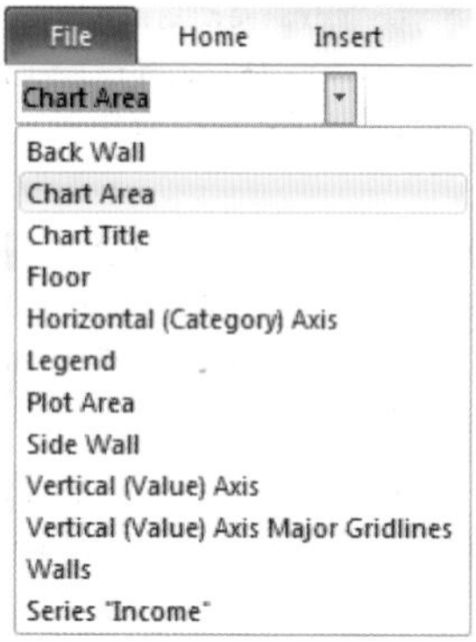

Fig. 6.7 The Chart Elements Box

To control what is selected, click the arrow next to the **Chart Elements** box (below the **File** command button) in the **Current Selection** group of the **Format** tab, and then click the chart element that you want, as shown in Fig. 6.7.

On the **Layout** tab, we suggest you click the label layout option that you want in the **Labels** group, select what chart axes you want in the **Axes** group, and what layout option you want in the **Background** group.

In the **Current Selection** group, clicking **Format Selection**, opens a Format control box like that shown in Fig. 6.8 on the next page, in which you select the formatting options you want for the selected chart element.

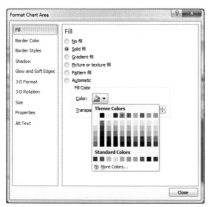

Fig. 6.8 Setting Format Options for Chart Elements

You can also apply a quick style to individual elements, or use the **Shape Fill**, **Shape Outline**, and **Shape Effects** buttons in the **Shape Quick Styles** group on the **Format** tab. These are our favourite ways of formatting our charts.

Try it, then change the May income (on the Quarter 2 sheet) from £16,000 to £26,000, and watch how the change is reflected on the redrawn graph. Finally, revert to the original entry for the May income, and if you like, change your chart back to its original column type, and then save your work again under the filename **Project 7** by clicking the **Save** button on the Quick Access toolbar. Your current work will be saved to disc replacing the previous version.

When Excel creates a chart, it plots each row or column of data in the selected range as a 'data series', such as a group of bars, lines, etc. A chart can contain many data series, but Excel charts data according to the following rules:

1. If the selected range contains more rows than columns of data, Excel plots the data series by columns.

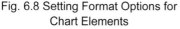

X-axis labels   1st data series   2nd data series   3rd data series

2. If the selected range contains more columns than rows of data, or the same number of columns and rows, Excel plots the data series by rows.

Legend labels   X-axis labels   ⟶
                 1st data series ⟶
                 2nd data series ⟶

If you select a range to chart which includes column and row headings, and text above or to the left of the numeric data, Excel uses the text to create the axis labels, legends, and title.

Saving Charts

When you save a workbook, the chart or charts you have created are saved with it. It is, therefore, a good idea not only to give each chart a title (select it then use the **Chart Tools**, **Layout** tab, **Properties**, and rename **Chart 1** to **Income Column** and press **Enter**).

It is also a good idea to locate charts on a separate sheet. To do this, click the Insert Worksheet tab at the bottom of the screen, move the new sheet in front of the Summary tab and rename it Charts. Use **Cut** and **Paste** to move the chart from its present position to the Charts tab sheet, and save the workbook as **Project 7**.

Predefined Chart Types

To select a different type of chart, click the **Design**, **Type**, **Change Chart Type** button shown here. Excel 2010 uses 11 basic chart types, and with variations of these has 73 type options in all. These chart-types are normally used to describe the following relationships between data:

Area	for showing a volume relationship between two series, such as production or sales, over a given length of time.
Bar	for comparing differences in data (noncontinuous data that are not related over time) by depicting changes in horizontal bars to show positive and negative variations from a given position.

 for showing a type of XY (scatter) chart. The size of the data (radius of the bubble) indicates the value of a third variable.

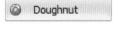 for comparing separate items (noncontinuous data which are related over time) by depicting changes in vertical bars to show positive and negative variations from a given position.

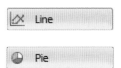 for comparing parts with the whole. Similar to pie charts, but can depict more than one series of data.

 for showing continuous changes in data with time.

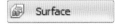 for comparing parts with the whole. You can use this type of chart when you want to compare the percentage of an item from a single series of data with the whole series.

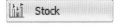 for plotting one series of data as angle values defined in radians, against one or more series defined in terms of a radius.

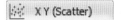 for showing optimum combinations between two sets of data, as in a topographic map. Colours and patterns indicate areas that are in the same range of values.

for showing high-low-close type of data variation to illustrate stock market prices or temperature changes.

for showing scatter relationships between X and Y. Scatter charts are used to depict items which are not related over time.

Drawing a Multiple Column Chart

As an exercise, we will consider a new column chart which deals with the quarterly 'Costs' of Adept Consultants. To achieve this, first select the Summary sheet of workbook **Project 7**, then highlight the cell range A3:E3, press the **Ctrl** key, and holding it down, use the mouse to select the costs range A6:E11.

Next, click the **Insert**, **Charts**, **Column** button, select Clustered Cylinder from the gallery as pointed to below. The 6 different quarterly costs will be drawn automatically, as displayed in the composite 'before and after' screen dump in Fig. 6.9.

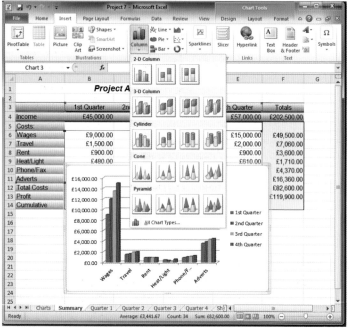

Fig. 6.9 Creating a Costs Column Chart

Because the selected range contains more rows than columns of data, Excel follows the 1st rule of data series selection, which is not really what we want.

To have the 'quarters' appearing on the x-axis and the 'costs' as the legends, we need to tell Excel that our data series is in rows by clicking the **Design**, **Data**, **Switch Row/Column** button on the Ribbon. Immediately this is done the column chart changes to:

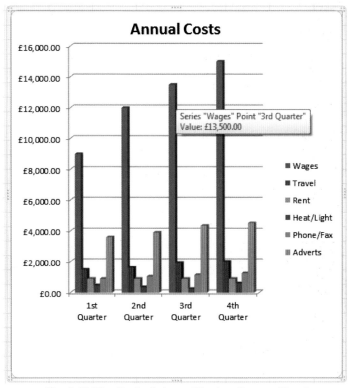

Fig. 6.10 The Costs Column Chart on its own Sheet

The chart title was added by clicking the **Layout**, **Labels**, **Chart Title** button, selecting **Above Chart** and then typing the heading in the object space provided on the chart.

Finally we moved the chart to the Chart Tab sheet, as before, and renamed it **Costs Column** using the **Chart Tools**, **Layout** tab, **Properties** command buttons. Save the workbook under its existing name by clicking the **Save** button on the Quick Access toolbar.

Changing Titles and Labels

To change a title, an axis label or a legend within a chart, click the appropriate area on the chart. This reveals that these are individual objects (they are surrounded by small green circles and squares called 'handles') and you can edit, reposition, or change their font and point size. You can even rotate text within such areas in any direction you like.

To demonstrate some of these options, we will use the **Costs Column** chart saved in **Project 7**, so get it on screen if you are to follow our suggestions.

To change the font size of a chart title, click in the Chart Title area to select it and select the existing title text. Then simply click the **Home** tab and use any of the **Font** group buttons. Below, in Fig. 6.11, we show what happens when you select to change the colour of the chart title by clicking on the **Font Color** 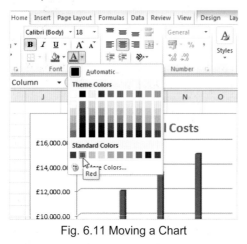 button.

You can also change the colour of the chart title by using the options on the **Format**, **WordArt Styles** group and clicking the **Text Fill** button. Either way can make your chart or axis titles really stand out. There are also options to apply a gradient or a texture to a title.

Fig. 6.11 Moving a Chart

The **WordArt Styles** group also has the **Text Outline** and **Text Effects** buttons, which include Shadow, Reflection and Glow effects. The possibilities are almost limitless!

Drawing a Pie Chart

Change
Chart Type

To change the chart type, simply select the chart, click the **Design**, **Type**, **Change Chart Type** button, shown here, and choose from the gallery.

As a last example in chart drawing, we used the data ranges A6:A11 and F6:F11 of the Summary worksheet to plot an **Exploded Pie in 3-D** chart, as shown in Fig. 6.12 below.

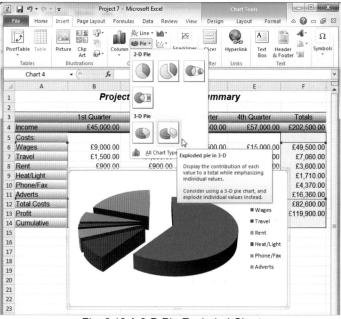

Fig. 6.12 A 3-D Pie Exploded Chart

Next, copy the chart to the Chart Tab of the workbook, and use the **Chart Tools**, **Layout**, **Labels**, **Data Labels** button and in the **More Data Label Options** section check the **Category name**, **Percentage** and **Show Leader Lines** check boxes. Then just drag things around and re-size them to obtain the pie chart shown in Fig. 6.13 on the next page. We chose to copy rather than move the chart from its original place, so that a copy of it is available in case of mistakes!

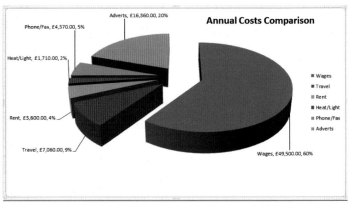

Fig. 6.13 The Final 3-D Pie Exploded Chart

This chart tells us, for example, that Wages for the whole year amount to 60% of the total yearly costs. Other cost categories are also displayed with their appropriate percentages. Pointing to any pie slice, opens a pop-up showing the actual data series, its value and its percentage of the whole.

Sparklines

New to Excel 2010 is the ability to examine trends in data by providing a tiny chart representation of the data in one cell. In this way, you can see at a glance the trend in the underlying data.

To illustrate how you can use sparklines, we copied the **Heat/Light** costs from each quarter and pasted them into the Summary sheet of our **Project 7** workbook, as shown in Fig. 6.14 on the next page. To make it easy to show you what we are doing, we copied the data from each quarter, but pasted them into two six-monthly rows.

Next, select the range of the first six-monthly data (A19 to F19) and click the **Insert**, **Sparklines**, **Lines** button. This opens the Create Sparklines dialogue box in which the **Data Range** is already inserted, but you need to provide the **Location Range** which in this case is G19.

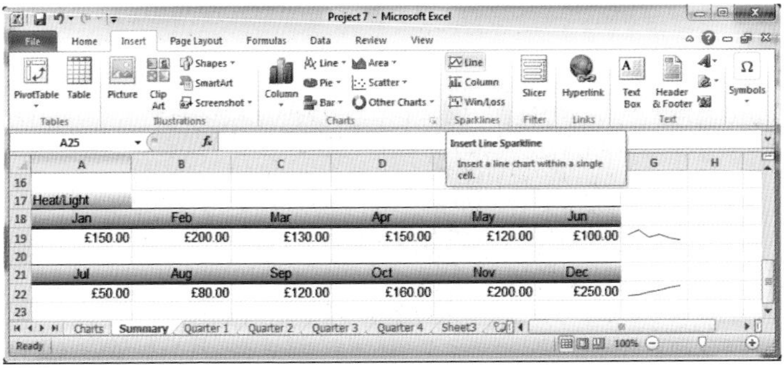

Fig. 6.14 Illustrating Sparklines

Obviously this example is rather too feeble, but it is the technique that matters.

Excel Web App

Just as with Word Web App, Excel Web App is part of Microsoft Web Apps which allows you to create Word, Excel, PowerPoint and OneNote documents on Windows Live. This allows you to work with documents directly on the Web site where they are stored.

To use this facility, you must set up a Windows Live ID, which is very easy to do and is free! If you already use Hotmail, Messenger, or Xbox Live, then you already have a Windows Live ID. If not, do the following:

Use your Internet Explorer and go to the www.live.com Web site. In the displayed screen, click the **Sign up** link and fill in the required information, then click the **I accept** button. It is as easy as that!

You can now start using Excel Web App by saving your latest workbook (**Project 7**) to Windows Live SkyDrive. Use the **File**, **Save & Send** command button, then click **Save to Web**, and select **My Documents**. You can also use the **File**, **Save & Send** command to publish an Excel workbook to a Blog site, send it as an attachment to an e-mail, or as a PDF.

To retrieve an Excel workbook from SkyDrive (from anywhere in the World), use your Internet Explorer and go to www.live.com, sign in with your Live ID and Password, click on **Office** and select **Your Documents**, then **My Documents**.

Now, by clicking the required workbook on SkyDrive, it is loaded into Excel Web App, as shown in Fig. 6.15, and then you can use the **File** command button to display a menu of options, such as Open in Excel, Print, Share, etc.

Fig. 6.15 Loading a Workbook into Excel Web App for Viewing or Printing

Clicking the **Edit in Browser** button in Fig. 6.15 above, opens the Excel Web App and loads your workbook as shown in Fig. 6.16. As you can see, although the options available on the Ribbon are a limited version to those in Excel, they are quite adequate. We leave it to you to explore.

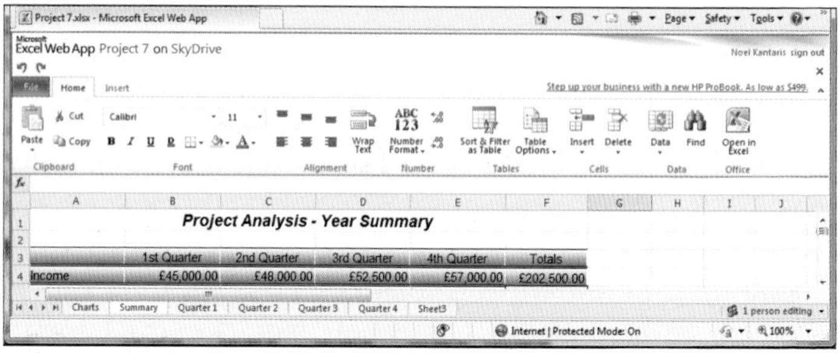

Fig. 6.16 Loading a Document into Excel Web App for Editing

* * *

In the next few chapters we shall discuss Excel's database and also explore its various tools, such as Formula Auditing, What-if Analysis, Scenarios, Goal Seek, Solver and how to share information with other Office 2010 Applications.

7

The Excel Database

An Excel database table is a worksheet range which contains related information, such as 'Customer's Name', 'Consultancy Details', 'Invoice No.', etc. A phone book is a simple database table, stored on paper. In Excel each record is entered as a worksheet row, with the fields of each record occupying corresponding columns.

A database table is a collection of data that exists, and is organised, around a specific theme or requirement. It is used for storing information so that it is quickly accessible. To make accessing the data easier, each row (or **record)**, of data within a database table is structured in the same fashion, i.e. each record will have the same number of columns (or **fields**).

We define a database and its various elements as follows:

Database table A collection of related data organised in rows and columns in a worksheet file which can contain many different database tables.

Record A row of information relating to a single entry and comprising one or more fields.

Field A single column of information of the same type, such as people's names.

Creating a Database

In order to investigate the various database functions, such as sorting, searching, etc., we first need to set up a database table in the form shown on the next page.

Note that in creating a database table, the following rules must be observed:

1. The top row of the database table must contain the field labels, one per column, which identify the fields in the database table. The second and subsequent rows of such a database table must contain records; no blank rows should be inserted between the field labels and the records, or indeed anywhere between records.

2. Field labels must be unique within a given database table.

3. Entries under each field must be of the same type.

4. The size of a database table must be limited within the design criteria of the package.

We suggest that the 'Invoice Analysis' of Adept Consultants is designed and set out as shown below with the listed field titles and field widths.

Column	Title	Width	Type
A	NAME	21	General or Text
B	DETAILS	20	General or Text
C	No.	8	General or Text
D	ISSUED	11	Short Date, dd/mm/yy
E	PAID?	7	General or Text
F	VALUE	8	Currency, 2 decimals

These widths were chosen so that the whole worksheet could be seen on the screen at once (Fig. 7.1 on the next page).

If you cannot see all the rows of this database on your screen at once (it depends on the configuration of your display under Windows), either adjust the zoom level on the Zoom slide, shown here and located on the bottom right of the screen, or select the **View** tab on the Ribbon, then click the **Zoom** icon in the **Zoom** group and set the **Custom** zoom level to say 90%, as shown in Fig. 7.2, also shown on the next page.

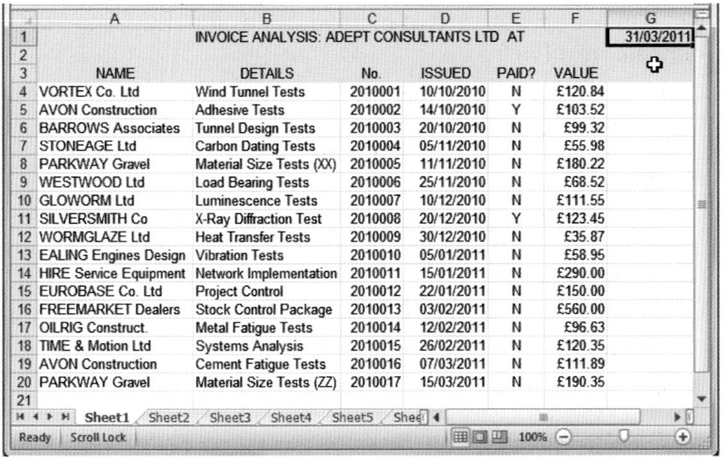

	A	B	C	D	E	F	G
1		INVOICE ANALYSIS: ADEPT CONSULTANTS LTD AT					31/03/2011
2							
3	NAME	DETAILS	No.	ISSUED	PAID?	VALUE	
4	VORTEX Co. Ltd	Wind Tunnel Tests	2010001	10/10/2010	N	£120.84	
5	AVON Construction	Adhesive Tests	2010002	14/10/2010	Y	£103.52	
6	BARROWS Associates	Tunnel Design Tests	2010003	20/10/2010	N	£99.32	
7	STONEAGE Ltd	Carbon Dating Tests	2010004	05/11/2010	N	£55.98	
8	PARKWAY Gravel	Material Size Tests (XX)	2010005	11/11/2010	N	£180.22	
9	WESTWOOD Ltd	Load Bearing Tests	2010006	25/11/2010	N	£68.52	
10	GLOWORM Ltd	Luminescence Tests	2010007	10/12/2010	N	£111.55	
11	SILVERSMITH Co	X-Ray Diffraction Test	2010008	20/12/2010	Y	£123.45	
12	WORMGLAZE Ltd	Heat Transfer Tests	2010009	30/12/2010	N	£35.87	
13	EALING Engines Design	Vibration Tests	2010010	05/01/2011	N	£58.95	
14	HIRE Service Equipment	Network Implementation	2010011	15/01/2011	N	£290.00	
15	EUROBASE Co. Ltd	Project Control	2010012	22/01/2011	N	£150.00	
16	FREEMARKET Dealers	Stock Control Package	2010013	03/02/2011	N	£560.00	
17	OILRIG Construct.	Metal Fatigue Tests	2010014	12/02/2011	N	£96.63	
18	TIME & Motion Ltd	Systems Analysis	2010015	26/02/2011	N	£120.35	
19	AVON Construction	Cement Fatigue Tests	2010016	07/03/2011	N	£111.89	
20	PARKWAY Gravel	Material Size Tests (ZZ)	2010017	15/03/2011	N	£190.35	
21							

Fig. 7.1 A Set of Invoices for Adept Consultants

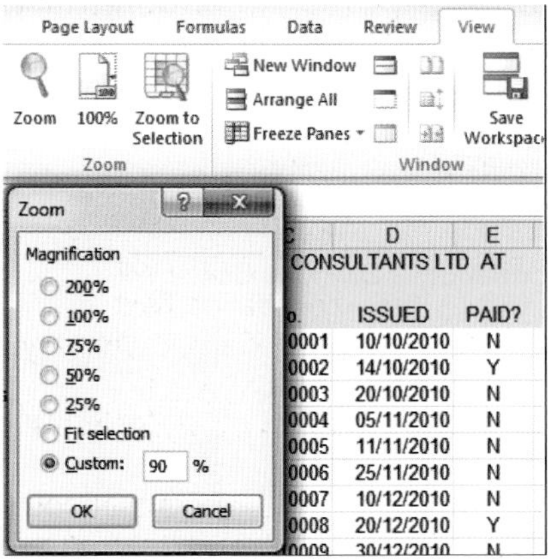

Fig. 7.2 Using the Zoom Button to Set the Zoom Level

To change the width of the various columns to those given on the previous page, use the mouse to drag the vertical separators of the column borders. Next, enter the abbreviated titles, centrally positioned, in row 3, as shown in the worksheet above (Fig. 7.1).

Excel automatically formats entries for you appropriately. For example, if you type 15/3/11, it assumes that this is a date entry and turns it to 15/03/2011. However, if you want to change entries, first click a column letter to select a whole column, then click the down-arrow in the **Number** group, shown in Fig. 7.3 on the next page, and select the appropriate format style from the displayed drop-down list.

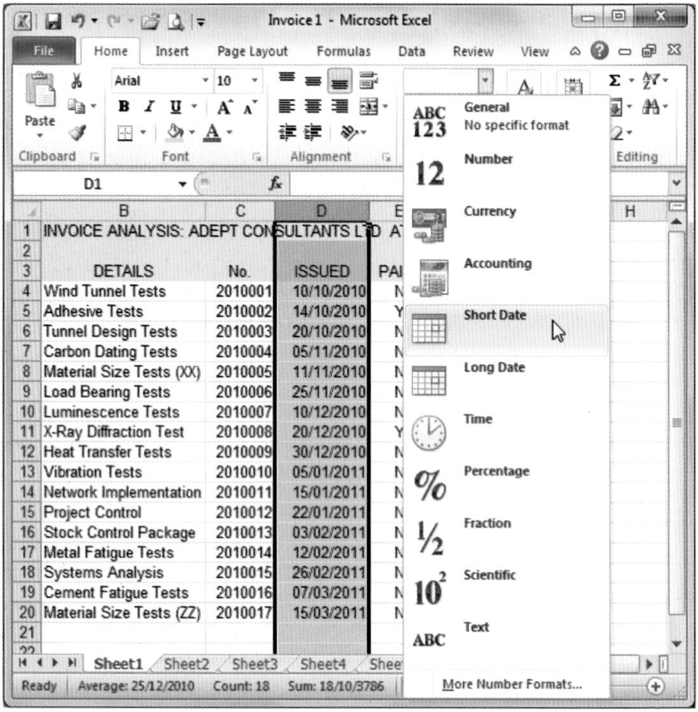

Fig. 7.3 The Format Cells Dialogue Box

The format of columns A, B, C and E should appear in the **Number** group as **General**, with column D as **Date** (which would be the same had you select the **Short Date** category format). Column F is automatically formatted to a **Currency** format with 2 decimal places, if you typed, say £12.55 in a cell (with the preceding currency sign).

Finally, enter the numeric information in your worksheet as shown in Fig. 7.1 and save the worksheet under the filename **Invoice 1**.

You could format your database further by freezing the range A1:G3, then clicking the **Home**, **Font**, **Fill Color** icon to shade the background of the selection to, say, a pale shade of blue. However, we leave this to you, as it is entirely a matter of personal choice.

Sorting a Database List

The records within our database list are in the order in which they were entered, with the invoice 'No.' shown in ascending order. However, we might find it easier to browse through the information if it was sorted in alphabetical order of customer's name. Excel has an easy way to do this.

To use it, highlight the database list (data range A4:F20; don't include the field names in the range to be sorted) and click the **Home**, **Editing**, **Sort & Filter** Ribbon icon and select the **Sort A to Z** option, which displays the sorted results shown in Fig. 7.4 below.

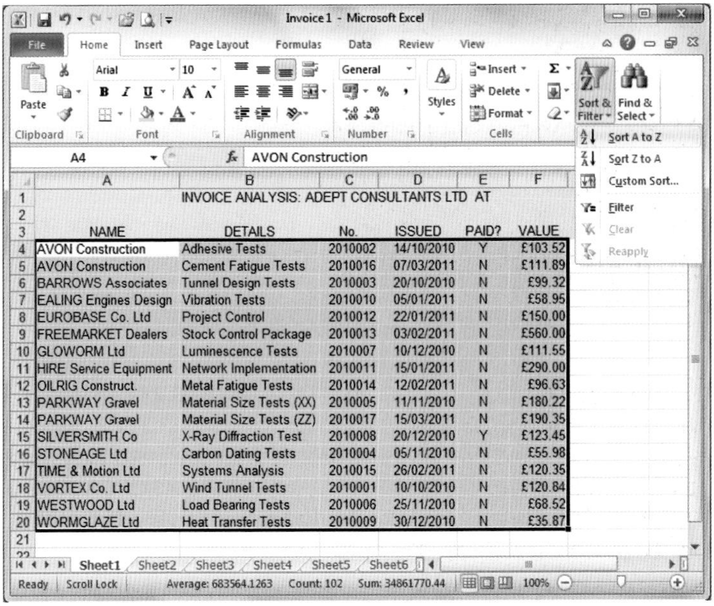

	A	B	C	D	E	F
3	NAME	DETAILS	No.	ISSUED	PAID?	VALUE
4	AVON Construction	Adhesive Tests	2010002	14/10/2010	Y	£103.52
5	AVON Construction	Cement Fatigue Tests	2010016	07/03/2011	N	£111.89
6	BARROWS Associates	Tunnel Design Tests	2010003	20/10/2010	N	£99.32
7	EALING Engines Design	Vibration Tests	2010010	05/01/2011	N	£58.95
8	EUROBASE Co. Ltd	Project Control	2010012	22/01/2011	N	£150.00
9	FREEMARKET Dealers	Stock Control Package	2010013	03/02/2011	N	£560.00
10	GLOWORM Ltd	Luminescence Tests	2010007	10/12/2010	N	£111.55
11	HIRE Service Equipment	Network Implementation	2010011	15/01/2011	N	£290.00
12	OILRIG Construct.	Metal Fatigue Tests	2010014	12/02/2011	N	£96.63
13	PARKWAY Gravel	Material Size Tests (XX)	2010005	11/11/2010	N	£180.22
14	PARKWAY Gravel	Material Size Tests (ZZ)	2010017	15/03/2011	N	£190.35
15	SILVERSMITH Co	X-Ray Diffraction Test	2010008	20/12/2010	Y	£123.45
16	STONEAGE Ltd	Carbon Dating Tests	2010004	05/11/2010	N	£55.98
17	TIME & Motion Ltd	Systems Analysis	2010015	26/02/2011	N	£120.35
18	VORTEX Co. Ltd	Wind Tunnel Tests	2010001	10/10/2010	N	£120.84
19	WESTWOOD Ltd	Load Bearing Tests	2010006	25/11/2010	N	£68.52
20	WORMGLAZE Ltd	Heat Transfer Tests	2010009	30/12/2010	N	£35.87

Fig. 7.4 The Sorted Invoices by Ascending Name

Above, we show the action to be taken and the result of that action.

Another method of sorting data, which allows more control over the sorting options, is to select the **Custom Sort** from the **Sort & Filter** list. This opens the Sort dialogue box displayed in Fig. 7.5, in which we show a composite of the available options for the **Sort by** fields and the **Sort On** items.

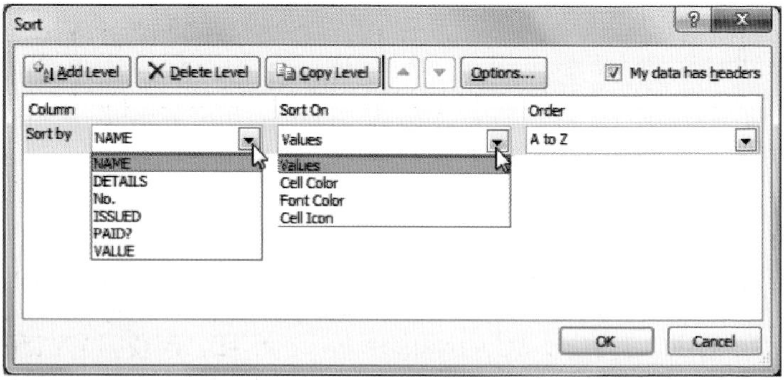

Fig. 7.5 The Sort Dialogue Box

Note that in the **Sort On** list you can choose to sort your database on **Values**, **Cell Color**, **Font Color**, or **Cell Icon**. In the **Sort By** box you can choose the name of the field on which you want to sort the database (in this case NAME). This will be the primary sort key. Clicking the **Add Level** button pointed to in Fig. 7.6, adds another sort level, as shown below.

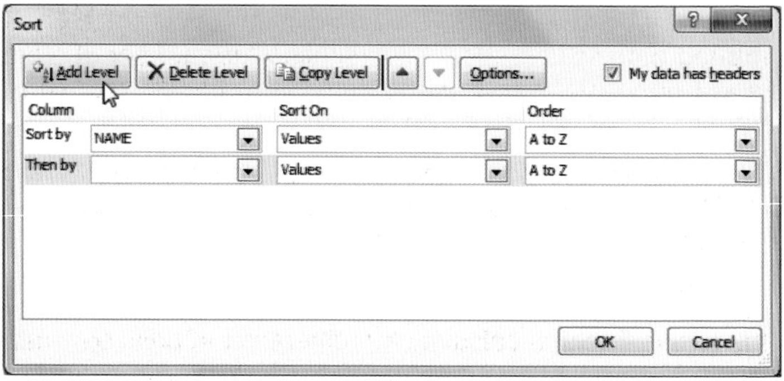

Fig. 7.6 A Two Level Sort

The second sort level allows you additional control over the sorting options, by the selection of a secondary sort key (in this case No.) in the **Then by** list (see the drop-down menu in Fig. 7.5). In this case this ensures that the lowest number invoices appear first, if a company has been issued with more than one invoice. You even have the choice of a third sort key, if you needed one.

The easiest way to return the database to its original sort order is to re-sort it in ascending order of Invoice No. However, for the time being leave it in alphabetical order.

Date Arithmetic

There are several date functions which can be used in Excel to carry out date calculations. For example, if the cell is formatted as **General**, typing the function =DATE(2011,2,25) returns the date 25/02/2011 and changes the format of the cell to 'Date'. The function =DATEVALUE("25/2/2011"), returns the date 25/02/2011 provided the cell is formatted as a **Short Date** category (type dd/mm/yy). If the cell in which you have typed such a function is formatted as **General** or **Number**, then Excel would return the number of days since 1 January 1900.

Typing the function =NOW( ), returns the current date and time as given by your computer's internal clock. The cell is formatted automatically as **Custom** (type dd/mm/yy hh.mm). If the cell was formatted as **Number**, then Excel would have returned a decimal number representing the number of days since 1 January 1900, with the digits after the decimal point representing a fraction of a day.

With Excel 2010 you don't need to use the DATE and DATEVALUE functions when entering dates. You could, for example, write in a cell the formula:

=NOW()–D4

This allows Excel to calculate the difference in days between now and the mentioned date, provided the cell was formatted as **Number**.

We could use this formula to work out the number of overdue days of the unpaid invoices in our example, by typing it in cell G4. However, if you want to compare the numbers you get with those displayed in this book, use instead the following formula:

=$G$1–D4

where $G$1 causes an 'absolute' reference to be made to the contents of cell G1. If the record in row 4 refers to AVON Construction, then the result should be 168 days, provided the cell is formatted as **General**.

However, before we proceed to copy the above formula to the rest of the G column of the database list, we should take into consideration the fact that, normally, such information is not necessary if an invoice has been paid. Therefore, we need to edit the above formula in such a way as to make the result conditional to non-payment of the issued invoice.

The IF Function

The IF function allows comparison between two values using special 'logical' operators. The logical operators we can use are listed below.

Operator	Meaning
=	Equal to
<	Less than
>	Greater than
<=	Less than or Equal to
>=	Greater than or Equal to
<>	Not Equal to

The general format of the IF function is as follows:

IF(Comparison,Outcome-if-true,Outcome-if-false)

which contains three arguments separated by commas.

The first argument of the IF function is the 'logical comparison', the second is what should happen if the outcome of the logical comparison is 'true', while the third is what should happen if the outcome of the logical comparison is 'false'.

Thus, we can incorporate the IF function in the formula we entered in cell G4 to calculate the days overdue only if the invoice has not been paid, otherwise a blank string "   " should be written into the appropriate cell, should the contents of the corresponding E column of a record be anything else but N. The final version of the formula in cell G4 should now correspond to:

=IF(E4="N",$G$1–D4,"   ")

Now copy this formula to the range (G5:G20) and compare your results with those shown in Fig. 7.7 below.

	G4	▾	fx	=IF(E4="N",$G$1-D4," ")			

	A	B	C	D	E	F	G
1		INVOICE ANALYSIS: ADEPT CONSULTANTS LTD AT					31/03/2011
2							
3	NAME	DETAILS	No.	ISSUED	PAID?	VALUE	OVERDUE
4	AVON Construction	Adhesive Tests	2010002	14/10/2010	Y	£103.52	
5	AVON Construction	Cement Fatigue Tests	2010016	07/03/2011	N	£111.89	24
6	BARROWS Associates	Tunnel Design Tests	2010003	20/10/2010	N	£99.32	162
7	EALING Engines Design	Vibration Tests	2010010	05/01/2011	N	£58.95	85
8	EUROBASE Co. Ltd	Project Control	2010012	22/01/2011	N	£150.00	68
9	FREEMARKET Dealers	Stock Control Package	2010013	03/02/2011	N	£560.00	56
10	GLOWORM Ltd	Luminescence Tests	2010007	10/12/2010	N	£111.55	111
11	HIRE Service Equipment	Network Implementation	2010011	15/01/2011	N	£290.00	75
12	OILRIG Construct.	Metal Fatigue Tests	2010014	12/02/2011	N	£96.63	47
13	PARKWAY Gravel	Material Size Tests (XX)	2010005	11/11/2010	N	£180.22	140
14	PARKWAY Gravel	Material Size Tests (ZZ)	2010017	15/03/2011	N	£190.35	16
15	SILVERSMITH Co	X-Ray Diffraction Test	2010008	20/12/2010	Y	£123.45	
16	STONEAGE Ltd	Carbon Dating Tests	2010004	05/11/2010	N	£55.98	146
17	TIME & Motion Ltd	Systems Analysis	2010015	26/02/2011	N	£120.35	33
18	VORTEX Co. Ltd	Wind Tunnel Tests	2010001	10/10/2010	N	£120.84	172
19	WESTWOOD Ltd	Load Bearing Tests	2010006	25/11/2010	N	£68.52	126
20	WORMGLAZE Ltd	Heat Transfer Tests	2010009	30/12/2010	N	£35.87	91
21							

Fig. 7.7 Demonstrating the Use of the IF Function in the Overdue Column

Your results might differ from the ones shown above, if you have used the NOW( ) function in cell G1. Check your work, then save it under the file name **Invoice 2**.

Conditional Formatting

Excel 2010, just like its predecessor, has the ability to format cells according to certain conditions. The idea for this type of formatting is that normally it is very difficult to see patterns and trends in large data by just looking at numbers.

Referring to our small invoicing example, it is rather difficult to see at a glance which companies are behind with their payments by just looking at the numbers in the 'Overdue' column, particularly if the database has been left sorted in alphabetical order of company 'Name'.

In Fig. 7.8 below, we show how conditional formatting works. First, select the data you want to conditionally format; in our case cell range G4:G20. Then, on the **Home** tab click the **Conditional Formatting** button in the **Styles** group and select the **Data Bars** option from the displayed menu. We then chose the **Purple Data Bar** pointed to in Fig. 7.8 on the right of the display.

Note that as the mouse pointer hovers over the other bars, the data in the selected range changes colour. As you can see it is now very easy to identify the long overdue invoices.

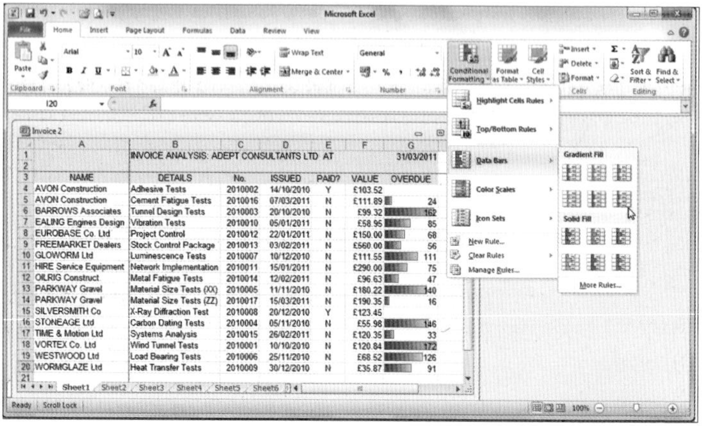

Fig. 7.8 Using Conditional Formatting with Data Bars

In Fig. 7.9, we show the effect of choosing the **Red to Black** from the **Icon Sets** option. This is shown together with the **Purple Data Bar** formatting, but you can choose to remove the latter by selecting the **Clear Rules** option before selecting to mark your data with an icon set.

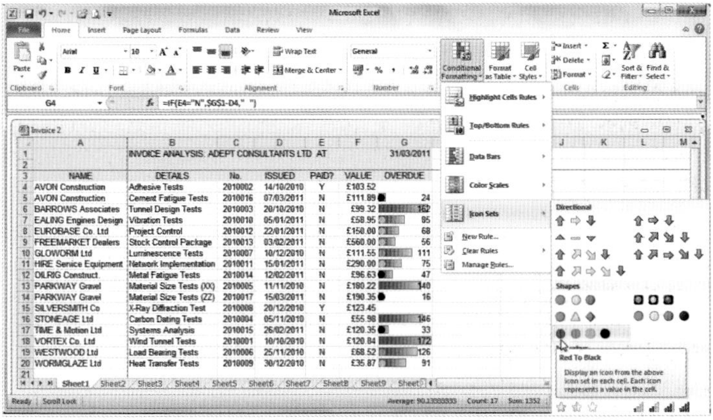

Fig. 7.9 Using Conditional Formatting with Data Bars and Icon Sets

Now save your work again under the filename **Invoice 2** before going on.

Managing Conditional Rules

Assuming that the database **Invoice 2** is on your screen, we will first remove the conditional formatting we had imposed on

it so far. To do this, select the range G4:G20, then click the **Home, Styles, Conditional Formatting** button and select **Clear Rules**, then **Clear Rules from Selected Cells**, as shown in Fig. 7.10.

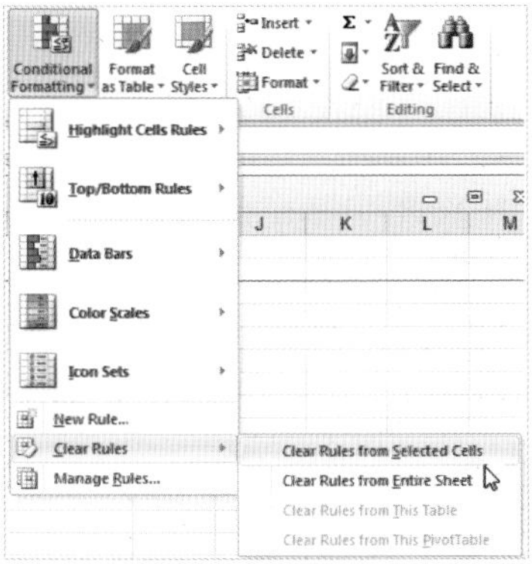

Fig. 7.10 Clearing Conditional Formatting

Next, and with the same range selected, click the **Conditional Formatting** button, but this time select the **New Rules** option from the drop-down menu which opens the **New Formatting Rule** window, the lower part of which is shown in Fig. 7.11, having accepted the default **Format all cells based on their values** on the upper part of the screen.

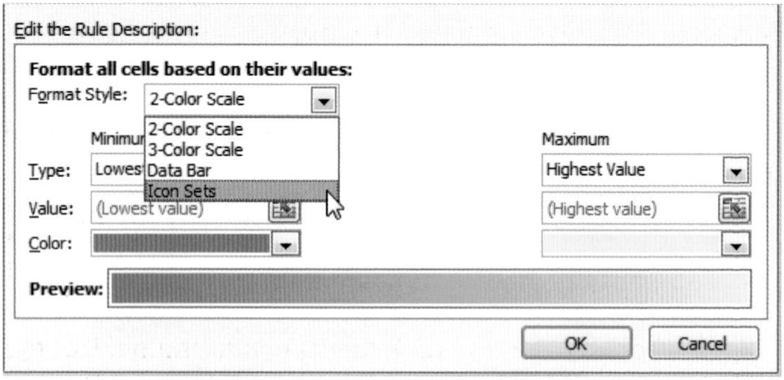

Fig. 7.11 The New Formatting Rule Screen (Lower Part)

We now need to go through a procedure outlined below before we can start querying the database.

- Click the down-arrow against the **Format Style** box and select **Icon Sets** from the drop-down menu pointed to in Fig. 7.11 above which changes the lower part of the screen, as shown in Fig. 7.12, to accommodate our new requirements.

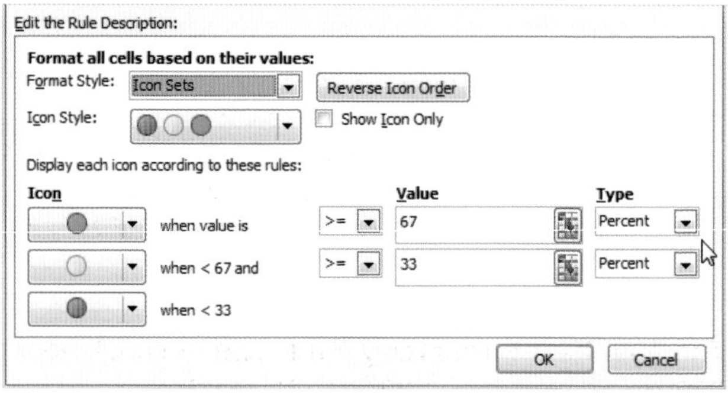

Fig. 7.12 The Changed Lower Part of the New Formatting Rule Screen

- On the changed screen, click the down-arrow against **Percent** and change both the **Type** values from the default to **Number** by choosing from the displayed drop-down menu.

The moment the **Type** is changed to **Number** the corresponding default numerical values of 67 and 33 disappear from their respective places on the window and you can enter your own numbers as follows:

- Click the 🔢 button at the far right of the first **Value** box to open the screen below.

- Type, say, 90 and click the button to the right of the box pointed to above. This causes the number you typed to be entered in the **New Formatting Rule** window.

- Repeat the above procedure, using the second **Value** box, but enter 60 in the displayed New Formatting screen.

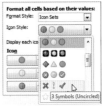

- Click the down-arrow against the **Icon Style** box and select the **3 Symbols (Uncircled)** option from the drop-down menu shown here.

- Check the **Reverse Icon Order** box, so that now the red cross ✖ icon represents **Number** values greater or equal to 90, the yellow exclamation mark ❗ represents values less than 90 but greater or equal to 60, and the green check mark ✔ represents values less than 60.

The final **New Formatting Rule** screen should look like the one shown in Fig. 7.13 on the next page.

Note: The numeric values of 90 and 60 were chosen randomly as an example. You, of course, could type your own values to reflect your specific needs. Explaining this procedure takes a lot longer than executing it, so don't be put off!

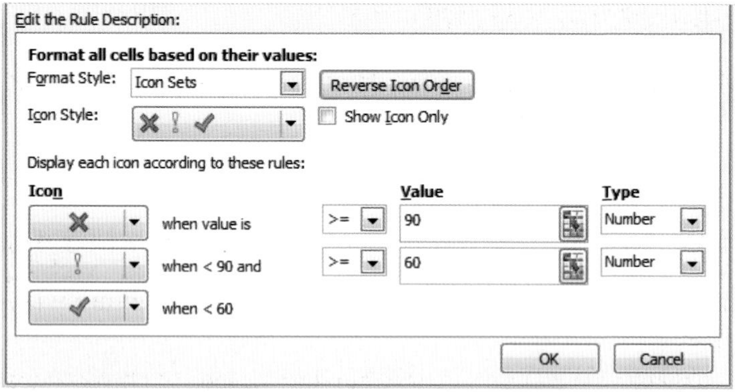

Fig. 7.13 The Final New Formatting Rule Screen (Lower Part)

Finally, click **OK** and on the reopened **Conditional Formatting Rules Manager** screen click **Apply** to see the icons appear on the selected range of cells and, if satisfied, click **OK** to fix them in place. Your screen should now look similar to ours below (Fig. 7.14).

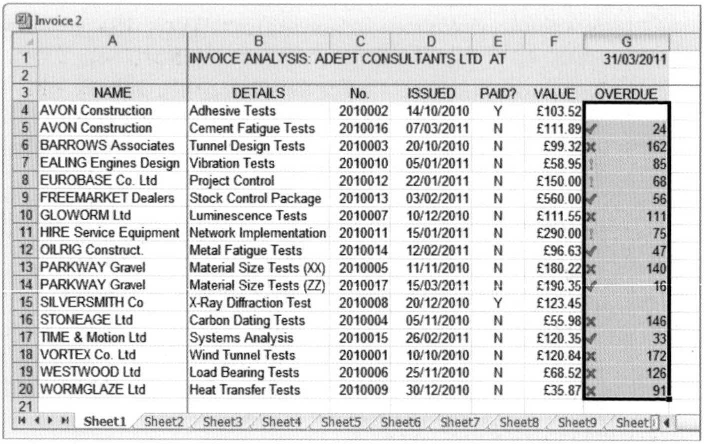

Fig. 7.14 The Excel Screen Showing 3 Conditional Symbols

Finally, to visually enhance the 'Overdue' column, add the **Purple Data Bar** option to it from the **Data Bars** list (see page 96), and save your work as **Invoice 3.**

Searching a Database

We will use the enhanced database of **Invoice 3** to find records with overdue payment.

Filtering Records

Excel 2010 and its predecessor, have a new, very easy way of finding specific records from within a database involving conditional formatting, whether this is by cell colour or by cell symbols (or icons).

To start the process, select the data range which you have

formatted conditionally, in our example this is G3:G20, as shown in Fig. 7.15. Note that we have included the heading 'Overdue' in the selected range.

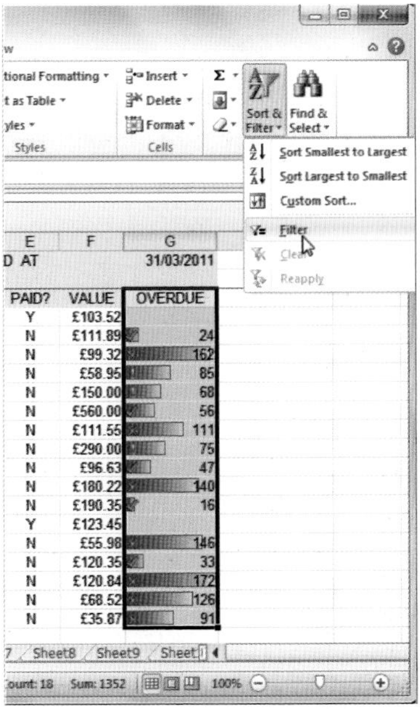

Next, click the **Home**, **Editing**, **Sort & Filter** button, and select **Filter** from the drop-down menu also shown in Fig. 7.15. Doing so, places a down-arrow button on the right of the cell 'Overdue', as shown in Fig. 7.16 on the next page. Clicking this down-arrow, displays a sub-menu, also shown in Fig. 7.16 on the next page.

Fig. 7.15 Preparing to Filter Records

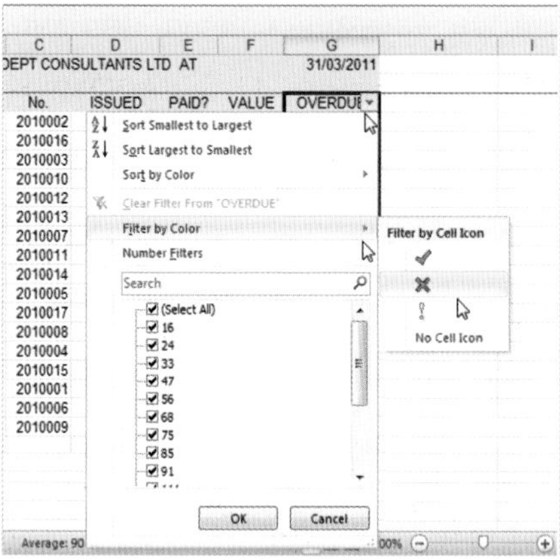

Fig. 7.16 Selecting a Filter

As you can see, you can either use **Number Filters**, in which case you'll have to provide the filter criteria, or **Filter by Color**. Choosing the latter displays a further sub-menu which lists the coloured cell icons you used to conditionally format your selected data range.

If you click the red cross symbol, pointed to above, Excel displays only the data marked with this symbol, as shown in Fig. 7.17 below.

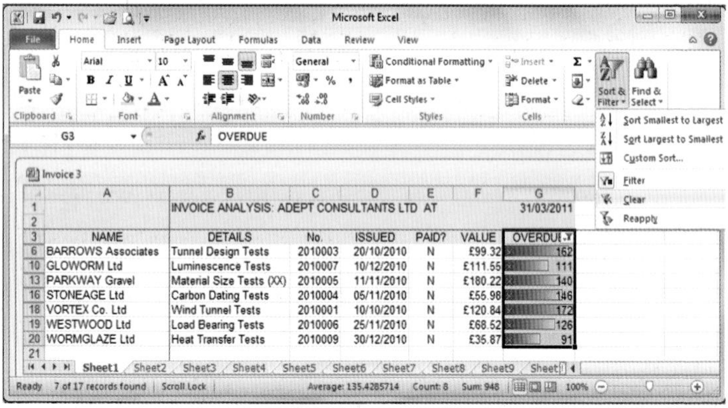

Fig. 7.17 Filtered Data by Symbol

To remove the filter, click the **Clear** option from the drop-down menu shown above. To filter the data with another symbol click the down-arrow in the 'Overdue' cell.

Finding Records

To find records that include specified text, conditional formatting or formulae, use the **Home**, **Editing**, **Find & Select** button, as shown in Fig. 7.18 below.

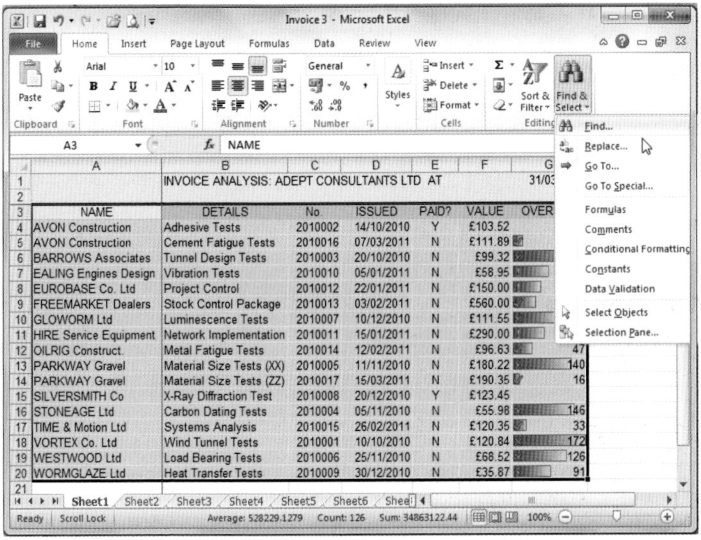

Fig. 7.18 Finding Records with Formulae or Conditional Formatting

It so happens that in our example the range G4:G20 is the only range that contains both conditional formatting and formulae, so the same range is highlighted when we select either of these two options from the drop-down menu shown above.

To find records that contain specified text, we need to select a wider range, in this case A4:G20, then choose the **Find** option from the above drop-down menu. This opens the Find and Replace dialogue box in which you type the text you are looking for in your data.

Now clicking the **Find All** button displays the ranges of the records containing the specified text at the bottom of the dialogue box, and highlights the first such record in the database, as shown in Fig. 7.19 on the next page.

Below, we display a composite showing what we typed in the Find and Replace dialogue box ('Control' in our example) and the result of the **Find All** action.

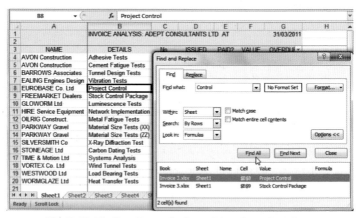

Fig. 7.19 Finding Records Containing Specified Text

Filtering and Removing Duplicate Records

Filtering for unique values and removing duplicate values are closely related operations which display the same results. However, there is a major difference – filtering for unique values only temporarily hides duplicate values, while removing duplicate values permanently deletes such values.

It is, therefore, a good idea to filter for unique values first before permanently removing duplicate values from a database, to confirm that indeed that is what you are intending all along.

To filter for unique values, we need to specify an area of the worksheet for setting our criteria for the search. To do this, follow the steps below very closely:

• First, copy the field names of the database (A3:G3) to an empty area of the worksheet, say, A23:G23 which will form the first line of the 'criteria range'.

- Next, type in cells E24 and F24 the actual criteria (N and >150), respectively.

- Click the **Data**, **Sort & Filter**, **Advanced** button pointed to in Fig. 7.20.

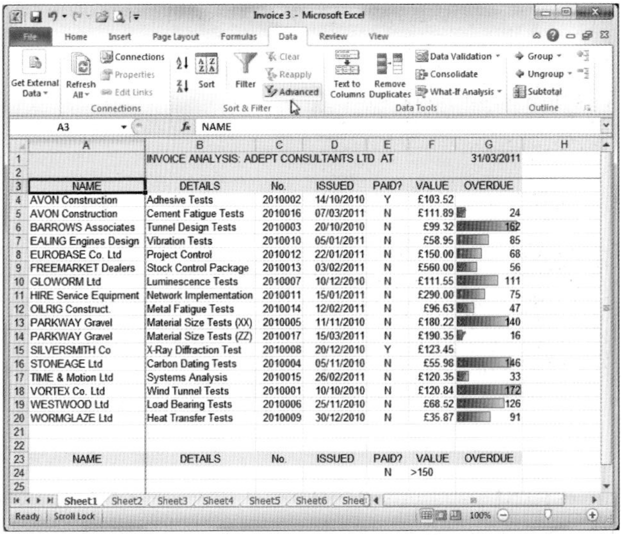

Fig. 7.20 Using the Data, Advanced Filter to Search a Database

- This opens the Advanced Filter dialogue box shown here. Next, click the button pointed to on the right of the **List Range**.

- An Advanced Filter - List range dialogue box opens. Now point to cell A3 and click, then with the **Shift** key pressed down point to cell G20, click and release the **Shift** key. This specifies the **List range** in the dialogue box as $A$3:$G$20 and places a dotted line around the database data, including the field names, as shown in Fig. 7.21 on the next page.

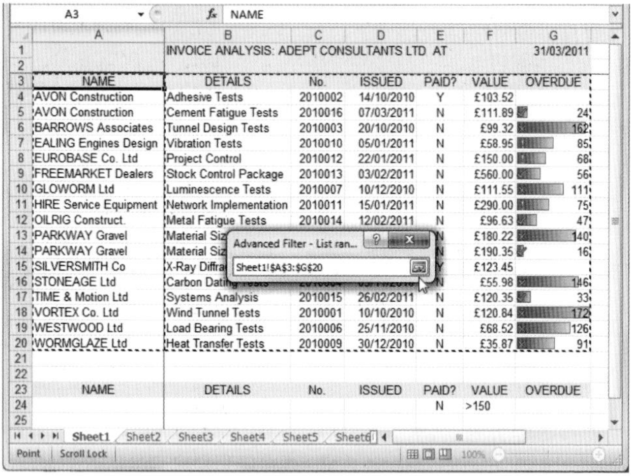

Fig. 7.21 Specifying the Data Range

- Clicking the button pointed to above (to the right of the **Data range** in Fig. 7.21) reopens the Advanced Filter dialogue box, shown here, ready for you to enter the **Criteria range**.

- Now click the button to the right of the **Criteria range** (pointed to above) to open the Advance Filter - Criteria range dialogue box.

- Next, point to cell A23 and click, then with the **Shift** key pressed down, point to cell G24, click and release the **Shift** key. This enters the **Criteria range** as $A$23:$G$24 (including the field names) in the Advanced Filter - Criteria range dialogue box, as shown here. Clicking the button pointed to above, reopens the Advanced Filter dialogue box with the **Criteria range** filled in, as shown at the lower half of Fig. 7.22 on the next page.

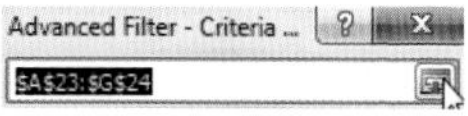

- Finally, clicking the **OK** button, pointed to below, causes Excel to **Filter the list, in-place** by hiding the rows that do not meet the criteria, as shown in the upper-half of Fig. 7.22.

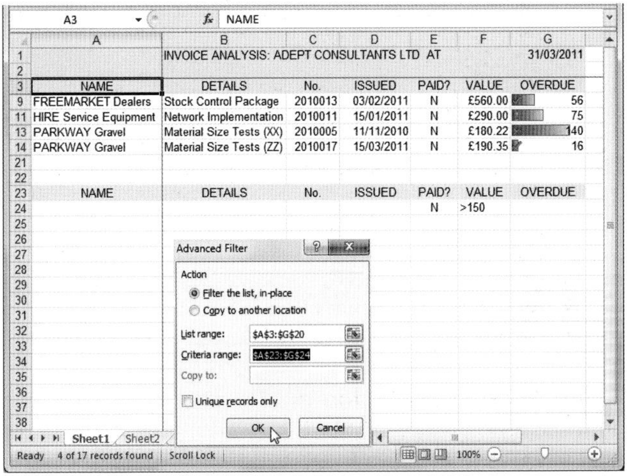

Fig. 7.22 The Filtered Data

As we mentioned previously, the above screen dump is a composite – it shows what action you have to take and the result of that action. To return your display to the full database list, click the `Clear` button in the **Data**, **Sort & Filter** category.

Note: Do not specify an empty line as part of the criterion range, as this has the effect of searching the database for **all** records. The criteria must be entered in the second and subsequent rows of the criterion range, with each entered below the copy of the appropriate field name. A label (text) or a value may be entered exactly as it appears in the database.

In the case of searching a database for label (text), such as under the fields 'NAME' and 'DETAILS' in our example, you can use the two special characters ? and * (known as 'wildcard characters') to match any single character of a label or all characters to the end of the label, as shown in Fig. 7.23 on the next page.

	A	B	C	D	E	F	G	
1		INVOICE ANALYSIS: ADEPT CONSULTANTS LTD AT					31/03/2011	
2								
3	NAME	DETAILS	No.	ISSUED	PAID?	VALUE	OVERDUE	
13	PARKWAY Gravel	Material Size Tests (XX)	2010005	11/11/2010	N	£180.22	140	
14	PARKWAY Gravel	Material Size Tests (ZZ)	2010017	15/03/2011	N	£190.35	16	
21								
22								
23	NAME	DETAILS	No.	ISSUED	PAID?	VALUE	OVERDUE	
24	PARK*				N	>150		
25								

Ready   Filter Mode   100%

Fig. 7.23 Using Wildcard Characters in a Search

To search a database for values, either enter the value as the exact criterion or use a simple numeric comparison, such as >90, in which the logical operators (<, <=, >, >=, <>) can be used. The logical formula generates a value of 1 if the condition is TRUE or a value of 0 if the condition is FALSE.

Several criteria can be entered, either in the same row, or one per row. You choose the former if you want Excel to search for records that match every criterion (i.e. criteria entered are linked with the logical AND), or the latter, if you want Excel to search records that satisfy any of the criteria (i.e. criteria entered are linked with the logical OR). You can also choose a combination of the two, as shown in Fig. 7.24 below. Remember to increase the criteria range to accommodate the extra row.

	A	B	C	D	E	F	G	
1		INVOICE ANALYSIS: ADEPT CONSULTANTS LTD AT					31/03/2011	
2								
3	NAME	DETAILS	No.	ISSUED	PAID?	VALUE	OVERDUE	
9	FREEMARKET Dealers	Stock Control Package	2010013	03/02/2011	N	£560.00	56	
11	HIRE Service Equipment	Network Implementation	2010011	15/01/2011	N	£290.00	75	
13	PARKWAY Gravel	Material Size Tests (XX)	2010005	11/11/2010	N	£180.22	140	
14	PARKWAY Gravel	Material Size Tests (ZZ)	2010017	15/03/2011	N	£190.35	16	
21								
22								
23	NAME	DETAILS	No.	ISSUED	PAID?	VALUE	OVERDUE	
24	PARK*				N			
25						>150		
26								

Ready   4 of 17 records found   100%

Fig. 7.24 Demonstrating the Logical AND and OR Operators

Finally, don't forget to click the **Data, Sort & Filter**, **Clear** button to display the full database list before re-specifying your data and criteria ranges each time you embark on a new search.

To remove duplicate records, first filter them using the method discussed above, but with the criteria given below.

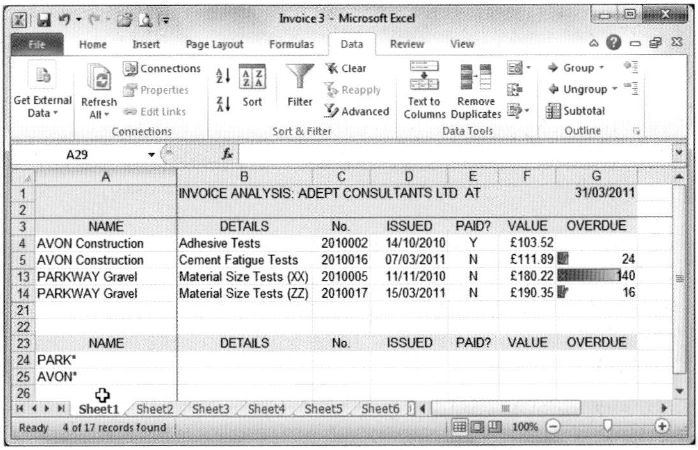

Fig. 7.25 Searching for Duplicates with the Logical OR Operator

If these are the duplicate records found and you want to remove one of each, then click the **Data**, **Data Tools**, **Remove Duplicates** button, and in the displayed dialogue box select the NAME as the only column for the search criteria. Clicking the **OK** button, removes all duplicates from the database – one AVON and one PARKWAY. Try it, then click the **Undo** button to recover the original database.

Extracting Records

To extract records and have them copied into another area of the worksheet, we need to select the **Copy to another location** option in the Advanced Filter dialogue box. But first, we need to set up a second area – the 'output range'. To do this, copy the field names to the cell range $A$28:$G$28 and label it as *OUTPUT RANGE* in cell A27. At the same time, add the label *CRITERIA RANGE* in cell A22. Both of these additions are shown in Fig. 7.26 on the next page.

The screen dump in Fig. 7.26 is a composite – it shows what action you have to take and the result of that action.

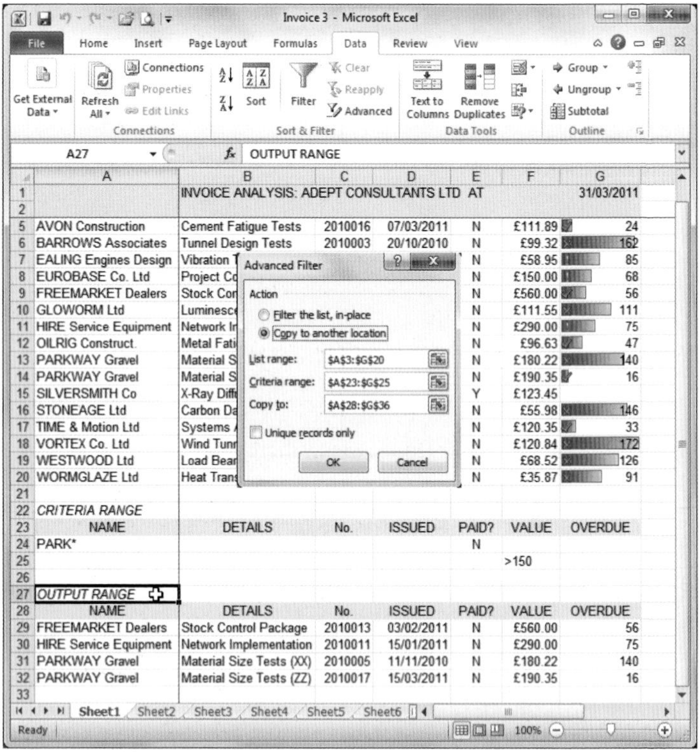

Fig. 7.26 Extracting Data into an Output Range

Note that in our example we have chosen to put the criteria and output ranges in rows below the actual database (perhaps not the best position), rather than on the side of it. This avoids the errors that might ensue should we later decide to insert a row in our database, which will also insert a row in the criteria/output range. For a more structured worksheet layout, see below.

Finally, save the worksheet under the filename **Invoice 4**, before going on.

Structuring a Workbook

In a well designed workbook, areas of calculations using formulae should be kept on a separate sheet from the data entry sheet. The reason for this is to prevent accidental overwriting of formulae that might be contained within the data entry sheet.

As an example, we will use the **Invoice 4** file, but instead of extracting data into the same sheet, we will use another sheet into which to copy the extracted records. To do this, first open file **Invoice 4**, then click the **View**, **Window**, **New Window** button, followed by the **Arrange All** button and in the displayed Arrange Windows dialogue box click the **Horizontal** radio button and click **OK**, as shown in the composite below.

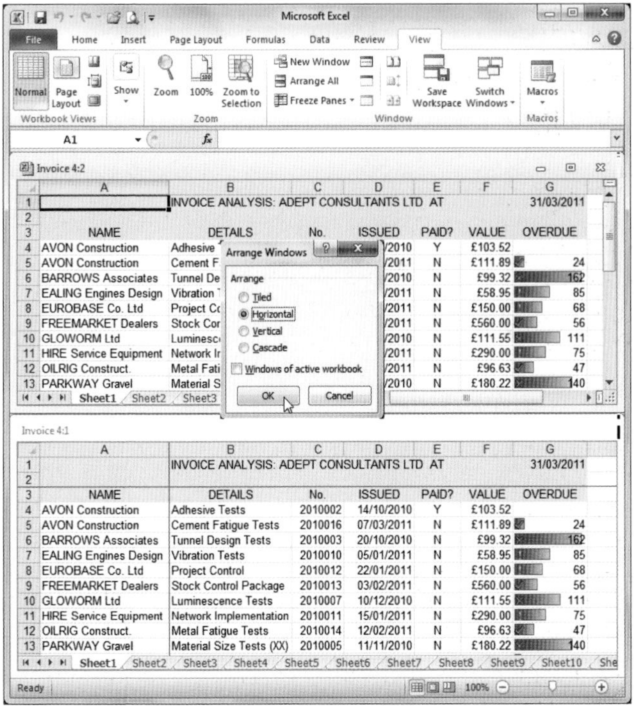

Fig. 7.27 Arranging Windows Horizontally

Next, activate the lower window and click on the Sheet2 tab to display an empty worksheet at the bottom half of the screen, as shown in Fig. 7.28 below.

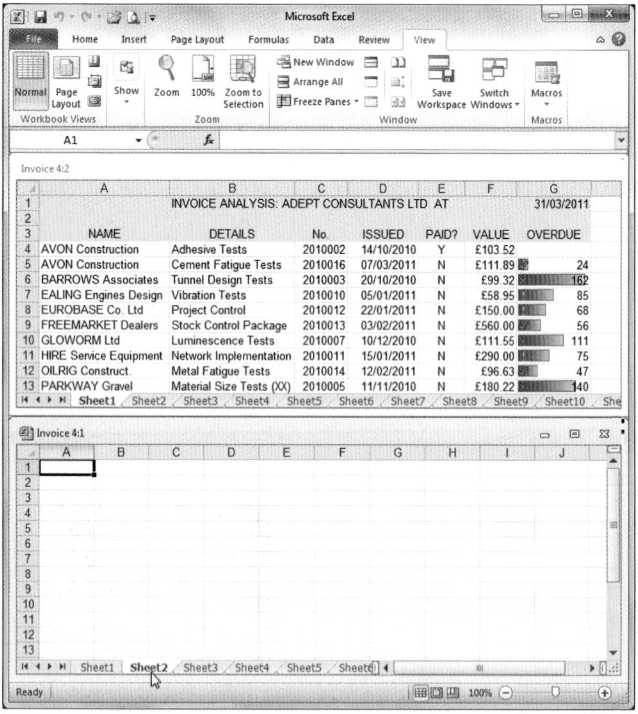

Fig. 7.28 Structuring a Workbook

Now use the **Cut** (Ctrl+X) and **Paste** (Ctrl+V) commands to transfer cell range A22:G28 of Sheet1 to a range starting at cell A1 of Sheet2 and adjust the widths of the various columns to match those of Sheet1 (also, don't forget to delete from Sheet1 any extracted data from a previous search).

Note: Excel only extracts data into an active sheet. Therefore, you must make Sheet2 the active sheet and since the program also requires to know which are the database field labels, place the cell pointer in cell A7, before you use the **Data, Sort & Filter, Advanced** command.

The address in the **List range** box of the Advanced Filter dialogue box must be specified (you can either type it in or use the buttons to the right of the entry box to point to the required range) to indicate the correct address for the database list which is

Sheet1!$A$3:$G$20

The **Criteria range** and the **Copy to** address locations should be similarly prefixed with Sheet2 for correct data extraction. To access the entry box of the latter, click the **Copy to another location** radio button on the Advanced Filter dialogue box, as shown in Fig. 7.29.

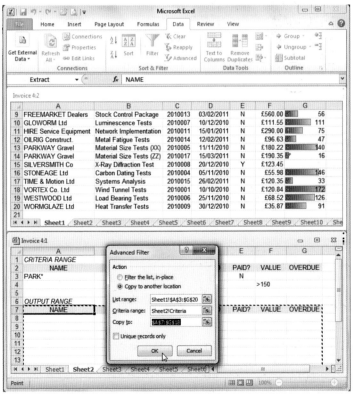

Fig. 7.29 Preparing to Extract Data into Another Location

Pressing the **OK** button causes the records that match the specified criteria to be extracted from Sheet1 and copied into Sheet2, as shown in Fig. 7.30 below.

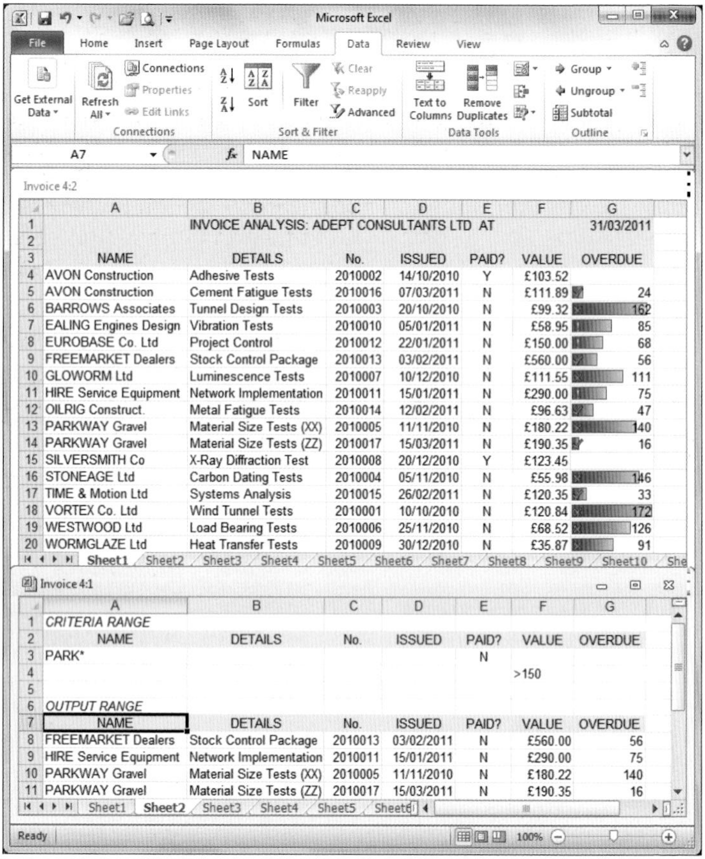

Fig. 7.30 Extracted Data into Sheet2 of Workbook

Save the workbook under the file name **Invoice 5**.

Another aspect of structuring is the provision of a screen with technical information about the contents of the particular workbook; a kind of overview of the function of the worksheet application. This area should also contain instructions for the use of the particular application at hand.

Information on structuring can help you in the future, or help others to learn and use an application easily and effectively. If you use range names, then include a range name table in your information screen(s).

Finally, provide a separate sheet within a workbook, or a separate worksheet altogether, for macros (discussed in Chapter 10), which are in a programming language that allows you to chain together commands. Sensitive sheets or indeed whole workbooks can be protected using the **Review** tab, then clicking either the **Protect Sheet** or the **Protect Workbook** button in the **Changes** group, according to your application needs, to restrict cell entries to unprotected cells. This prevents accidental changes being made to cells containing formulae.

A good spreadsheet design, using the 3-dimensional ability of Excel could be as shown in Fig. 7.31 below, but bearing in mind that the headings of the various workbook sheets could be different. They would largely depend on the application.

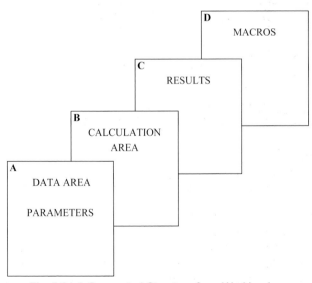

Fig. 7.31 A Suggested Structure for a Workbook

8

Other Tools and Capabilities

As well as the **Spelling** and **Thesaurus** tools, to be found under the **Proofing** group of the **Review** tab of the Ribbon, Excel includes a **Formula Auditing** capability (to be found in the **Formulas** tab) and tools to carry out What-If Analysis (to be found in the **Data** tab), used to solve problems such as the **Goal Seek**, **Data Tables**, and **Scenarios**. A short description of each of these is given below.

Formula Auditing

You use the Formula Auditing capability of Excel to analyse the way your worksheet is structured, or for locating the source of errors in formulae. You will find everything you need in the **Formula Auditing** group of the **Formulas** tab of the Ribbon, as shown in Fig. 8.1.

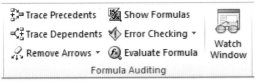

Fig. 8.1 The Formula Auditing Group

In this you can specify what you want to audit on the current file. For a description of the options see below.

The Formula Auditing options have the following functions:

Option	Function
Trace Precedents	Identifies with arrows all cells that affect the currently selected cell.

Trace Dependents	Identifies with arrows all cells that are affected by the value of the currently selected cell.
Remove Arrows	Removes the identifying arrows placed on the worksheet as a result of invoking the previous options.
Show Formulas	Displays the actual formulae you have entered in cells with the effective range of their arguments marked in blue outline.
Error Checking	Identifies all cells involved in the production of an error, such as a circular reference.
Evaluate Formula	Launches the Evaluation Formula dialogue box to debug a formula by evaluating each part of the formula in the selected cell.
Watch Window	Watch cells and their formulae on the Watch Window, as changes are made to the worksheet even when the cells are out of view.

As an example, in Fig. 8.2 on the next page, we show an audit on the file **Project 3**, for the first two options. For the first option, select cell E11, then click the **Formulas**, **Formula Auditing**, **Trace Precedents** ⟬Trace Precedents⟭ button, while for the second option, select cell B12, then click the **Trace Dependents** ⟬Trace Dependents⟭ button.

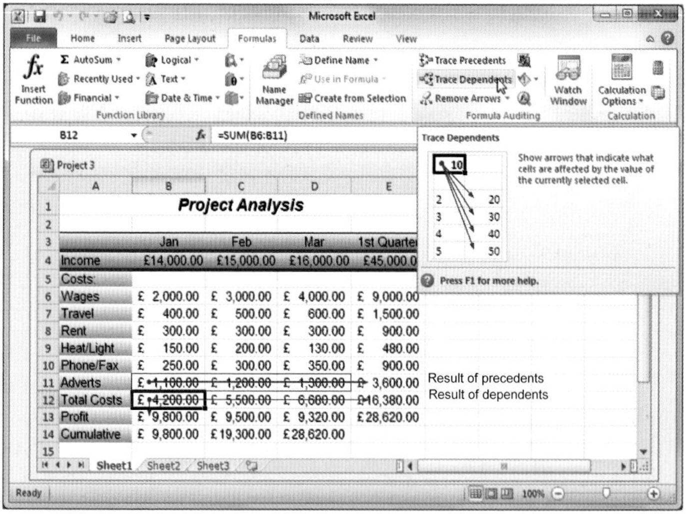

Fig. 8.2 Illustrating the Trace Precedents and Trace Dependents
Options

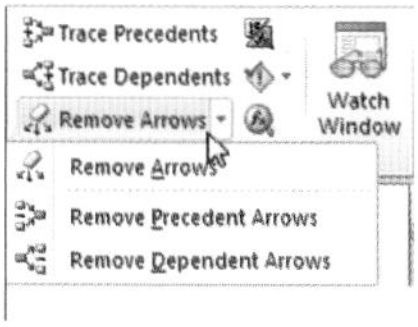

To remove the arrows resulting from the above choice of auditing options, click the **Remove Arrows** button, shown here, then click the **Show Formulas**  button, or use the key combination (**Ctrl+`**) to display Fig. 8.3 (` is the Grave sign on the key board, to be found below the ESC key).

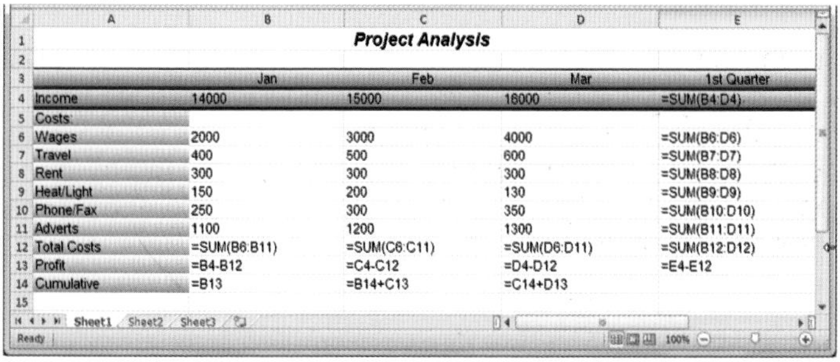

Fig. 8.3 Illustrating the Show Formulas Option

To return to normal viewing, click the **Show Formulas** button, or use **Ctrl+`** again – they act as a toggle switch.

As an example of evaluating a formula step by step, select cell D14 then click the **Formulas**, **Formula Auditing**, **Evaluate Formula** ![Show Formulas] button to open the Evaluate Formula dialogue box displaying the formula C14+D13 with the first section of the formula underlined, as shown in Fig. 8.4 below.

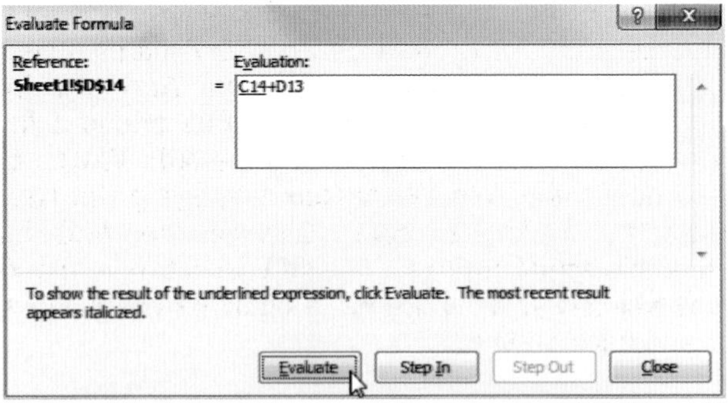

Fig. 8.4 The Evaluate Formula Dialogue Box

Clicking the **Evaluate** button at the bottom of the dialogue box displays its value and moves the underline to the next section of the formula, as shown in Fig. 8.5 below.

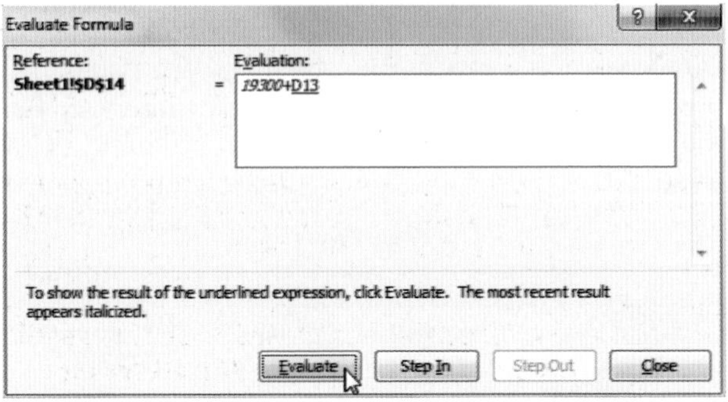

Fig. 8.5 Evaluating the First Part of the Formula

Clicking the **Evaluate** button again, displays the value of the second section of the formula and underlines the two displayed values. Clicking the **Evaluate** button yet again, displays the result that is also shown in cell D14 in the worksheet. Clicking the **Evaluate** button once more, starts the process all over again.

The Watch Window

The adoption of the Watch Window allows the calculated values of specified cells to be displayed in a window as you work so that you can see the results even if you are working on another, faraway part of the worksheet or workbook.

In the composite display in Fig. 8.6 below, we have first selected cells E11, E12, and E13 of the **Project 3** file, then clicked the **Formulas**, **Formula Auditing**, **Watch Window** button shown here. This opens a floating Watch Window, and clicking the **Add Watch** button opens the Add Watch box displaying the range of the selected worksheet cells. Clicking the **Add** button, transfers this selection from the Add Watch box to the Watch Window which now remains visible on screen even when you select another worksheet.

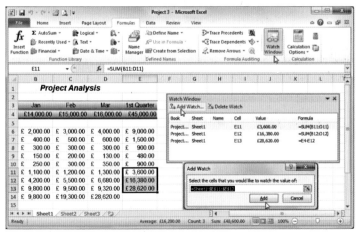

Fig. 8.6 Illustrating the Use of the Watch Window

You can remove individual parts of what you were watching, by clicking their entry in the Watch Window dialogue box and then clicking the **Delete Watch** button which is situated on the same dialogue box and to the right of the **Add Watch** button. To remove all watched items at once, click the **Formulas**, **Formula Auditing**, **Watch Window** button again – it acts as a toggle switch.

What-If Analysis

Excel allows you to create and manage Scenarios for What-If Analysis. A scenario is a set of values that Excel saves and can substitute automatically on your worksheet. You can use scenarios to forecast the outcome of a worksheet model.

Creating a Scenario

We will use **Project 3** to find out what the effect on the first quarter's 'Profit' of Adept Consultants would be if the 'Wages' in the month of January were increased (a) to the level of February, and (b) to the level of March.

To start, select cell B6 then click the **Data**, **Data Tools**, **What-If Analysis** button and select the **Scenario Manager** from the drop-down list, as shown here in Fig. 8.7 to the left, to open the dialogue box shown in Fig. 8.8 below.

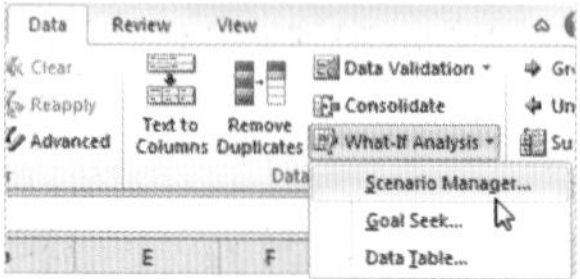

Fig. 8.7 The What-If Options

Next, click the **Add** button on the displayed Scenario Manager box to open the **Add Scenario** dialogue box, shown in Fig. 8.9 on the next page. In this newly displayed box, we gave the name of our first scenario as 'Equal to Feb', as shown, and pressed the **OK** button.

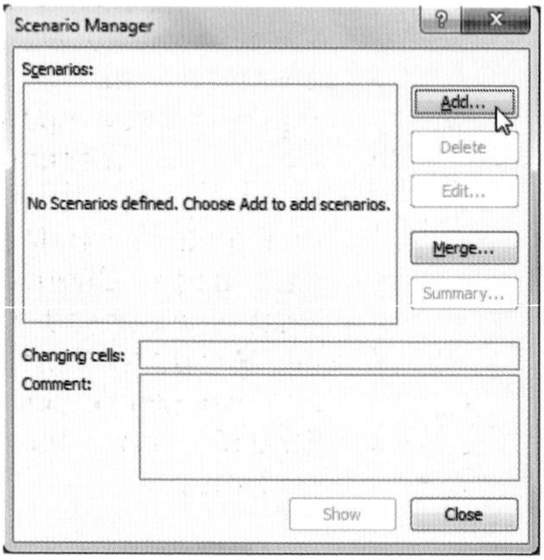

Fig. 8.8 Illustrating the Scenario Manager

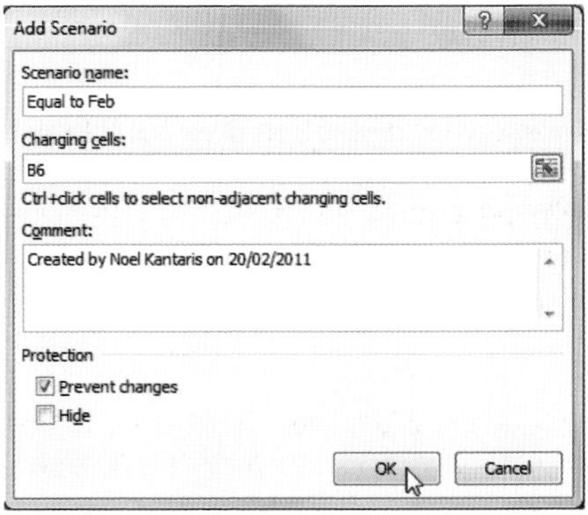

Fig. 8.9 The Add Scenario Dialogue Box

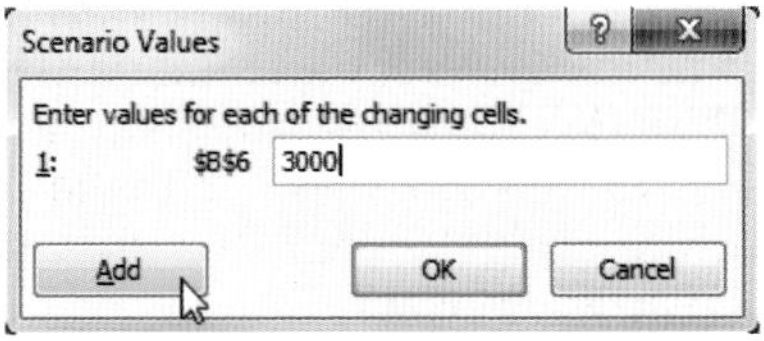

Fig. 8.10 The Scenario Values
Dialogue Box

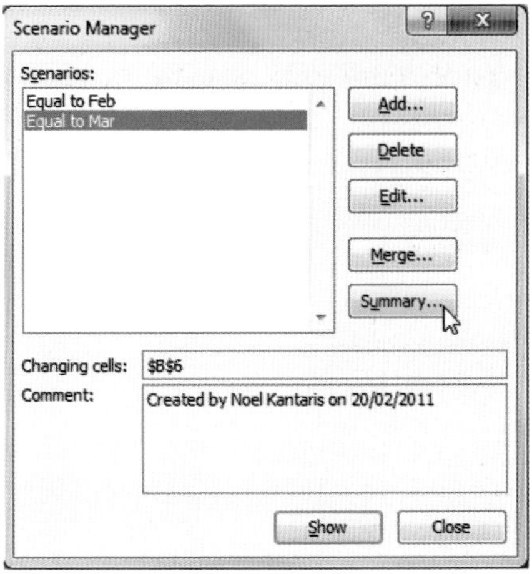

Fig. 8.11 The Scenario Manager Screen

This opens the Scenario Values box shown in Fig. 8.10, in which we typed the value of 3000, being the value we want cell $B$6 to change to.

Next, click the **Add** button to open the Add Scenario dialogue box once more to add the name of our second scenario as 'Equal to Mar' and give it a value of 4000 by repeating the process described above.

Now, clicking the **OK** button, causes these scenarios to transfer into the Scenario Manager window as shown in Fig. 8.11.

Next, click the **Summary** button, pointed to in Fig. 8.11, to open the Scenario Summary box shown in Fig. 8.12 on the next page. Change what is displayed in the **Result cell** box by selecting cells E6,E13 on your worksheet.

This displays the selected worksheet cells with a dotted outline, as shown below.

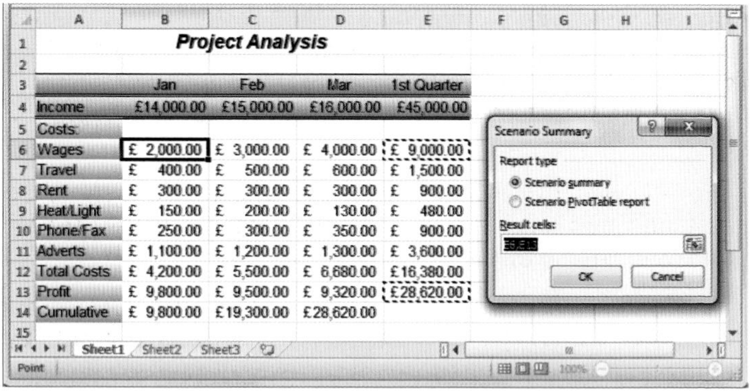

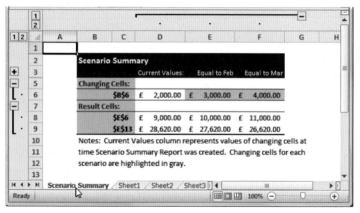

Fig. 8.12 The Scenario Summary Box

Clicking the **OK** button, opens the Scenario Summary sheet as shown in Fig. 8.13 below.

Fig. 8.13 The Scenario Summary Sheet

Excel displays all three results; 'Current Values', 'Equal to Feb', and 'Equal to Mar' for you to compare at a glance. Save this workbook under the filename **Tools 1**.

If you wanted to remove the Scenario Summary sheet from your workbook, right-click it and select **Delete** from the drop-down menu.

The Goal Seek

You use **Goal Seek** to fine-tune a formula that gives you the required result by changing one of the variables that affect the final value. As an example, we will use the information in the **Tools 1** file. If you don't have this file, use the **Project 3** file.

To effectively use Goal Seek, first type the formula to be fine-tuned by Excel in a cell. We will use the **=sum(B4:D4)** formula in cell E4 of **Sheet1** of our example.

Next, click the **Data**, **Data Tools**, **What-If Analysis** button and select **Goal Seek** from the drop-down menu to display the Goal Seek dialogue box as shown in Fig. 8.14.

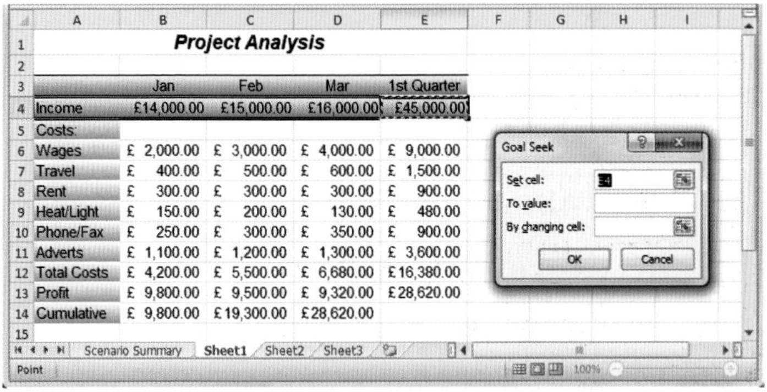

Fig. 8.14 Using the Goal Seek

In this dialogue box you can specify in the **Set cell** box the address or range name of the cell that contains the formula you want to fine-tune, E4 in our example. In the **To value** box you type the value you want the formula in the formula cell to equate to when Goal Seek solves the problem, 40000 in our example, while in the **By changing cell** box you type the address of the cell whose value Goal Seek can change, $B$4 in our example.

Click the **OK** button to find an answer to the problem, displayed in Fig. 8.15 on the next page – it changed the contents of B4 from £14,000 to £9,000. If it can't be done, you will be informed.

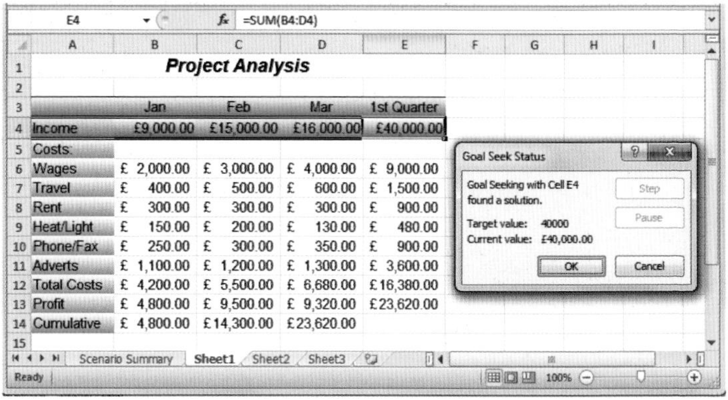

Fig. 8.15 Goal Seek Finding a Solution

If you don't want to lose the original values in the adjustable cell, then press the **Cancel** button.

What-if Data Tables

What-if data tables are used if you require to calculate and display the results of substituting different values for one or more (up to three) variables in a formula.

For example, suppose we wanted to examine the effect to the quarterly profits of Adept Consultants if we varied the quarterly income from £35,000 to £55,000, in steps of £5,000. This problem is rather trivial, but suppose at the same time we expected a wage award increase of between 0% to 3%, while all other costs were tied to inflation which could change from 3% to 5%. This becomes rather more difficult to analyse. However, using what-if tables reduces the problem to something more manageable.

A Two-Input What-if Data Table

To illustrate the above problem, but simplifying it by forgetting inflation, we will use the **Tools 1** file. First select cell A4 and click the **View**, **Window, Freeze Panes** button, and select the **Freeze First Column** option, then fill in the range F2:K9, as shown in Fig. 8.16 and save the result as **Tools 2**.

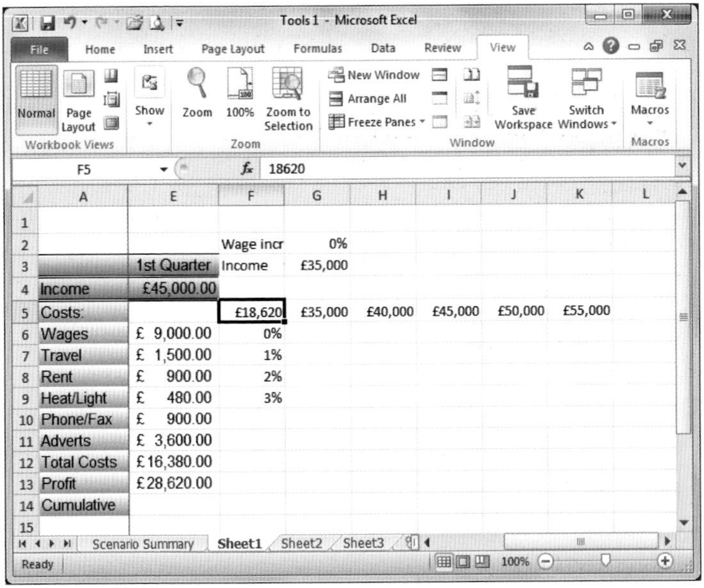

Fig. 8.16 Designing a Two-Input What-if Data Table

Note: A two-input what-if data table has two input cells – in our example these are: Input 1 in cell G2 (which refers to the rows) and input 2 in cell G3 (which refers to the columns), representing 'Wage increases' and 'Income', respectively. The value in each of these cells is the first value in their respective ranges, which are F6:F9 and G5:K5. Thus, income varies from £35,000 to £55,000, while wage increases vary from 0% to 3%.

Finally, a formula is required in cell F5 which represents profits and which refers to the two input cells defined above. The formula used is:

=G3-(E6*(1+G2)+SUM(E7:E11))

To verify that this formula is correct, change the input in the 'Income' cell (G3) to £45,000, which should give you the same profit in cell F5 as that shown in cell E13.

The formula in a two-input what-if table must be placed in the top-left corner of the table (F5 in our example). Which cell is declared as a 'row input' and a 'column input' in the Table dialogue box is very important.

In the case of a one-input what-if table, Excel expects the input range to be either in one column, with the formula placed in the row above the first value and one cell to the right of the input range, or in one row, with the formula placed in the column to the left of the first value and one cell below the row of the input range.

Before going on, save your work under the filename **Tools 2**, then select the effective table range F5:K9. Next, click the **Data**, **Data Tools**, **What-If Analysis** button, select the **Data Table** option and enter $G$3 in the **Row input cell** box of the displayed dialogue box, and $G$2 in the **Column input Cell** box as shown in Fig. 8.17.

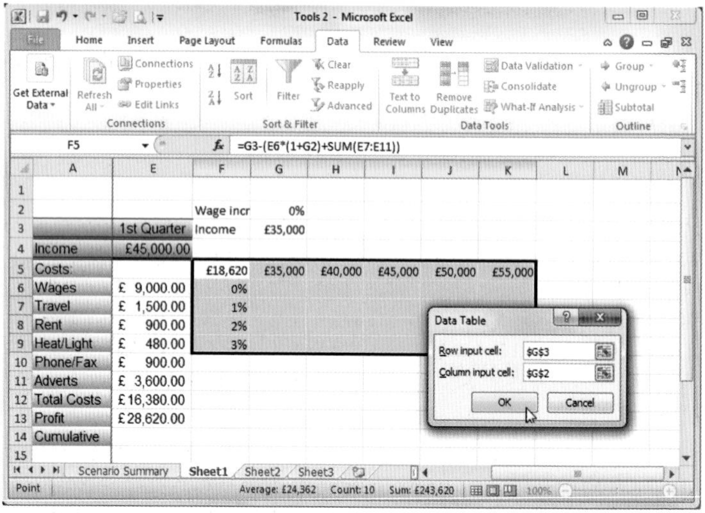

Fig. 8.17 Allocating Parameters to a Two-Input What-if Table

Pressing the **OK** button displays the results shown in Fig. 8.18 on the next page.

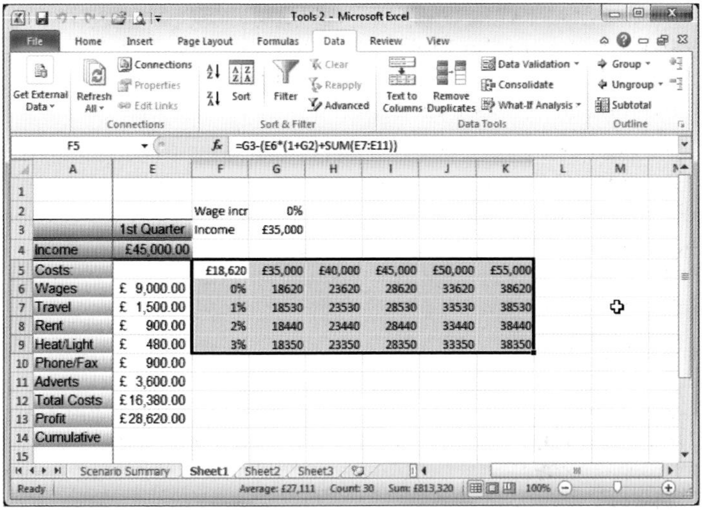

Fig. 8.18 The Results of a Two-Input What-if Data Table

You could now save this example under the file name **Tools 3**.

Editing a Data Table

The input values and formula in the top leftmost column of a data table can be edited at any time. However, the actual results calculated within the data table cannot be edited individually, because they are an array. Some editing operations require you to select the entire data table, while others require you to select only the resulting values. For example:

- To clear the resulting values from a data table, select the resulting values only (G6:K9 in our example) and press the **Del** key. Individual resulting values cannot be cleared separately.

- To copy resulting values from a data table, select them and use the **Copy** (**Ctrl+C**) command. Doing this results in copying the values only, not the formulae for those values.

Subsequent use of the **Paste Special** command converts the resulting values array into a range of constant values.

• To move, delete, or modify a table, first select the entire data table (F5:K9 in our example). If you are moving the table, having selected it, then click the border of the selection and drag it to a new location on your worksheet.

The Solver

You use the Solver if you want to analyse data in a worksheet and solve 'what-if' type problems. Solver is ideal for problems that have more than one answer. It can investigate different options and present you with alternative solutions, including the best match to your requirements.

Before you can use the Solver, you might need to install it, as it is an add-in and it might not have been installed automatically by **Setup** – you will know if it is installed already as its name will then appear on the **Data** tab of the Ribbon in the **Analysis** group. If it does not, you will need to install it by clicking the 🗀 File button, then **Options** pointed to in Fig. 8.19.

Fig. 8.19 The File Options Button

In the displayed Excel Options dialogue box, click the **Add-Ins** option in the left pane, select **Solver Add-in** in the **Inactive Applications Add-ins**, as shown in Fig. 8.20, and click **Go**.

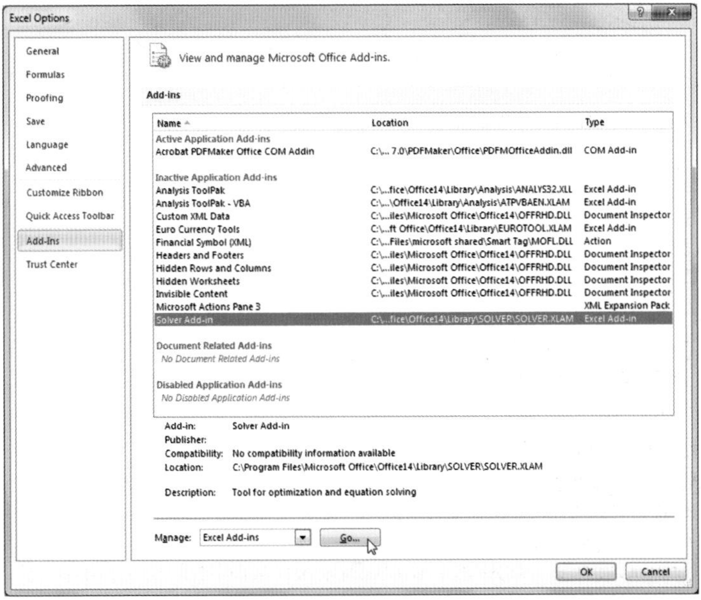

Fig. 8.20 The Add-Ins in the Excel Options Dialogue Box

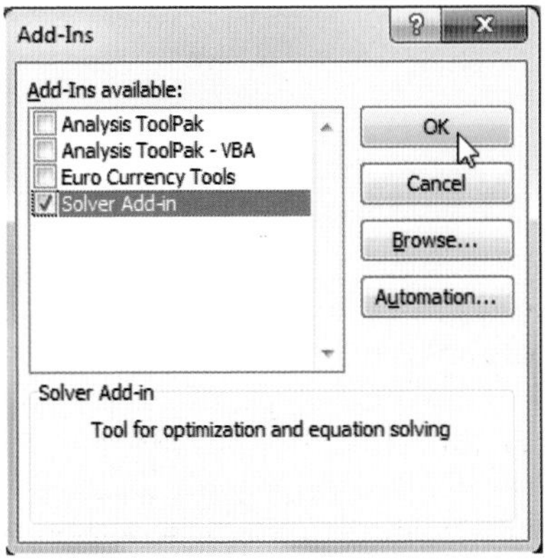

In the displayed Add-Ins dialogue box shown here in Fig. 8.21, select the **Solver Add-in** check box, and then click **OK**. The program will then automatically install it for you.

Fig. 8.21 The Available Add-ins in the Add-ins box

To use the Solver option, you start with a worksheet model. Solver problems can be set up in one or more worksheet files in memory, by selecting which cells to adjust, adding logical formulae and defining the limits of the required answers.

As an example, let us analyse more closely Adept Consultants' 1st Quarter results. We use the information held in Sheet1 of the **Tools 1** file.

On Sheet2 of the file, add the text and equations shown in Fig. 8.22 below and save the resultant workbook under the file name **Tools 4**.

	A	B	C	D	E
2					
3		Type	Home	Abroad	Total
4					
5	Number		30	20	
6	Income/consultancy		=Sheet1!E4/50*2/3	=Sheet1!E4/50*3/2	=C5*C6+D5*D6
7	Costs/consultancy		=Sheet1!E12/50*2/3	=Sheet1!E12/50*3/2	
8	Hours/consultancy		60	160	
9					
10	Total Income		=C5*C6	=D5*D6	=C10+D10
11	Total Costs		=C5*C7	=D5*D7	=C11+D11
12	Total Hours		=C5*C8	=D8*D5	=C12+D12
13	Profit/Hour		=(C10-C11)/C12	=(D10-D11)/D12	
14	Total Profit		=C12*C13	=D13*D12	=C14+D14
15					
16	Constraints				
17	Maximum hours available<=6000				
18	Minimum Home Consultancies >=25				
19	Minimum Abroad Consultancies >=15				
20	Minimum Profit >=28600				
21					

Fig. 8.22 The Solver Exercise Entered in Sheet2 of the Workbook

What we assume in this exercise is that Adept Consultants operate both at home and abroad. In the first quarter they undertook 30 consultancies at home and 20 consultancies abroad. We also assume that the income per consultancy for 'Home' is equal to 2/3 of the total income for the 1st quarter, while the income per consultancy for 'Abroad' is equal to 1/3 of the total income for the 1st quarter.

Similarly the costs per consultancy for 'Home' and 'Abroad' are assumed to be in the same ratio as those for the income. However, the time spent (hours per consultancy) are set for 'Home' and 'Abroad' to be 60 and 160 respectively, because of extra travelling time.

In the range C10:D14 of the worksheet we proceed to work out the 'Total Profit' in terms of 'Profit per hour'. The reason for this is that later in this chapter we will examine what happens to profit/hour if the hours taken to complete a consultancy were to be varied.

Below we show the actual values that should appear in the worksheet if all formulae are entered correctly. The values in column E either summate the two types of consultancies or contain crosschecks of our workings. Remember that you can use the **Ctrl+`** key combination (see page 123) to return to the formula screen (Fig. 8.22), if you need to make any corrections so that you get the correct values shown below.

	Type	Home	Abroad	Total
5 Number		30	20	
6 Income/consultancy		£ 600.00	£ 1,350.00	£ 45,000.00
7 Costs/consultancy		£ 218.40	£ 491.40	
8 Hours/consultancy		60	160	
10 Total Income		£ 18,000.00	£ 27,000.00	£ 45,000.00
11 Total Costs		£ 6,552.00	£ 9,828.00	£ 16,380.00
12 Total Hours		1,800.00	3,200.00	5,000.00
13 Profit/Hour		6.36	5.37	
14 Total Profit		£ 11,448.00	£ 17,172.00	£ 28,620.00
16 Constraints				
17 Maximum hours available<=6000				
18 Minimum Home Consultancies >=25				
19 Minimum Abroad Concultancies >=15				
20 Minimum Profit >=28600				

Fig. 8.23 The Results of the Solver Exercise Entered in Sheet2 of the Workbook After Entering All Constraints

Cells E12 and E14 hold the total time spent in consultancies and the total profit made, respectively, which is very important information.

What we would like to do now is to increase the consultancies to make up the maximum available time in the three month period, which is 6000 hours, while maximising the profit. The question is 'what mixture of consultancies (home or abroad) is more profitable?'

Starting the Solver

?₊ Solver   To start Solver click the **Data**, **Analysis**, **Solver** button, shown here, which displays the Solver Parameters dialogue box shown in Fig. 8.24.

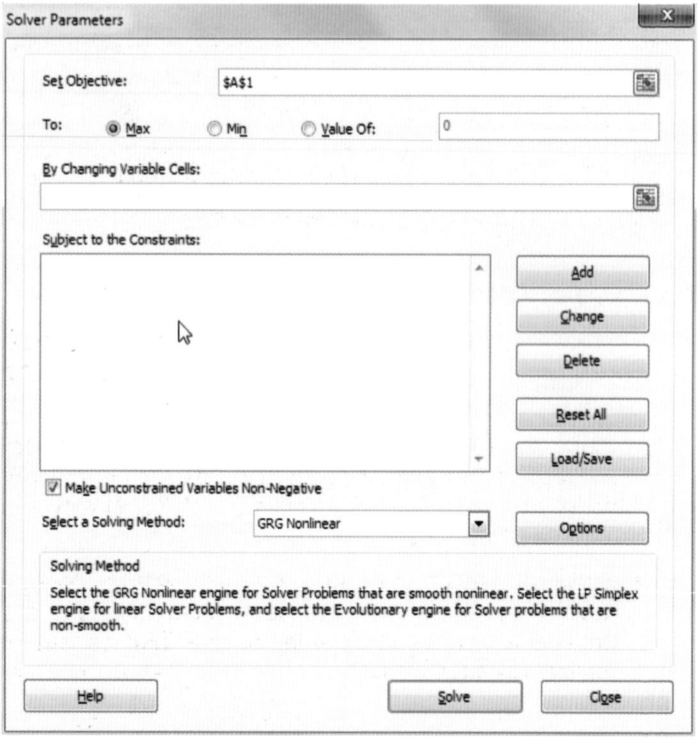

Fig. 8.24 The Solver Parameters Box

Next, we enter the constraints under which we will impose a solution to our problem. These can be added, changed or deleted using the three buttons at the bottom of the Solver Parameters dialogue box.

Entering Constraints

At the bottom of the worksheet we have included certain constraints, discussed below. These are entered as logical formulae using the Add Constraint dialogue box, shown in Fig. 8.25 below, opened by clicking the **Add** button on the Solver Parameters dialogue box to enter the first constraint. Then by clicking the **Add** button on the Add Constraint box to add subsequent constraints.

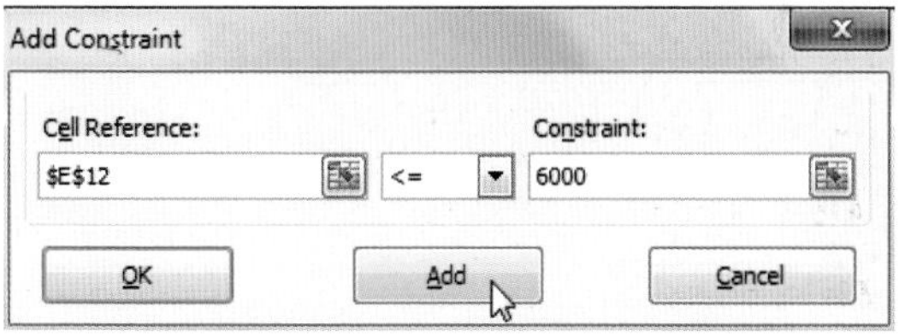

Fig. 8.25 The Add Constraint Box

The logic behind these constraints is as follows:

- Since the maximum available hours in a quarter must remain less than or equal to 6000, we enter as the first constraint the formula **$E$12<=6000**.

- Since a long-term contract with the government requires that at least 25 consultancies are undertaken at home, we enter as the second constraint the formula **$C$5>=25**.

- Since a similar long-term contract with a foreign government requires that at least 15 consultancies are undertaken abroad, we enter as the third constraint the formula **$D$5>=15**.

Solving a Problem

Once the last constraint is inserted into the Add Constraint dialogue box, clicking the **OK** button opens the Solver Parameters box, shown in Fig. 8.26 below.

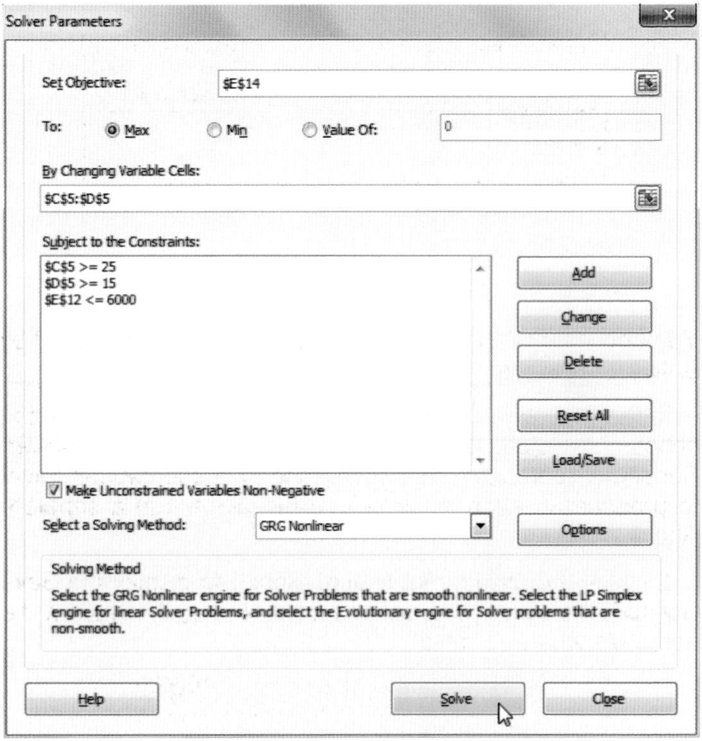

Fig. 8.26 The Solver Parameters Box

Next, specify the **Set Objective** as $E$14, then the adjustable cells in the **By Changing Variable Cells** box as $C$5:$D$5 (see page 129 on how to do that, or just type them in) – these are cells that contain values that Solver can adjust when it searches for an answer.

The final Solver Parameters dialogue box should look as displayed above, and clicking the **Solve** button, opens the Solver Results screen shown in Fig. 8.27 on the next page.

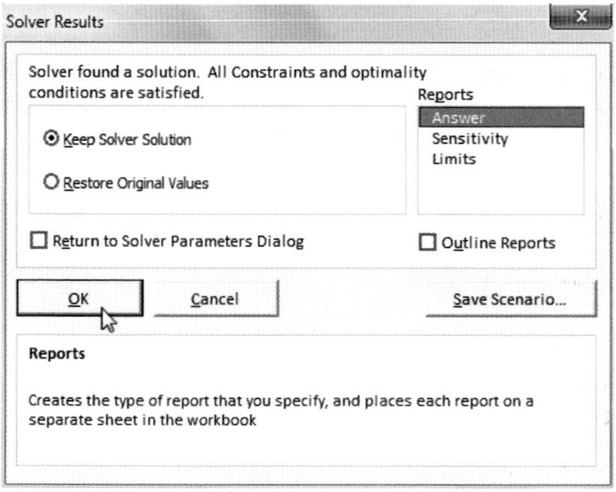

Fig. 8.27 The Solver Results Box

You now have a choice of either keeping the values found by Solver or reverting to the original worksheet values.

In the **Reports** section of the above dialogue box you can choose to create one of three report types: Answer, Sensitivity, and Limits. Selecting one of these causes Excel to produce an appropriate report and place it in a separate Sheet.

Clicking the **OK** button, causes Solver to display the Save Scenario box, asking for a **Scenario Name**. We gave it the name Maximising Profits.

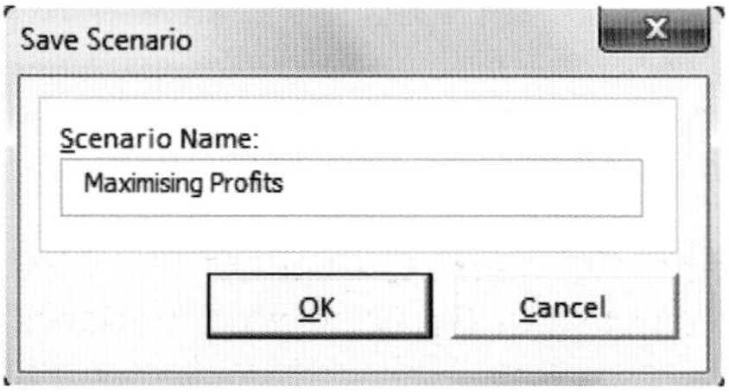

Fig. 8.28 The Save Scenario Box

Finally, clicking the **OK** button, lets Solver find a solution, placing the answer in the worksheet and displaying the Solver Results dialogue box, as shown in Fig. 8.29 on the next page.

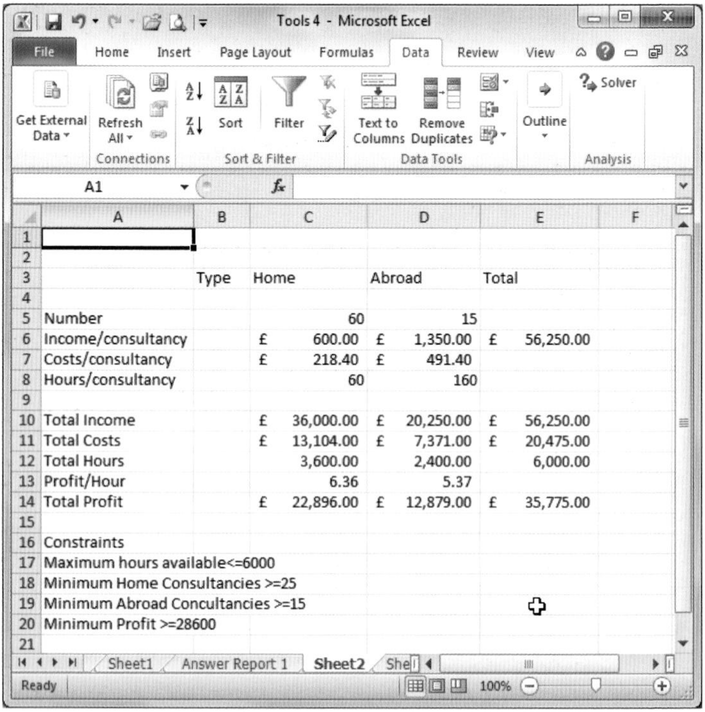

Fig. 8.29 The Solver Results

This is identical to the results shown in Fig. 8.23 on page 137, except that here Solver has inserted a sheet tab named **Answer Report 1**. Clicking this sheet tab opens the Answer Report 1, as shown in Fig. 8.30 on the next page.

If a problem is too complex for the default settings of Solver, then click the **Options** button on the Solver Parameters dialogue box (Fig. 8.26) to display the Solver Options dialogue box, in which you can change the time limit for solving a problem, the maximum iterations allowed, and even select the type of model to be used.

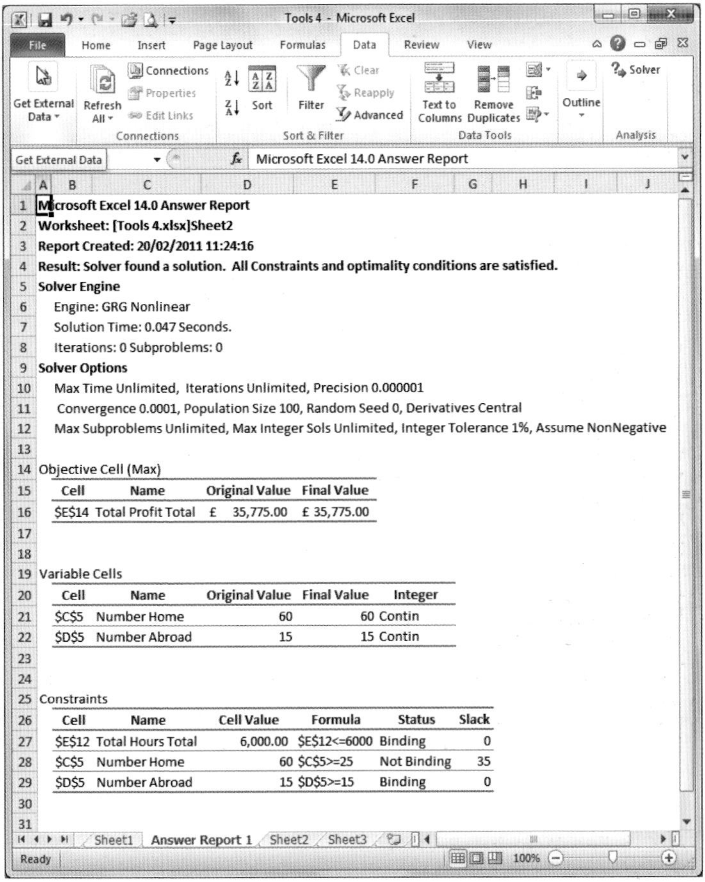

Fig. 8.30 The Solver Answer Report

Finally, save your work under the filename **Tools 5**.

Managing What-if Scenarios

There may be times when we would like to examine different what-if scenarios created from a single spreadsheet model. Normally, managers tend to copy the model to different parts of the spreadsheet so as to examine and display different assumptions. However, keeping track of all the different assumptions can become extremely problematic, confusing, and indeed wasteful of spreadsheet space and PC memory.

With Excel you can use the Scenario Manager to keep all the different versions of the same worksheet model together. In addition you can also give each version a meaningful name, such as 'Original Case', 'Best Case', and 'Worst Case'.

We will use the **Tools 5** example to illustrate the method. In addition, we assume that it is possible to reduce the number of hours it takes Adept Consultants to complete a consultancy at home or abroad, but if one is reduced the other is increased by the same amount.

The model looks as shown in Fig. 8.31 below, with '% Changes' added in columns F and G, the contents of cells C8 and D8 changed to =60*(1+F8) and =160*(1+G8) respectively, and the overall profit now also displayed in column H, by inserting in H5 the reference =E14.

	A	B	C	D	E	F	G	H
1								
2								
3		Type	Home	Abroad	Total		% Changes	Profit
4						Home	Abroad	
5	Number		60	15				£35,775.00
6	Income/consultancy	£	600.00	£ 1,350.00	£ 56,250.00			
7	Costs/consultancy	£	218.40	£ 491.40				
8	Hours/consultancy		60	160		0%	0%	
9								
10	Total Income	£	36,000.00	£ 20,250.00	£ 56,250.00			
11	Total Costs	£	13,104.00	£ 7,371.00	£ 20,475.00			
12	Total Hours		3,600.00	2,400.00	6,000.00			
13	Profit/Hour		6.36	5.37				
14	Total Profit	£	22,896.00	£ 12,879.00	£ 35,775.00			
15								
16	Constraints							
17	Maximum hours available<=6000							
18	Minimum Home Consultancies >=25							
19	Minimum Abroad Concultancies >=15							
20	Minimum Profit >=28600							
21								

Fig. 8.31 Designing a What-if Scenarios Worksheet

Obviously, since we will be optimising our solutions, you must learn to use Solver first.

Next, enter 0% change in the hours per consultancy on both the home and abroad input cells, which reflects the 'Original' state of our problem with an optimum answer on profits using the already defined constraints. This gives a profit of £35,775 – the no-change scenario.

Finally, save your model as **Tools 6** before going on. This ensures that you can go back to it if anything goes wrong when trying to run the **Scenarios** option.

Next, click the **Data**, **Data Tools**, **What-If Analysis**, **Scenarios** icon and select **Scenario Manager** from the drop-down menu to open its dialogue box which, at this point, contains the Maximise Profits scenario, shown in Fig. 8.32.

Fig. 8.32 The Scenario Manager Box

To start the process, first **Delete** the old scenario, then click the **Add** button to display the Add Scenario dialogue box shown in Fig. 8.33. Now add the description 'Original Version' in the **Scenario name** text box, then specify in the **Changing cells** F8:G8.

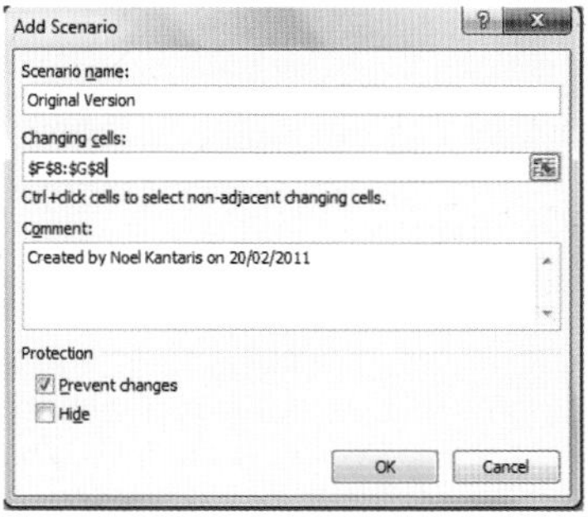

Fig. 8.33 The Add Scenario Box

Pressing the **OK** button, displays the Scenario Values dialogue box, shown in Fig. 8.33, with the values for both F8 and G8 showing as 0 (zero), as displayed in Fig. 8.34 on the next page.

Pressing the **OK** button on the Scenario Values dialogue box,

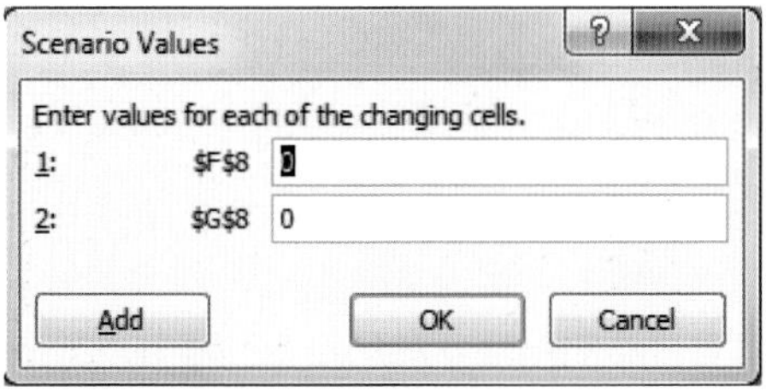

Fig. 8.34 The Scenario Values Box

returns you to the Scenario Manager with the recently created scenario appearing in the **Scenarios** list box.

Next, repeat the process by pressing the **Add** button on the Scenario Manager dialogue box to display the Add Scenario dialogue box in which you type a name for the second scenario, say 'Negative Home Change' and click the **OK** button.

In the displayed Scenario Values box, change the values for cells F8 and G8 to –5% and 5%, respectively (the actual values should be entered as -0.05 and 0.05).

Finally, repeat the process to create a 'Positive Home Change' with Scenario Values in F8 and G8 of 5% and –5%, respectively.

The final Scenario Manager box is shown in Fig. 8.35 in which you can select any one of the defined scenarios. To look at the results of one of these, simply highlight it and

Fig. 8.35 The Final Scenario
Manager Box

press the **Show** button. The only changes you'll see are those relating to hours spent consulting and profits per hour, as shown in Fig. 8.36 on the next page.

Finally, save your work under the file name **Tools 7**. In this way you always have **Tools 6** to revert to in case any errors occur in the final version of our example.

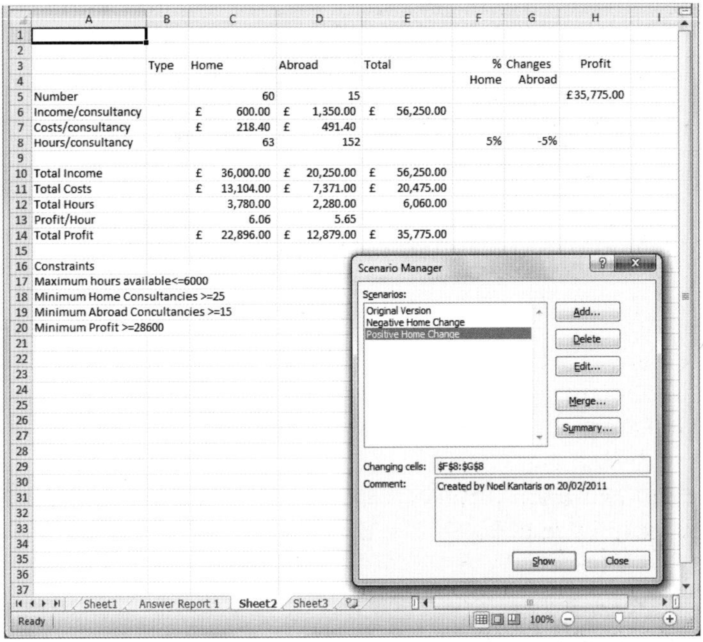

Fig. 8.36 Using The Scenario Manager to View Different Scenarios

Below we summarise the data you should get from these three scenarios.

Scenario	Consulting Hours		Profit/hour	
	Home	Abroad	Home	Abroad
Original Version	60	160	6.36	5.37
-ve Home Change	57	168	6.69	5.11
+ve Home Change	63	152	6.06	5.65

Last but not least, Scenario Manager allows you to merge several versions together and define them as a scenario, and also create a summary report – you have a choice of two. The first report is a 'scenario summary', while the second is a 'scenario pivot table'. With the pivot table you get an instant what-if analysis of different scenario combinations, as shown in Fig. 8.37 on the next page.

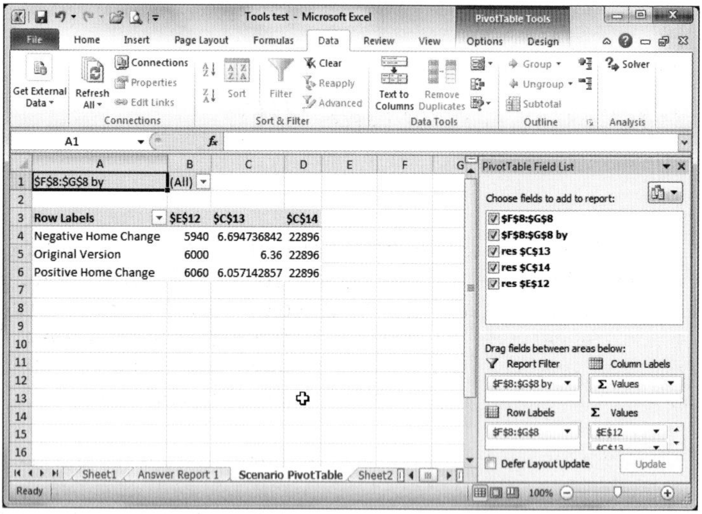

Fig. 8.37 The Scenario Pivot Table

As you can see, you could spend endless time exploring Excel's Tools and other capabilities, but we leave that to you! We shall, however, introduced Excel's Macro Basics, after discussing how to share information between Excel, and other Office 2010 applications, which is the subject of the next chapter.

9

Sharing Information

Office 2010 is an extremely integrated suite of applications. Just like its predecessor, Office 2010's **Themes** feature makes it easy to keep consistent colours, fonts, and special effects between Excel 2010, Word 2010, and PowerPoint 2010 documents, while **Office Styles** ensure a consistent appearance among the diagrams, tables, and shapes.

To transfer information between Office programs, or many other Windows programs for that matter, you copy, move, link, embed or hyperlink information depending on the imposed situation, as follows:

Imposed Situation	Method to Adopt
Inserted information will not need updating.	Copy or move
Inserted information needs to be automatically updated in the destination file as changes are made to the data in the source file, or Source file will always be available and you want to minimise the size of your file.	Link
Source file not always accessible, or Destination file needs to be edited without the changes showing in the source file.	Embed
To jump to a location in a document or Web page, or to a file in a different program.	Hyperlink

The improved charting capabilities in Excel are shared across the main Office 2010 applications, so you can create and interact with charts the same way, whichever program you are using. You can build tables, charts and create **SmartArt** in Excel with the same tools you use in Word and PowerPoint.

Copying or Moving Information

To copy or move information between Office 2010 applications is extremely easy. Most of the time you can just drag and drop a selection between programs. It is safer to do this with the right mouse button depressed, as you are usually given the option to **Move** or **Copy**. This prevents you actually deleting something from the source document, when you only wanted to copy it.

To illustrate the technique, we will copy the file **Project 3**, created in Excel, into a Word document.

Source File Available without its Application

Let's first assume that we only have the source file **Project 3** on disc, and don't have Excel on the computer. In such a situation, you can only copy the whole file into Word. To achieve this, do the following:

*   Start Word and minimise it on the Taskbar.

*   Click the **Computer** option on the **Start** menu and locate the file whose contents you want to copy into Word.

*   Left-click the filename that you want to copy, hold the mouse button down and point to Word on the Taskbar until the application opens.

*   While still holding the mouse button down, move the mouse pointer into Word's open document to where you want to insert the contents of **Project 3**.

*   Release the mouse button to place the contents of the Excel file into Word at that point.

The result of this operation is shown in Fig. 9.1 on the next page.

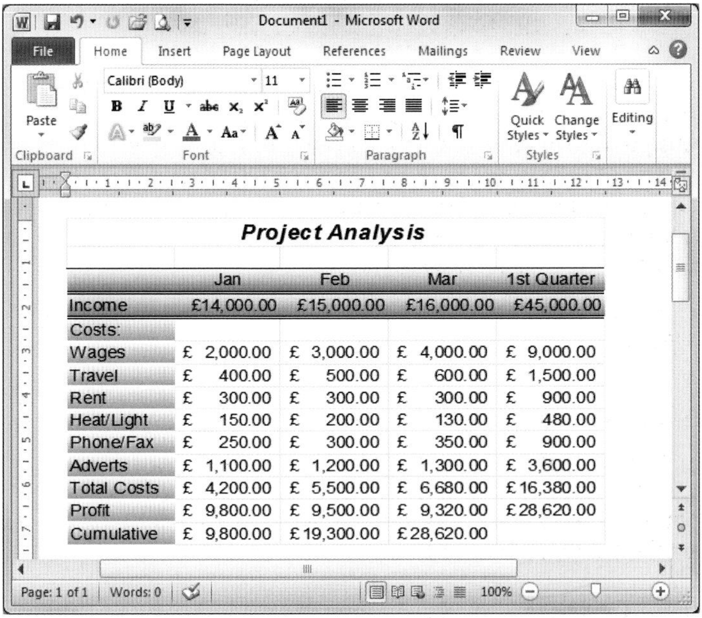

Project Analysis

	Jan	Feb	Mar	1st Quarter
Income	£14,000.00	£15,000.00	£16,000.00	£45,000.00
Costs:				
Wages	£ 2,000.00	£ 3,000.00	£ 4,000.00	£ 9,000.00
Travel	£ 400.00	£ 500.00	£ 600.00	£ 1,500.00
Rent	£ 300.00	£ 300.00	£ 300.00	£ 900.00
Heat/Light	£ 150.00	£ 200.00	£ 130.00	£ 480.00
Phone/Fax	£ 250.00	£ 300.00	£ 350.00	£ 900.00
Adverts	£ 1,100.00	£ 1,200.00	£ 1,300.00	£ 3,600.00
Total Costs	£ 4,200.00	£ 5,500.00	£ 6,680.00	£16,380.00
Profit	£ 9,800.00	£ 9,500.00	£ 9,320.00	£28,620.00
Cumulative	£ 9,800.00	£19,300.00	£28,620.00	

Fig. 9.1 A Copied Spreadsheet in Word 2010

Source File and Application Available

If you have Office 2010 installed you should have both Excel and Word on your PC, so you should have both the file and the application that created it on your computer. You can then copy all or part of the contents of the source file to the destination file, as follows:

- Start Excel and open **Project 6**, select the information to copy (we selected cells A1:F13 of the Summary sheet) and click the **Home**, **Clipboard**, **Copy** button.
- Start Word, locate where you want the insertion and click the **Home**, **Clipboard**, **Paste** button. Then select the first **Paste** icon which is the **Keep Source Formatting** option from the menu that opens when you click the Paste Options Smart Tag, as shown in the composite in Fig. 9.2.

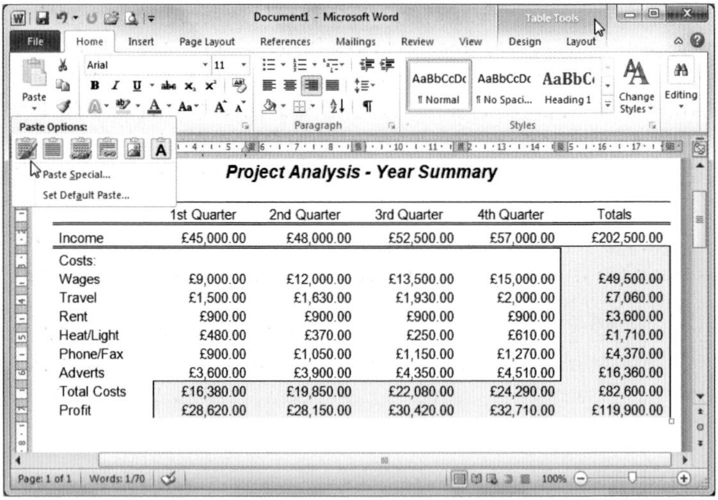

Fig. 9.2 Completing a Paste into Word 2010

The worksheet is pasted as a table in Word as shown above. Although formatting has been preserved, some colouring of cells has been lost.

Object Linking and Embedding

Object Linking is copying information from one file (the source file) to another file (the destination file) and maintaining a connection between the two files. When information in the source file is changed, then the information in the destination file is automatically updated. Linked data is stored in the source file, while the file into which you place the data stores only the location of the source and displays a representation of the linked data.

For example, you would use Object Linking if you wanted an Excel chart included in a Word document to be updated whenever the data in Excel was changed. The Excel worksheet containing the chart would be referred to as the source file, while the Word document would be referred to as the destination file.

Object Embedding is inserting information created in one file (the source file) into another file (the container file). After it is embedded, the object becomes part of the container file. When you double-click an embedded object, it opens in the application in which it was created in the first place. You can then edit it in place, and the original object in the source application remains unchanged.

Thus, the main differences between linking and embedding are where the data is stored and how it is updated after you place it in your file. Linking saves you disc space as only one copy of the linked object is kept on disc. Embedding a logo in the Word template used for your headed paper, would save the logo every time a letter was saved, whereas linking it would not.

Linking Selected Information

To link selected information from an existing Excel file into Word, do the following:

* Select the information in the source file you want to link and click the **Home**, **Clipboard**, **Copy** button, or **Ctrl+C**. As an example, we used the Excel **Quarter 1** sheet (range A1:E4) of **Project 6**. The selection has to be contiguous – you cannot use the **Ctrl** key to select non-contiguous parts of a worksheet.

* In Word 2010, locate where you want the insertion placed and click the **Home**, **Clipboard**, **Paste** button. Then select the **Paste Special ...** option pointed to here to open the dialogue box shown in Fig. 9.3 on the next page. Unfortunately, the third icon under **Paste Options** shown  above (the **Link & Keep Source Formatting** icon) does not always work correctly, particularly for wide selections – most of the times it resulted in an elongated and distorted display, hence the alternative method used here.

- In the display dialogue box of Fig. 9.3, select the options shown, i.e., the type of object involved in the **As** list as shown below, then click the **Paste Link** radio button, followed by **OK**.

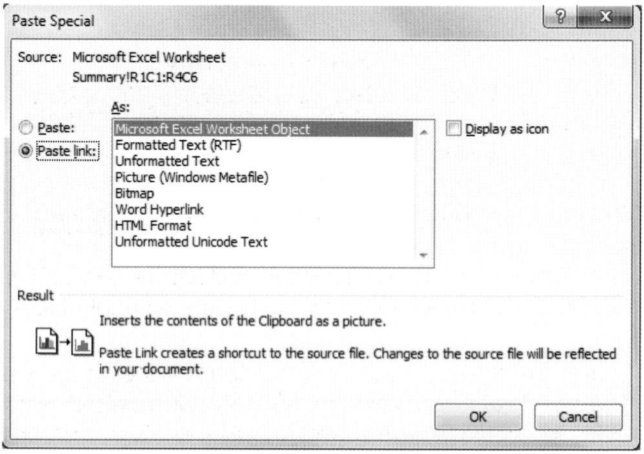

Fig. 9.3 Using Paste Special to Link an Object

Embedding Selected Information

To embed selected information from an existing Excel file, repeat the above (we chose the same range of the same worksheet as previously and embedded it in Word below the linked range), but this time with the **Paste** radio button selected.

The Result of Linking and Embedding

The result (in our example) for both the linked and embedded Excel selections in Word is shown in Fig. 9.4 on the next page. However, before we captured this screen, we checked that changing an entry in, say, cell B4 in Excel of **Quarter 1** of **Project 6**, from £14,000 to £16,000, it changed the linked sheet selection in Word, but not the embedded sheet selection.

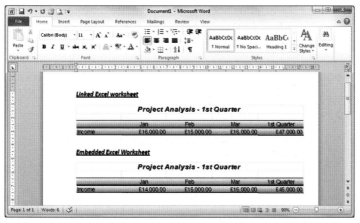

Fig. 9.4 Linked and Embedded Excel Selections into Word 2010

If you now close Excel, then double-click the *linked* selection in Word, it opens Excel and displays the linked worksheet, while double-clicking the *embedded* selection, opens a table within Word for you to edit.

An Excel Chart in PowerPoint

As an example, we will link an Excel chart into a PowerPoint presentation, to be shown, say, in a slide show. Furthermore, if the chart data changes, the chart in PowerPoint will be updated automatically. To achieve this, do the following:

- Select the chart in Excel (as an example use the Pie chart in **Project 7**) and click the **Home**, **Clipboard**, **Copy** button, or **Ctrl+C**.

- Next, open PowerPoint 2010, create an empty slide (**New Slide**, **Blank** command) and click the **Paste** button, or **Ctrl+V**, to paste the chart onto it.

- In the lower-right corner the **Paste Options** button should appear, as shown in Fig. 9.5 on the next page. Click this and select the **Keep Source Formatting & Link Data** option to ensure that any changes in Excel will be reflected in PowerPoint.

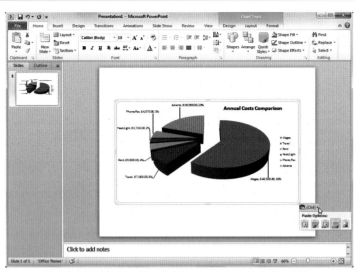

Fig. 9.5 Linking an Excel Chart to a PowerPoint Slide

Hypertext Links

All the Office 2010 applications support hyperlinks. A hyperlink causes a jump to another location in the current document or Web page, to a different document or Web page, or to a file that was created in a different program. For example, you can jump from an Excel worksheet to a Word document or to a PowerPoint slide, to see more detail.

A hyperlink is represented by a 'hot' image or by display text (which is often blue and underlined) that you click to jump to a different location. To insert a hyperlink into Excel, Word, or PowerPoint, select the display text or image in the application, and click the **Insert**, **Links**, **Insert Hyperlink** button, shown here, to open the dialogue box shown in Fig. 9.7 on the next page, in which you can browse for the destination file, or enter a Web site URL address.

To illustrate the procedure, start Excel, open the **Project 3** file, and type in cell B16 the words 'Yearly Costs', as shown in Fig. 9.6 below.

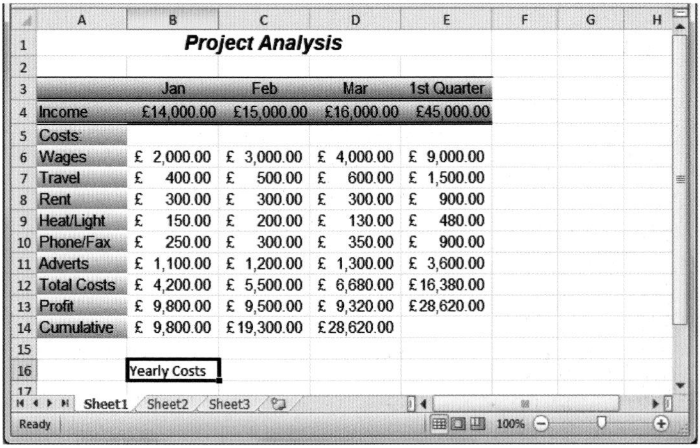

Fig. 9.6 Creating a Hyperlink in an Excel Worksheet

While cell B16 is the active cell, click the **Insert**, **Links**, **Hyperlink** button and locate the **Project 7** file in the displayed Insert Hyperlink dialogue box shown in Fig. 9.7 below. Once you have located the file, its name is inserted in the **Address** box, and pressing the **OK** button inserts a hyperlink to that location.

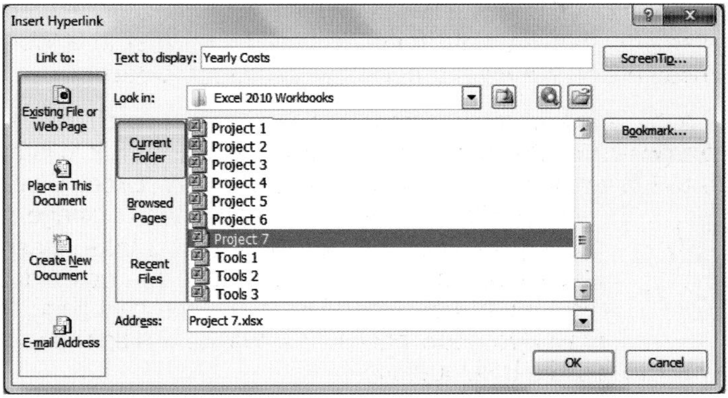

Fig. 9.7 Locating the Address for a Hyperlink

Fig. 9.8 The Select Place in
Document Dialogue Box

Should you want to jump to a specific sheet or defined name within a workbook, click the **Bookmark** button shown in Fig. 9.7, which opens the Select Place in Document dialogue box shown here in Fig. 9.8. In the latter case, when you jump to the specified document, the cell range of the selected defined name will be highlighted automatically, a rather useful feature.

Pressing the **OK** button of each dialogue box, underlines the text in B16, as shown in Fig 9.9 below, and changes its colour to blue.

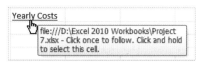

Fig. 9.9 The Hyperlink Address

Pointing to such a hyperlink changes the mouse pointer to a hand, as shown here in Fig. 9.9. Left-clicking it opens the 'Charts' sheet of the **Project 7** file. When you have finished looking at this file, click the **Close** icon on the worksheet, shown in Fig. 9.10 below, for the program to return you automatically to the hyperlinked Excel workbook.

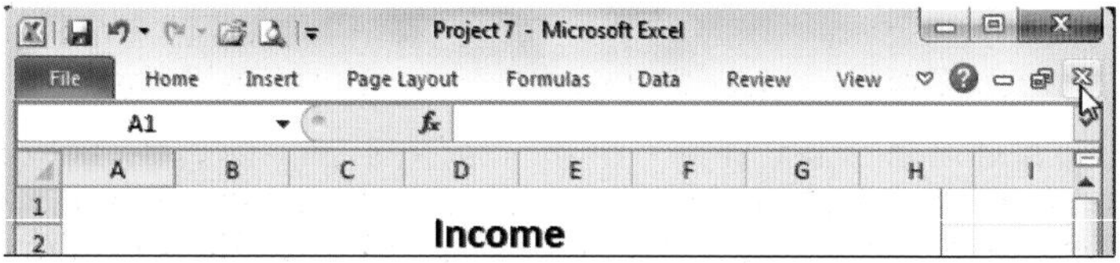

Fig. 9.10 The Close Button in the Excel Window

If the location of the file you wanted to hyperlink to is incorrect, then errors will obviously occur.

To remove unwanted hyperlinks, right-click the hyperlinked cell, then select the **Remove Hyperlink** option from the displayed menu.

As you can see from the above discussion, hyperlinks can just as easily be created and used on Web pages, provided you have Internet access. The procedure is identical to creating a hyperlink between two files on your hard disc.

Hypertext links on a Web page are elements that you can click with the left mouse button to jump to another Web document. You are actually fetching another file to your PC, and the link is an address that uniquely identifies the location of the target file, wherever it may be. This address is known as a Uniform Resource Locator (URL for short).

How to use Excel on the Internet is the subject of the rest of this chapter.

Sharing with Others

Microsoft has integrated Excel 2010 with the Internet and the Web by allowing the creation of the following:

- Non-interactive data or charts.

- Interactive spreadsheets, PivotTable lists, and charts.

- Combination Web pages.

The first one of these lets users view data as they would in Microsoft Excel, including tabs for each worksheet that they can click to switch between worksheets. It is like publishing a 'snapshot' of the data, but users cannot interact with the data.

To view non-interactive data or charts on the Web, users only need a Web browser – there are no restrictions on the type of browser. Also, they don't need Excel 2010 on their computer.

The last two items on the list above allow the user to interact with all or some of the data on your Web page. Such a Web page is created from an Excel worksheet, or items from it, by saving the data with 'spreadsheet functionality'.

Publishing in this way allows users to enter, format, calculate, analyse, sort and filter data.

Interactive Web pages allow users to change the data and layout of Web page items. They are used if you have data that users want to recalculate. For example, if you are supplying a program to calculate the repayments on loans based on particular interest rates (to be discussed shortly).

To view interactive (or partially interactive) data on the Web, users need to have installed on their computer one of the latest versions of the Microsoft Internet Explorer (preferably version 8 or later), or Google Chrome.

Creating Excel Static Web Pages

Most Web pages are written in HTML (Hypertext Markup Language), which can be used by Web browsers on any operating system, such as Windows, Macintosh, and UNIX.

Entire Workbook on a Web Page

Excel allows you to put an entire workbook on a Web page. As an example, we will use the **Project 7** file which has several worksheets, including three charts saved in a Chart sheet. To do this, start Excel, then

- Open **Project 7**, and use the **File** button and select the **Save As** option. In the **Save as type** box of the displayed dialogue box select **Web Page** which changes the displayed dialogue box.

- In the **Address Bar** at the top of the window, locate the drive, folder, Web folder, Web server, or File Transfer Protocol (FTP) location where you want to save your Web page (we chose our **Workbooks** folder).

- Make sure that the **Entire Workbook** radio button is selected, then click the **Change Title** button to display the Enter Text dialogue box, as shown in Fig. 9.11 on the next page. Type a description which will be displayed in the Title bar of the browser.

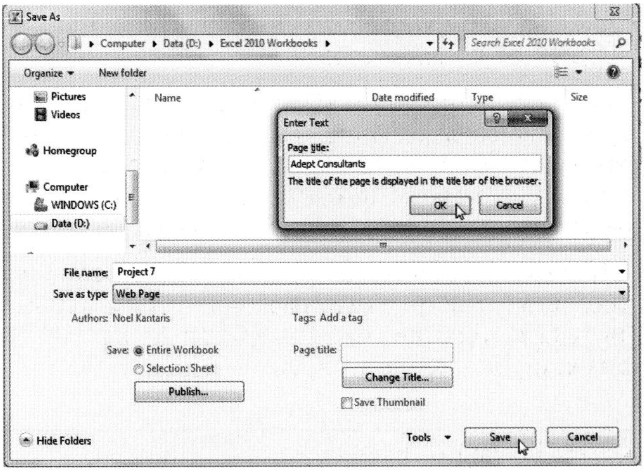

Fig. 9.11 Saving a Workbook as a Web Page

• Finally, press the **Save** button. To see the result of your efforts, then locate the **.htm** file produced by the save command. In our case this file was called **Project 7.htm** by default, as shown in Fig. 9.12 below.

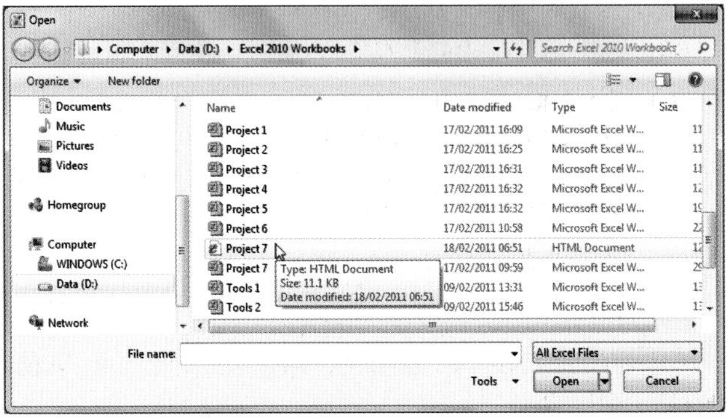

Fig. 9.12 Opening the Saved .htm File in Internet Explorer

• Double-clicking the HTML file, opens the screen in Fig. 9.13 on the next page.

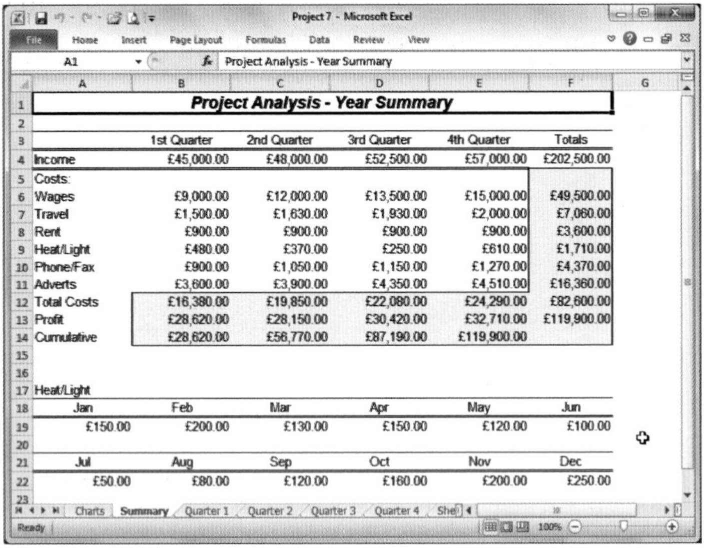

Fig. 9.13 The Saved .htm File in Internet Explorer

Most, but not all, features and formatting in your workbook are retained when you open your Web page (**.htm**) file later. These are held in a **_files** folder, called the 'supporting files folder' (in our case **Project 7_files**). If you ever move the Web page (**.htm**) from the place it was saved in the first place, you must also move the supporting files (**_files**) folder, otherwise you will lose all features and formatting when viewing your work on your browser.

Also, if you want to change data in your Web site, update the original **.xlsx** file in Excel and then republish it. We will discuss how to do this automatically shortly.

Single Worksheet on a Web Page

Excel allows you to put a single worksheet on a Web page. As an example, we will use the **Project 6** file, then use the **File** button and select the **Save As** option. In the **Save as type** box of the displayed dialogue box select **Single File Web Page** which changes the displayed dialogue box, as shown in Fig. 9.14 on the next page, then:

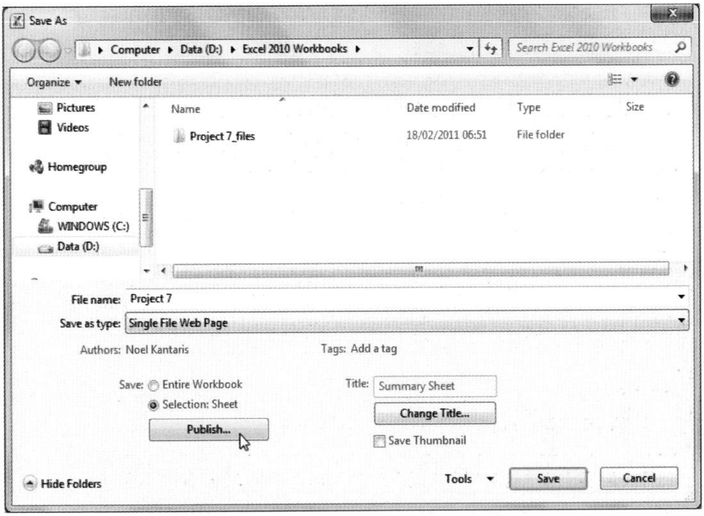

Fig. 9.14 Saving a File in Single Sheet Format

- Make sure that the **Selection: Sheet** radio button is selected. Next, click the **Change Title** button to display the Enter Text dialogue box and type a description. In the **Choose** text box, select, **Items on Summary** from the drop-down menu, click the **Open published web page in browser** check box, and click **Publish** button.

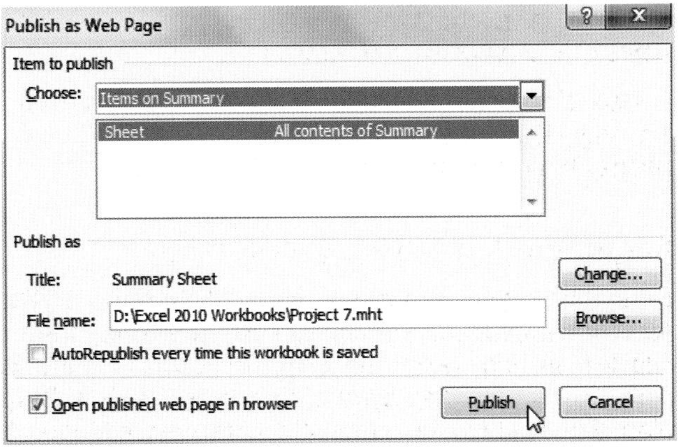

Fig. 9.15 Publishing a Single File as a Web Page

- Excel formats your chosen worksheet into a Web page and displays it in your browser, as shown in Fig. 9.16.

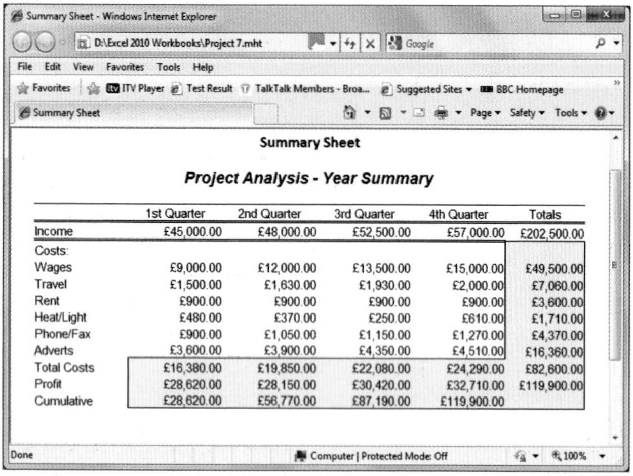

Summary Sheet

Project Analysis - Year Summary

	1st Quarter	2nd Quarter	3rd Quarter	4th Quarter	Totals
Income	£45,000.00	£48,000.00	£52,500.00	£57,000.00	£202,500.00
Costs:					
Wages	£9,000.00	£12,000.00	£13,500.00	£15,000.00	£49,500.00
Travel	£1,500.00	£1,630.00	£1,930.00	£2,000.00	£7,060.00
Rent	£900.00	£900.00	£900.00	£900.00	£3,600.00
Heat/Light	£480.00	£370.00	£250.00	£610.00	£1,710.00
Phone/Fax	£900.00	£1,050.00	£1,150.00	£1,270.00	£4,370.00
Adverts	£3,600.00	£3,900.00	£4,350.00	£4,510.00	£16,360.00
Total Costs	£16,380.00	£19,850.00	£22,080.00	£24,290.00	£82,600.00
Profit	£28,620.00	£28,150.00	£30,420.00	£32,710.00	£119,900.00
Cumulative	£28,620.00	£56,770.00	£87,190.00	£119,900.00	

Fig. 9.16 Displaying a Saved Web Page in Internet Explorer

Auto-Republishing Web Pages

To illustrate this procedure, first construct an Excel example suitable for Web page auto-republishing. We chose below to create a loans repayment worksheet using the compound interest formula given as

$$A = P * (1+R/100)^Y$$

where P is the principal (original money) lent, and A is what it amounts to in time Y years at an interest rate R% per annum.

We carry out the calculation on a yearly basis to the full period of the loan of 15 years which cannot be varied, with a value of Principal of £30,000 and with an interest rate of 5%, both of which can be varied by the user in cells C4 and C3 respectively. Cells A9:A23 hold the period of the loan, while cells C9:C23 hold the result of the calculation. Hint – type in C9 the Excel formula =\$C\$4*(1+\$C\$3/100)^A9, then copy it into C10:C23.

The resultant Excel worksheet, including a line chart of the repayment amount at the end of each year, is shown in Fig. 9.17 below.

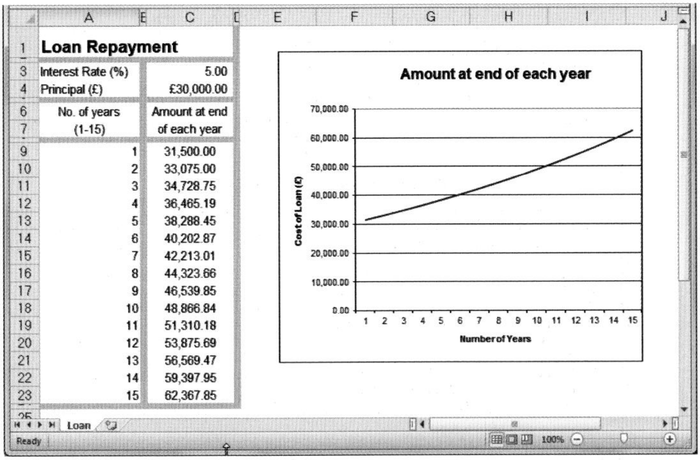

Fig. 9.17 Creating an Interactive Excel Web Page

Next, use the **File** button and select the **Save As** option. In the **Save as type** box of the displayed dialogue box select **Web Page** which changes the displayed dialogue box, as shown in Fig. 9.18.

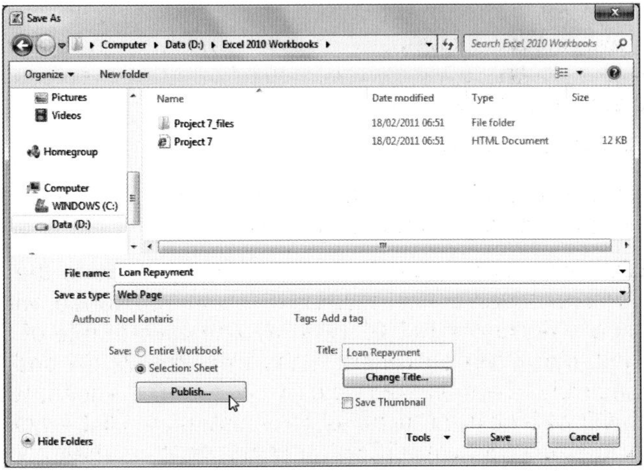

Fig. 9.18 Saving an Interactive Web Page

Make sure that the **Selection: Sheet** radio button is selected, and press the **Publish** button. Finally, in the displayed Publish as Web Page dialogue box, shown in Fig. 9.19, check both the **AutoRepublish every time this workbook is saved** box and the **Open published web page in browser** box, and press the **Publish** button.

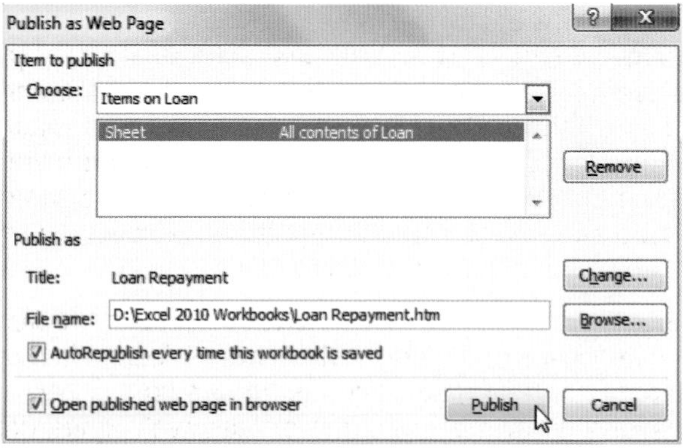

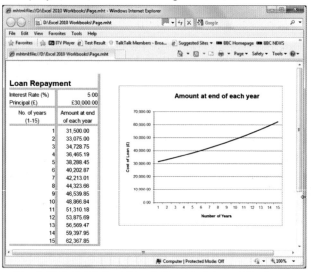

Fig. 9.19 The Publish as Web Page Dialogue Box

What displays next, is shown in Fig. 9.20 below.

Fig. 9.20 A Published Excel Sheet in Internet Explorer

10

Excel Macro Basics

A macro is simply a set of instructions made up of a sequence of keystrokes, mouse selections, or commands stored in a macro file. After saving or writing, a macro and attaching a quick key combination to it, you can run the same sequence of commands whenever you want. This can save a lot of time and, especially with repetitive operations, can save mistakes creeping into your work.

In Excel there are two basic ways of creating macros. The first one involves using Microsoft Visual Basic, the programming language that is common to all Office applications. With this method, you can write quite complex macro programs directly into a macro file using the Visual Basic editor which allows you, amongst other facilities, to edit, copy, or rename macros. Understanding Visual Basic also makes it easier to program with other Microsoft applications that use the language.

For simple work however, you don't really have to learn to program in Visual Basic, as Excel includes a Macro Recorder which provides you with the second method of generating macros. The Macro Recorder stores the actions you take, including mouse clicks, and the commands you use while working with Excel, which can then be played back (run) to repeat the recorded actions and commands.

Before you record or write a macro, plan the steps and commands you want the macro to perform. This is essential, because if you make a mistake while recording the macro, corrections you make will also be recorded, which might lead to a rather confused code!

Using the Macro Recorder

We will now use the worksheet saved under **Project 3** to show how we can use Excel's Macro Recorder to create a macro to perform 'what-if' type of projections by, say, increasing the 'Wages' bill by 15%.

If you haven't saved **Project 3** on disc, it will be necessary for you to enter the information shown in Fig. 10.1 into Excel so that you can benefit from what is to be introduced at this point. If you have saved **Project 3**, click the **File** button on the Ribbon, select the **Open** option from the displayed menu, locate the file and double-click it to open it. Your display should look similar to the one below.

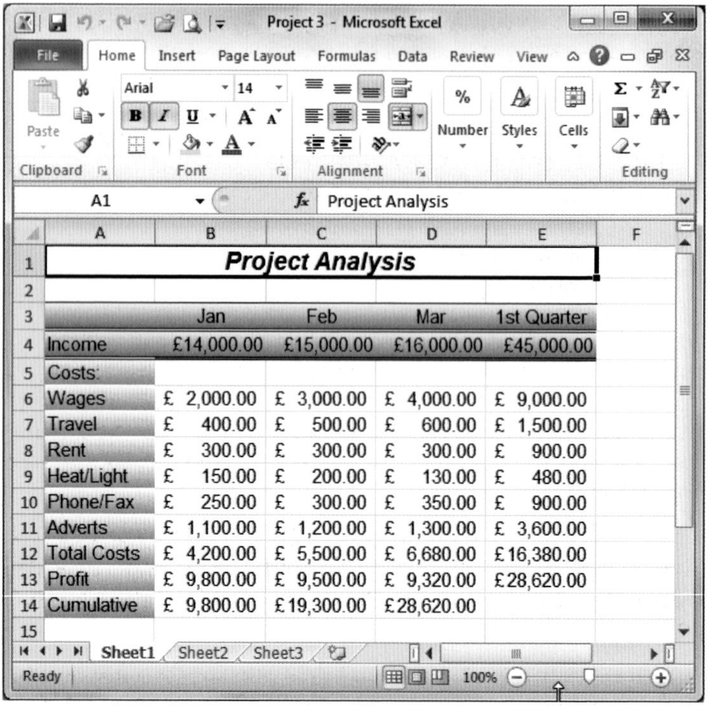

Fig. 10.1 An Example to Demonstrate Using the Macro Recorder

What we would like to do now is to edit the entry in cell B6 in 'Jan Wages' so that it can be increased by 15%. One way of doing this would be to multiply the contents of the cell value by 1.15. But please don't do anything to your worksheet yet, just read.

To change the value in cell B6 by 15%, we would start by changing its contents into a formula, by pressing the **F2** function key to 'Edit' the value in it by adding an equals sign at the beginning of the entry and then typing ***1.15** at the end of it, which has the effect of multiplying the contents of the cell by 1.15, thus increasing its contents by 15%. We would then press the **Enter** key which would cause the cell pointer to drop to B7, press the ⬆ arrow key to move back to cell B6, then press the ⇒ arrow key to move to cell C6.

The exact steps you will have to take in creating this macro, after highlighting cell B6, are as follows:

Press **F2** to 'Edit' cell
Press the **Home** key to move to beginning of entry
Type **=** to change entry to a formula
Press **End** to move to the end of the entry
Type ***1.15**
Press the **Enter** key
Press ⬆arrow key
Press ⇒ arrow key.

However, before starting to record a macro, and before you open the file in which this macro is to be created, we need to carry out two operations: (a) customise the Ribbon so that the Developer tab is visible, and (b) examine the macro security in Excel.

To customise the Ribbon, start Excel then click the **File** button, select the **Customize Ribbon** option and click the **Developer** check box, as shown in Fig. 10.2 on the next page.

To examine the macro security in Excel, start Excel then click the **File** button, select the **Trust Center** option and click the **Trust Center Setting** button, as shown in Fig. 10.3, also on the next page.

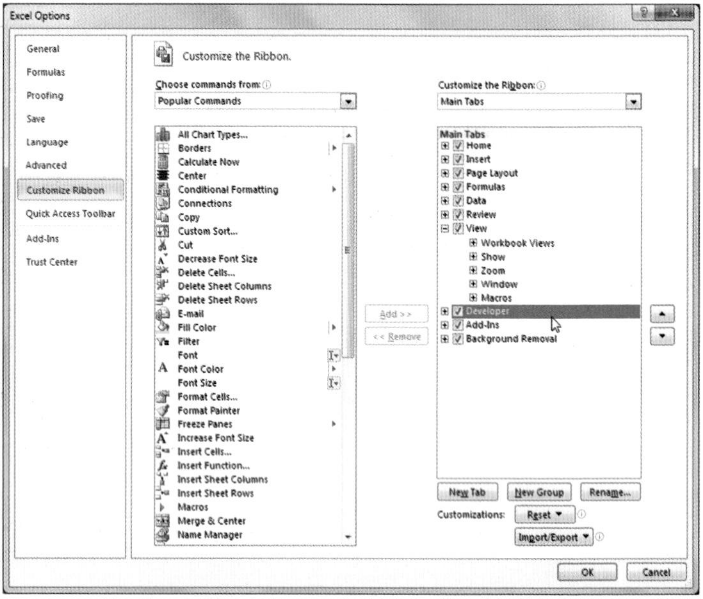

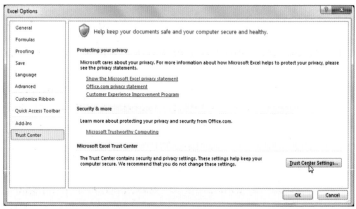

Fig. 10.2 Activating the Developer Ribbon Tab

Clicking **OK** displays the Developer tab on the Ribbon.

Fig. 10.3 Examining the Macro Settings

Clicking the **Trust Center Settings** displays the available options, as shown in Fig. 10.4 on the next page.

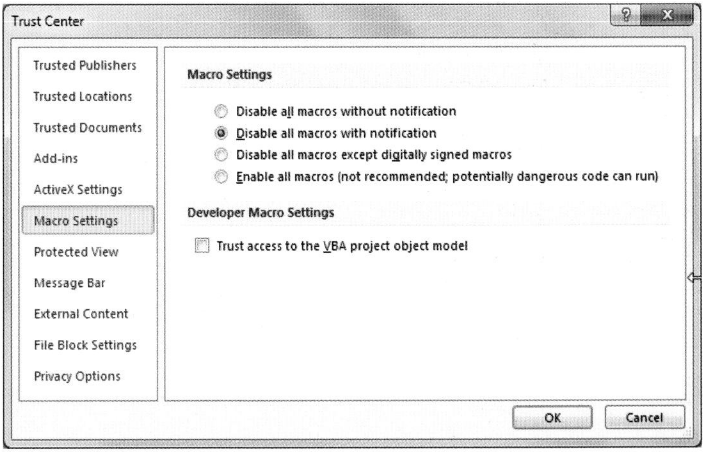

Fig. 10.4 The Available Macro Settings

The various options under Macro Settings have the following effect:

- **Disable all macros without notification:** Select this option if you don't trust macros. All macros in documents and security alerts about macros are disabled.

- **Disable all macros with notification**: This is the default setting. It alerts you if a macro is present and gives you a chance to enable those macros on a case by case basis.

- **Disable all macros except digitally signed macros:** It alerts you if a digitally signed macro is present. Those macros who are digitally signed <u>and</u> you have already specified that its publisher is to be trusted, will run without notification. All unsigned macros are disabled without notification.

- **Enable all macros (not recommended; potentially dangerous code can run):** This option allows all macros to run, but it makes your computer vulnerable to potentially malicious code and is not recommended.

Now, since we are about to develop a macro, select the **Enable all macros** option, but make sure you disconnect from the Internet while we discuss and design macros, to avoid any unwanted macros running on your PC.

Similarly, check the last option of Macro Security which allows you to **Trust access to the VBA project object model**. This setting provides a security option for code that is written to automate an Office application using a programmed VBA code.

Recording an Excel Macro

Having opened the **Project 3** file, select cell B6 - the first cell we want to operate on. Then, click the **Developer**, **Code**, **Macros** button, pointed to below, to open the Record Macro dialogue box with the default **Macro name** given as **Macro1**, as shown in the composite display in Fig. 10.5.

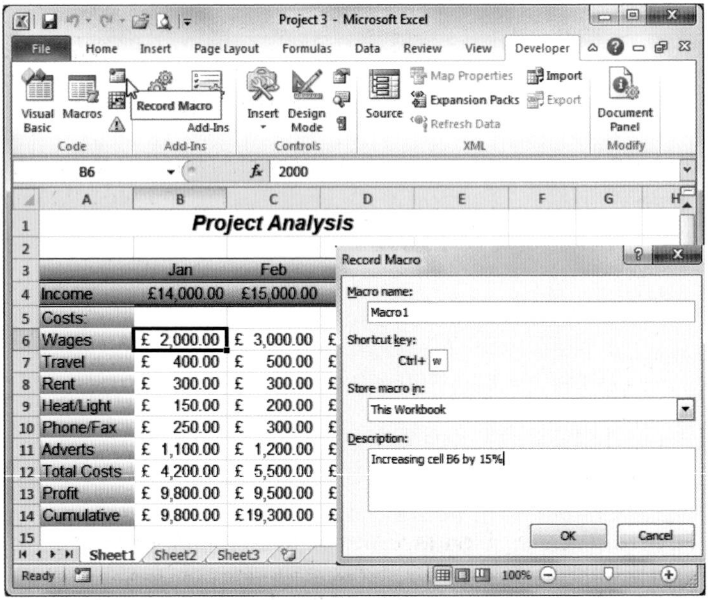

Fig. 10.5 Starting the Recording of a Macro

The macro name in the Record Macro dialogue box can be changed by you to some more meaningful name, if you so wish. We then specified that the **Shortcut key** in the Record Macro dialogue box should be **Ctrl+w** (**w** for wages), as shown in Fig. 10.5 on the previous page.

You can also type an appropriate message in the **Description** box so you know what the macro does. In this case we typed 'Increasing cell B6 by 15%', because our macro is designed to only change the first wages cell.

Pressing the **OK** button, starts Macro Recording, and puts a **Macros** button on the **Status Bar** shown here, as well as changing the **Record Macro** button on the Ribbon to a **Stop Recording** button, as shown in Fig. 10.6.

Fig. 10.6 The Stop Recording Button

Everything you type from now on becomes part of the macro. To start recording our macro, press/type the appropriate key/information, as shown below.

F2
Home
=
End
*1.15
Enter
Press ⇧arrow key
Press ⇒arrow key

To stop recording the macro, click either the **Macro** button on the **Status Bar**, or the **Stop Recording** button on the Ribbon. You will immediately notice that the value in cell B6, has now changed to 2,300.

To see the Visual Basic code of your macro, click the **View**, **Macros**, **Macros** button and select the **View Macros** option from the drop-down menu (or use the **Alt+F8** shortcut), specify which macro you want to edit by highlighting it, and press the **Edit** button on the Macro dialogue box to display the code shown below in Fig. 10.7.

However, before executing this macro, activate worksheet **Project 3** and change the entry in cell B6 back to its original value of 2000 (it was changed by 15% while you were typing the latest macro commands).

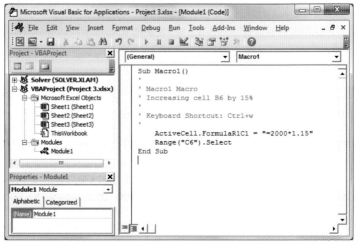

Fig. 10.7 The Visual Basic Code of our Macro

Next, use the **File** button on the Ribbon and give the worksheet the name **Auropro 1**, but select the **Excel Macro-Enabled Workbook** extension .xlsm in the **Save as type** box. Should you close the workbook **Project 3**, DO NOT save it when asked. In this way, should things go wrong when you execute your macro, you can reopen the original **Project 3** worksheet and start again rather than attempting to correct the **Autopro 1.xlsm** file.

To run the first macro, place the cell pointer on cell B6, then press **Ctrl+w**. The shortcut key starts the macro and automatically changes the entry in B6 by 15% from 2000 to 2300.

Visual Basic Programming Advantages

When the macros you write become more complicated there are many advantages to using Visual Basic rather than using the macro command language that much earlier versions of Excel and other spreadsheet packages used.

In Visual Basic you can assign values directly to variables instead of storing a value in a name as you would have to do in the macro command language. Variables can be made available to all procedures, to just the procedure in a module, or to just a single procedure, thus being far more flexible than names. In addition, in Visual Basic you can define constants to hold static values that you refer to repeatedly.

Reading Visual Basic Code

Referring to our simple example, you can see that Visual Basic has created a macro that is preceded by comment statements (that start with an apostrophe (')) in which you are informed of the name of the macro, the comment you typed in, and the keyboard shortcut.

The macro commands are placed in between the two keywords **Sub** and **End Sub** which mark the beginning and end of a macro. In general, keywords, variables, operators, and procedure calls are referred to as statements which are instructions to perform an action.

The statement

ActiveCell.FormulaR1C1 = "=2000*1.15"

is the way that Visual Basic enters the formula **=2000*1.15** into the active cell. In Visual Basic terminology; it uses the **Range** object to identify the range you want to change and sets the **Formula** property of the range to assign a formula to the range.

An 'object' is something you control in Visual Basic. Each object has characteristics called 'properties' which control the appearance of the object. Objects also have 'methods' which are actions that they can take. In Visual Basic you use:

- Objects (such as Workbooks, Worksheets, Ranges, Charts) to perform a task. Each object has characteristics, called properties, that make that object useful by controlling the appearance or behaviour of an object.

- Properties (such as ActiveCell, ActiveSheet, Value, Selection, ColumnWidth, RowHeight) to examine the condition of an object by returning the value of one of the object's properties (such as a numeric value for ColumnWidth, True, or False).

- Methods which are actions that objects can do (such as Calculate, Clear, Copy, Justify or Table). Methods are a part of objects just like properties. The difference between them is that properties have values which are set or returned, while methods are actions you would like an object to perform.

Should you want to learn to program in Visual Basic, then may we suggest you start with the book *Using Visual Basic* (BP498), also published by BERNARD BABANI (publishing) Ltd.

Editing a Macro

A macro can be edited by opening the file that contains it and pressing **Alt+F8** to display the Macro dialogue box, then selecting the required macro and pressing the **Edit** button, as discussed earlier.

Since each of the three months in our worksheet is to be changed we can edit all Macro1 references by copying the highlighted entries and pasting them twice before the **End Sub** statement as shown in Fig. 10.8 on the next page, where we have also changed references made to the amount of wages in the **ActiveCell.Formula** command, and typed the correct cell reference in **Range().Select** command. We then saved the workbook under the filename **Autopro 2**. Doing so also saves the new **Macro1** within the **Autopro 2** file.

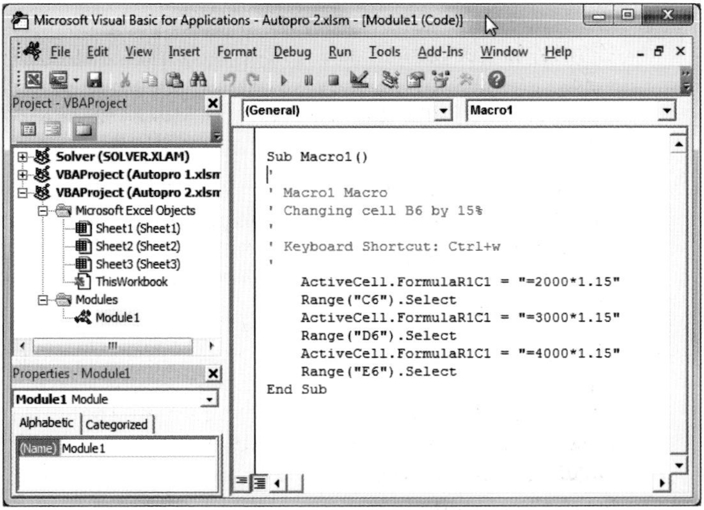

Fig. 10.8 Editing a Macro

If your macro is correct, activating cell B6 and pressing **Ctrl+w** runs it and increases by 15% the values of the wages entries for the three months from those shown on the original worksheet in Fig. 10.1 on page 168.

We could use the same macro to find out the effect of increasing wages by different percentages by editing it, but this would be rather inefficient. A better method is to allocate a cell for the % increase, say cell G5, and edit the macro so that reference to that cell is made in the R1C1 absolute format.

In our example, from cell B6 we would have to refer to R[-1]C[5] (Row 1 above present position, Column 5 from present position) which is the reference to cell G5 from B6.

Finally, edit all macro references and save the worksheet under the file name **Autopro 3**. Running the macro now changes the worksheet entries to those shown in Fig. 10.9 on the next page.

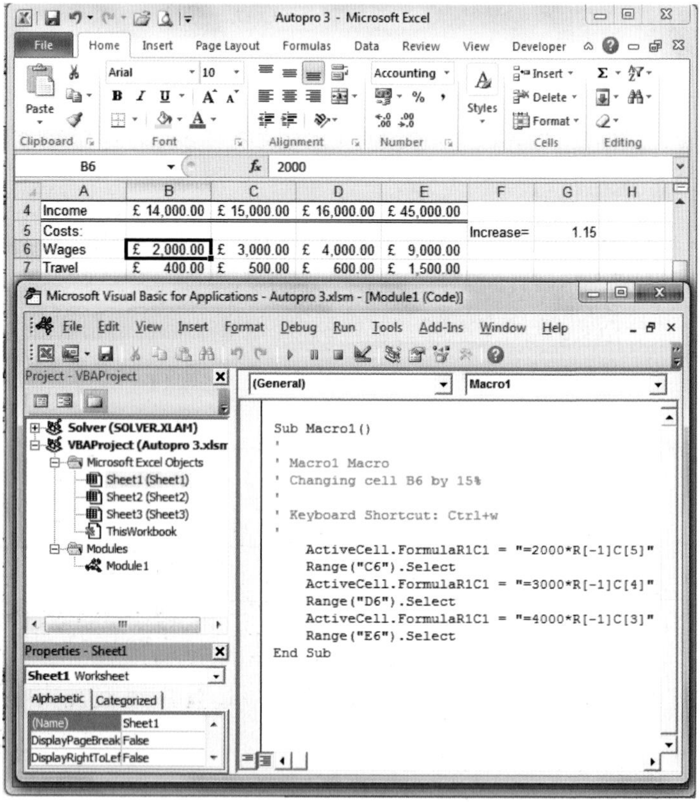

Fig. 10.9 A Macro Incorporating a Percentage Increase Cell

Macro Interaction with Keyboard

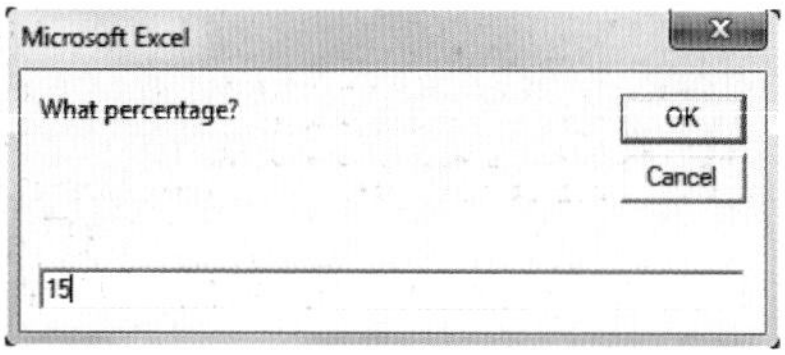

A further addition to the above macros could be made to allow for user entry of the 'increment' value from the keyboard, rather than having to edit cell G5. This can be achieved by using the **InputBox()** macro command, which creates a dialogue box, as shown here, and returns the information entered into it.

The general format of this macro command is:

Variable = InputBox("message")

and it returns the value typed on the keyboard into the *variable*.

In the macro shown in Fig. 10.10, we have tried to show the power of Visual Basic without making the example too complicated.

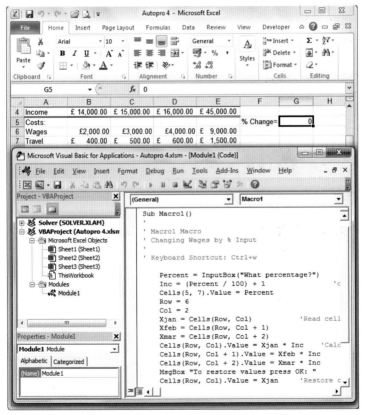

Fig. 10.10 A Macro Incorporating an Input Box

First, you are asked to give a percentage rate, then the macro calculates the increment and places the value of rate in G5 and stores the original contents of B6:D6 into the three variables, Xjan, Xfeb, and Xmar.

Next, the calculations take place and the results are entered in cell range B6:D6. Finally, a dialogue box is displayed (it can be moved out of the way) asking you to press the **OK** button in order to restore the original contents to the 'Wages' cell range, and change the contents of G5 to 0 (zero).

Finally, save this workbook as **Autopro 4** before attempting to run it. To start the macro, activate cell B6 and press **Ctrl+w**.

Visual Basic has many more statements, commands and functions which can be used to build and run your application in special ways. What we have tried to do here is to introduce you to the subject and give you some idea of the power of this programming language.

Note: When you finish experimenting with Excel macros, don't forget to undo the two changes in the Macro Security, before reconnecting to the Internet!

* * *

That is about it. We hope you have enjoyed reading this book as much as we have enjoyed writing it. Of course Excel 2010 is capable of a lot more than we have discussed here, but what we have tried to do is to give you enough information so that you can forge ahead and explore by yourself the rest of its capabilities.

What follows next is a chapter of exercises with enough guidance to help you get going on your own, followed by a chapter that lists all the functions available to Excel 2010 with an explanation of their required parameters.

11

Exercises Using Excel

The following exercises will help you to get going on your own and might be of interest to you. We give you as much guidance as we think is needed for you to complete them by yourself. Good luck!

Compound Interest

To illustrate the behaviour of interest rates, set up an Excel worksheet as shown in Fig. 11.1 below, to calculate the compound interest of money lent over a certain period of time. Plot the resultant yearly interest against time, on the same graph, for three different values of interest rates.

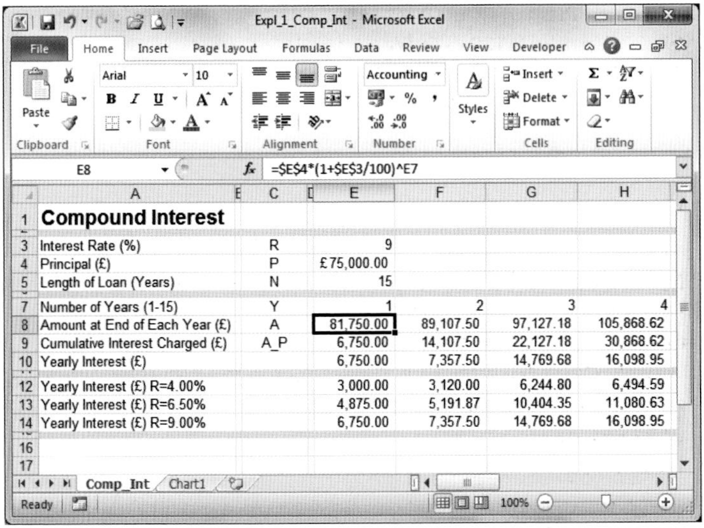

	A	C	E	F	G	H
1	**Compound Interest**					
3	Interest Rate (%)	R	9			
4	Principal (£)	P	£75,000.00			
5	Length of Loan (Years)	N	15			
7	Number of Years (1-15)	Y	1	2	3	4
8	Amount at End of Each Year (£)	A	81,750.00	89,107.50	97,127.18	105,868.62
9	Cumulative Interest Charged (£)	A_P	6,750.00	14,107.50	22,127.18	30,868.62
10	Yearly Interest (£)		6,750.00	7,357.50	14,769.68	16,098.95
12	Yearly Interest (£) R=4.00%		3,000.00	3,120.00	6,244.80	6,494.59
13	Yearly Interest (£) R=6.50%		4,875.00	5,191.87	10,404.35	11,080.63
14	Yearly Interest (£) R=9.00%		6,750.00	7,357.50	14,769.68	16,098.95
16						
17						

Fig. 11.1 The Layout of the Compound Interest Example

Compound interest is calculated using the formula

$$A = P * (1+R/100)^Y$$

where P is the principal (original money) lent, and A is what it amounts to in time Y years at an interest rate R% per annum. The cumulative interest charged is $A - P$.

Carry out the above calculation on a yearly basis to the full period of the loan (N=15) years, with a constant value of Principal (P=£75,000), but with variable values of interest rate R, namely 4, 6.5 and 9%.

Type in your formulae in the worksheet in such a way (by making absolute reference to cells E3 to E5) as to allow you to copy these in the rows below the 'number of years' range that stretches from column E to column S, as shown in the Formula bar in Fig. 11.1. You should then only need to change the value of R for the required 'Yearly Interest' to be calculated automatically in row 10.

Use the **Home**, **Editing, Fill, Series** command to fill the 'Number of Years' range with incremental data, and the **Home**, **Clipboard, Copy** button and **Home**, **Clipboard**, **Paste**, **Paste Special, Values** button to copy the values of 'Yearly Interest' for each value of R to the bottom of the sheet for subsequent graphing. Copying by value is necessary to avoid changes to the data when R is changed.

Format your worksheet as shown in Fig. 11.1 on the previous page (or better), and use the information in cells A12:A14 plus E12:S14, by first highlighting the first cell block then pressing the **Ctrl** key down and, while keeping it depressed, highlighting the second cell block. Next, in the **Insert**, **Charts** group, select the chart of your choice and specify Sheet2 as the placement area.

Note that you might have to change the font size of the title, axes labels, and legends, and also re-size the chart to get what is shown in Fig. 11.2 on the next page.

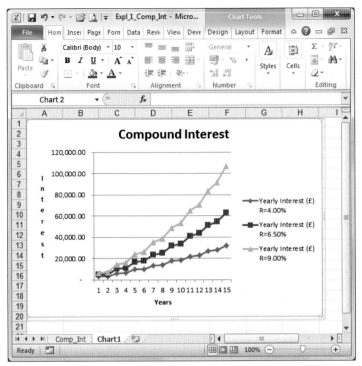

Fig. 11.2 A Graph of the Compound Interest Example

Product Sales Calculations

In this example, the first column shown below holds the part numbers which identify a product, while the second and third columns hold the cost price and % profit required from the sale of each product. The fourth column holds information on the number of items sold, as follows:

Part No.	Cost Price (£)	% Profit	No. Sold
127	5.6	110	2500
130	6.5	130	1300
133	7	115	2800
136	6.25	125	1900
139	7.25	118	2300
142	7.5	135	2550
145	6.75	120	1800
148	6	133	3200
151	6.55	128	2750
154	7.55	122	1750
157	5.95	119	1950
160	6.16	124	2850

Assuming that the VAT rate is 17.5%, but can be changed subsequently to some other value, like 20%, use Excel to calculate the following, assuming the relationships given below:

Sale price for each part,
VAT charged/unit,
Total income,
Sales cost,
Profit made.

Use the layout shown on the next page for the input data, and the calculated results. You will need to enter the following relationships in columns I to M, respectively:

Column I:
Sale Price_unit=Cost price_unit*(l+% profit_unit/100)*(l+VAT%/100)
(have a look at the Formula bar to see an example of the formula)

Column J:
VAT_Unit=Cost price_unit*(l+% profit_unit/100)*(VAT%/100)

Column K:
Total income=Sale Price_unit * No. sold

Column L:
Total sales cost=(Cost price_unit+VAT charged_unit)*No. sold

Column M:
Profit made=(Sale price_unit*No. sold)–Sales cost.

Format your worksheet as shown below (or better), and make provision for displaying the 'Total Profit Made' and 'Total VAT Charged' to also be displayed in cells C8 and C9 respectively.

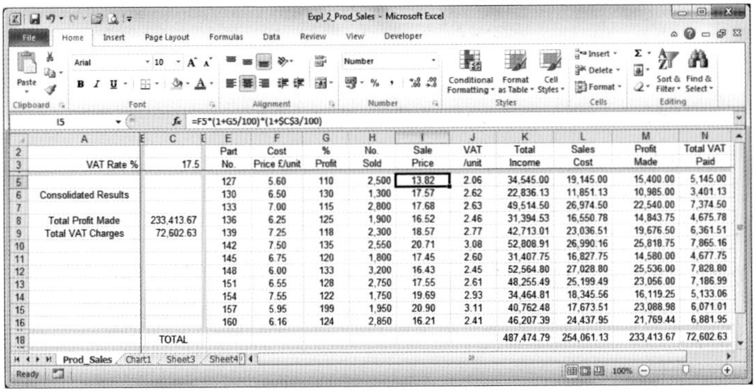

	A	C	E	F	G	H	I	J	K	L	M	N
2			Part	Cost	%	No.	Sale	VAT	Total	Sales	Profit	Total VAT
3	VAT Rate %	17.5	No.	Price £/unit	Profit	Sold	Price	/unit	Income	Cost	Made	Paid
5			127	5.60	110	2,500	13.82	2.06	34,545.00	19,145.00	15,400.00	5,145.00
6	Consolidated Results		130	6.50	130	1,300	17.57	2.62	22,836.13	11,851.13	10,985.00	3,401.13
7			133	7.00	115	2,800	17.68	2.63	49,514.50	26,974.50	22,540.00	7,374.50
8	Total Profit Made	233,413.67	136	6.25	125	1,900	16.52	2.46	31,394.53	16,550.78	14,843.75	4,675.78
9	Total VAT Charges	72,602.63	139	7.25	118	2,300	18.57	2.77	42,713.01	23,036.51	19,676.50	6,361.51
10			142	7.50	135	2,550	20.71	3.08	52,808.91	26,990.16	25,818.75	7,865.16
11			145	6.75	120	1,800	17.45	2.60	31,407.75	16,827.75	14,580.00	4,677.75
12			148	6.00	133	3,200	16.43	2.45	52,564.80	27,028.80	25,536.00	7,828.80
13			151	6.55	128	2,750	17.55	2.61	48,255.49	25,199.49	23,056.00	7,186.99
14			154	7.55	122	1,750	19.69	2.93	34,464.81	18,345.56	16,119.25	5,133.06
15			157	5.95	199	1,950	20.90	3.11	40,762.48	17,673.51	23,088.98	6,071.01
16			160	6.16	124	2,850	16.21	2.41	46,207.39	24,437.95	21,769.44	6,881.95
18		TOTAL							487,474.79	254,061.13	233,413.67	72,602.63

Fig. 11.3 The Layout of the Product Sales Calculations Example

Having done so, define a graph (see Fig. 11.4 on the next page) to plot profit made for each product and the corresponding volume of sales of each product versus the part number of the products. Annotate, title and save your graph on a separate worksheet of the workbook from that used for the calculations. See end of chapter for annotation method.

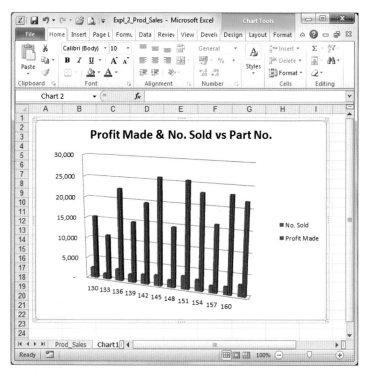

Fig. 11.4 A Graph of the Product Sales Calculations Example

Salary Calculations

A firm employs several people who are identified by a unique works number, as shown in the sample table below. The first column of the table holds the works number which identifies a person, while the second column holds the gross annual salary (£) of that person. The third and fourth columns of the table hold information relating to the overtime worked (hrs) per month, and the corresponding hourly rate (£), respectively.

Employee Works No.	Annual Income	Overtime (hrs/month)	Overtime rate (£/hr)
7001	18850	14	14
7002	48500	10	29
7003	69750	6	40
7004	12900	18	16
7005	24350	6	17
7006	11900	12	12
7007	21000	16	15
7008	34850	8	21
7009	28350	11	19
7010	25480	9	18
7011	16750	15	13
7012	53100	4	32

In addition to the above, the company would also like to hold the following information for each employee;

    Monthly Overtime Income,
    Total Monthly N.I.,
    Monthly Tax on Gross Yearly Income,
    Monthly Tax on Overtime,
    Total Monthly Income,
    Total Monthly Tax.

We propose to use an Excel worksheet to calculate and hold this information. For simplicity we will assume that a person pays 11% of their monthly gross salary (excluding the first £6,750 and overtime) towards National Insurance (N.I.), while what is left after personal allowance and N.I., is taxed at 22%. In addition, all earnings on overtime are taxed at 40%.

Use the layout, labels and formatting suggested in Fig. 11.5 (or better) to carry out these calculations. Devise your own formulae for the required calculations.

Type in your formulae in the worksheet in such a way (by making absolute reference to cells C2 to C4) as to allow you to copy these easily. You should then only need to change the values of tax rates and/or N.I., for the information in the consolidated area of the worksheet (C9 to C11) to be calculated automatically.

Use the following input values:

Tax Rate X = 22%,
Tax Rate Y = 40%,
National Insurance = 11%,
Personal Allowance = £6,750.

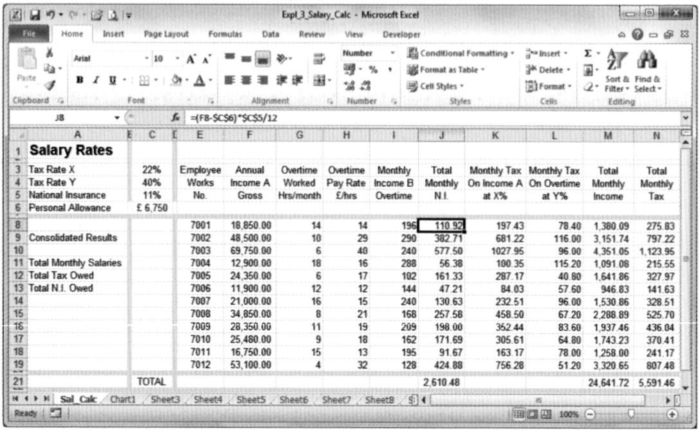

	A	C	E	F	G	H	I	J	K	L	M	N
1	Salary Rates											
3	Tax Rate X	22%	Employee	Annual	Overtime	Overtime	Monthly	Total	Monthly Tax	Monthly Tax	Total	Total
4	Tax Rate Y	40%	Works	Income A	Worked	Pay Rate	Income B	Monthly	On Income A	On Overtime	Monthly	Monthly
5	National Insurance	11%	No.	Gross	Hrs/month	£/hrs	Overtime	N.I.	at X%	at Y%	Income	Tax
6	Personal Allowance	£ 6,750										
8			7001	18,850.00	14	14	196	110.92	197.43	78.40	1,380.09	275.83
9	Consolidated Results		7002	48,500.00	10	29	290	382.71	681.22	116.00	3,151.74	797.22
10			7003	69,750.00	6	40	240	577.50	1027.95	96.00	4,351.05	1,123.95
11	Total Monthly Salaries		7004	12,900.00	18	16	288	56.38	100.35	115.20	1,091.08	215.55
12	Total Tax Owed		7005	24,350.00	6	17	102	161.33	287.17	40.80	1,641.86	327.97
13	Total N.I. Owed		7006	11,900.00	12	12	144	47.21	84.03	57.60	946.83	141.63
14			7007	21,000.00	16	15	240	130.63	232.51	96.00	1,530.86	328.51
15			7008	34,850.00	8	21	168	257.58	458.50	67.20	2,288.89	525.70
16			7009	28,350.00	11	19	209	198.00	352.44	83.60	1,937.46	436.04
17			7010	25,480.00	9	18	162	171.69	305.61	64.80	1,743.23	370.41
18			7011	16,750.00	15	13	195	91.67	163.17	78.00	1,258.00	241.17
19			7012	53,100.00	4	32	128	424.88	756.28	51.20	3,320.65	807.48
21		TOTAL						2,610.48			24,641.72	5,591.46

Fig. 11.5 The Layout of the Salary Calculations Example

Having achieved the Salary Calculation, define a stacked bar chart (see Fig. 11.6 below), to plot the Total Monthly Income, Total Monthly Tax, and Total Monthly N.I., versus Employee Works No. Annotate, title and save your chart within the workbook but on a different worksheet.

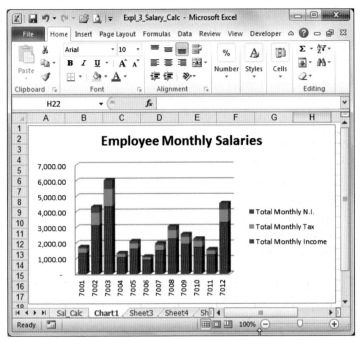

Fig. 11.6 A Graph of the Salary Calculations Example

Procedure for Annotating a Chart

To annotate a chart, select it, then click the **Design**, **Data**, **Select Data** button to display the Select Data Source dialogue box, then click the **Edit** button and select the range for the horizontal axis labels.

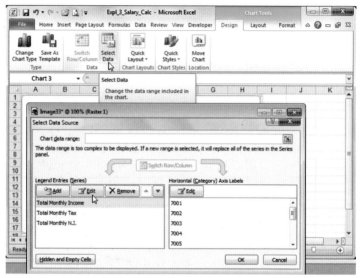

Fig. 11.7 The Select Data Source Dialogue box

Next, repeat this procedure to define the Legend labels. Having selected a data range, by clicking on it on the graph, you could use the **Home**, **Font**, **Font Color** button to add a bit of colour to your chart, as shown in the charts of our examples.

12

Excel 2010 Functions

Excel's functions are built-in formulae that perform specialised calculations. Their general format is:

name(arg1,arg2,...)

where 'name' is the function name, and 'arg1', 'arg2', etc., are the arguments required for the evaluation of the function. Arguments must appear in a parenthesised list as shown above and their exact number depends on the function being used. However, some functions do not require arguments and are used without parentheses. Examples of these are: FALSE, NA, NOW, PI, RAND, TODAY and TRUE.

There are four types of arguments used with functions: numeric values, range values, string values and conditions, the type used being dependent on the type of function. Numeric value arguments can be entered either directly as numbers, as a cell address, a cell range name or as a formula. Range value arguments can be entered either as a range address or a range name, while string value arguments can be entered as an actual value (a string in double quotes), as a cell address, a cell name, or a formula. Condition arguments normally use logical operators or refer to an address containing a logic formula.

Types of Functions

There are several types of functions in Excel 2010, namely, financial, date and time, mathematical and trigonometric, statistical, lookup and reference, database, text, logical, and information. Each type of function requires its own number and type of arguments.

Function arguments, also known as parameters, are listed on the next few pages under the various function categories. To find out in detail how these functions can be used, either click the **Formulas**, **Function Library**, **Insert Function** button, shown here, or the (f_x) button in front of the Formula bar, to display:

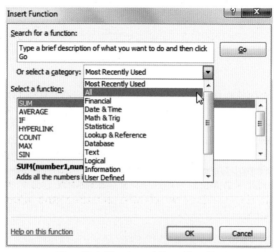

Fig. 12.1 The Insert Function Box

You can either type a brief description of what you want to do in the search box or you can click the down arrow to the right of the **Or select a category** box to reveal all the available functions in Excel. Selecting a function from the drop-down list and clicking the **Help on this function** link at the bottom-left of the box, provides detailed help on the chosen function.

In Fig. 12.2 on the next page, the various function categories appear as books when you maximise the Excel window. These function books when clicked display a drop-down menu of the actual functions in each category. The only function category that does not appear anywhere on this screen is the Database. We are sure this is an oversight carried forward from the previous version of Excel!

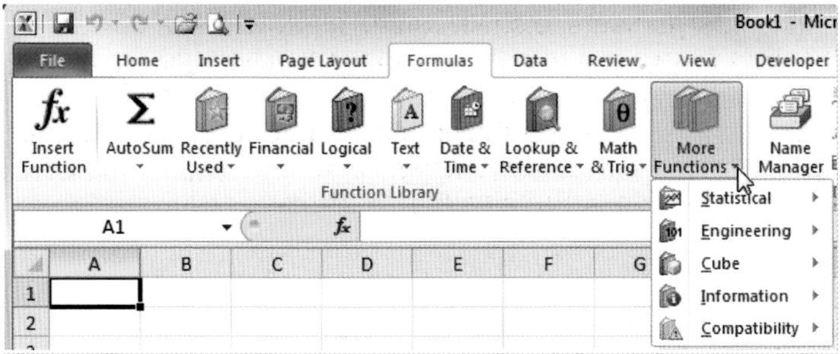

Fig. 12.2 The Function Library

In what follows, we list all the functions and what they return in a concise alphabetical order of category for ease of selection, and so that you can see at a glance what is available. Some statistical functions have been renamed, but there is a backward compatibility when using the old name. If you don't need backward compatibility, you should use the new function names. There are also some new functions added in Excel 2010, which are included and identified in what follows.

Cube Functions

Function	*Returns*
CUBEKPIMEMBER	A key performance indicator (KPI) property and displays the KPI name in the cell. A KPI is a quantifiable measurement, such as monthly gross profit or quarterly employee turnover, that is used to monitor an organisation's performance.
CUBEMEMBER	A member or tuple from the cube. Use to validate that the member or tuple exists in the cube.

CUBEMEMBERPROPERTY	The value of a member property from the cube. Use to validate that a member name exists within the cube and to return the specified property for this member.
CUBERANKEDMEMBER	The nth or ranked member in a set. Use to return one or more elements in a set, such as the top sales performer or the top 10 students.
CUBESET	A calculated set of members or tuples by sending a set expression to the cube on the server, which creates the set, and then returns that set to Excel.
CUBESETCOUNT	The number of items in a set.
CUBEVALUE	An aggregated value from the cube.

Database Functions

Database functions perform calculations on a database. The database, called the input range, consists of records, which include fields and field names, like Fd below. A criterion range must be set up to select the records from the database that each function uses.

Function	*Returns*
DAVERAGE(Db,Fd,Cr)	The average of the values in the field Fd that meet the criteria Cr in a database Db.
DCOUNT(Db,Fd,Cr)	The number of non-blank cells in the field Fd that meet the criteria Cr in a database Db.

DCOUNTA(Db,Fd,Cr)	Counts non-blank cells from a specified database and criteria.
DGET(Db,Fd,Cr)	The single value in the field Fd that meets the criteria Cr in a database Db.
DMAX(Db,Fd,Cr)	The maximum value in the field Fd that meets the criteria Cr in a database Db.
DMIN(Db,Fd,Cr)	The minimum value in the field Fd that meets the criteria Cr in a database Db.
DPRODUCT(Db,Fd,Cr)	The result of the product of the values in the field Fd that meet the criteria Cr in a database Db.
DSTDEV(Db,Fd,Cr)	The standard deviation based on the values in the field Fd that meet the criteria Cr in a database Db.
DSTDEVP(Db,Fd,Cr)	The standard deviation based on the entire population of the values in the field Fd that meet the criteria Cr in a database Db.
DSUM(Db,Fd,Cr)	The sum of the values in the field Fd that meet the criteria Cr in a database Db.
DVAR(Db,Fd,Cr)	The estimated variance based on the values in the field Fd that meet the criteria Cr in a database Db.
DVARP(Db,Fd,Cr)	The variance based on the population of the values in the field Fd that meet the criteria Cr in a database Db.

Date and Time Functions

These generate and use serial numbers with dates having integer serial numbers between 1 and 65380 to represent dates between 1 January 1900 and 31 December 9999, and time having decimal serial numbers starting with 0.000 at midnight and ending with 0.99999 next midnight. The various functions are:

Function	*Returns*
DATE(Yr,Mh,Dy)	The date number of argument Yr,Mh,Dy.
DATEVALUE(Ts)	The number of days from 1 January 1900 of date string Ts.
DAY(Dn)	The day of the month number (1-31) of date number Dn.
DAYS360(Sn,En)	The number of days between Sn and En, based on a year of 12 months, each of 30 days.
EDATE(Sd,Ms)	The serial number of the date that is the indicated number of months Ms before or after the start date Sd.
EOMONTH(Sd,Ms)	The serial number of the last day of the month before or after a specified number of months Ms from the start date Sd.
HOUR(Tn)	The hour number (0-23) of time number Tn.
MINUTE(Tn)	The minute number (0-59) of time number Tn.
MONTH(Dn)	The month number (1-12) of date number Dn.

NETWORKDAYS(Sd,Ed)   The number of whole workdays between a start date Sd and an end date Ed.

NETWORKDAYS.INTL(Sd,Ed,W)

The number of whole workdays between a start date Sd and an end date Ed, with W weekend days.

NOW()   The serial number for the current date and time.

SECOND(Tn)   The second number (0-59) of time number Tn.

TIME(Hr,Ms,Ss)   The time number of argument Hr,Ms,Ss.

TIMEVALUE(Ts)   The time number of string Ts.

TODAY()   The current date number.

WEEKDAY(Dn)   The day of the week from date number Dn in integer form; 0 (Monday) through 6 (Sunday).

WEEKNUM(Sn)   The number that indicates where the week falls numerically within a year of a specified date Sn.

WORKDAY(Sd,Ds)   The number that represents a date that is the indicated number of working days Ds before or after a starting date Sd.

WORKDAY.INTL(Sd,Ds,W)   The serial number of the date that is the indicated number of working days Ds before or after a starting date Sd, with W weekend days.

YEAR(Dn)	Returns the year number (0-199) of date number Dn.
YEARFRAC(Sd,Ed)	The year fraction representing the number of whole days between start date Sd and end date Ed.

Engineering Functions

Engineering functions mainly convert a number from one measurement system to another.

Function	*Returns*
BESSELI(X,N)	The modified Bessel function In(x) of order N evaluated at point X.
BESSELJ(X,N)	The Bessel function Jn(x) of order N evaluated at point X.
BESSELK(X,N)	The modified Bessel function Kn(x) of order N evaluated at point X.
BESSELY(X,N)	The Bessel function Yn(x) of order N evaluated at point X.
BIN2DEC(Nr)	The decimal number of a binary number Nr.
BIN2HEX(Nr)	The hexadecimal of a binary number Nr.
BIN2OCT(Nr)	The octal of a binary number Nr.
COMPLEX(Rn,In)	A complex number of real Rn and imaginary In coefficients.
CONVERT(Nr,Ut1,Ut2)	The conversion of a number Nr of units Ut1 of one measurement system to units Ut2 of another.

DEC2BIN(Nr)	The binary of a decimal number Nr.
DEX2HEX(Nr)	The hexadecimal of a decimal number Nr.
DEC2OCT(Nr)	The octal of a decimal number Nr.
DELTA(Nt1,Nt2)	Tests whether two values Nt1 and Nt2 are equal.
ERF(Ll,Ul)	The error function integrated between lower limit Ll and upper limit Ul.
ERF.PRECISE(X)	The error function integrated between 0 and X.
ERFC(X)	The complementary error function.
ERFC.PRECISE(X)	The complementary ERF function integrated between X and infinity.
GESTEP(Nr,Sp)	Tests whether a number Nr is greater than a threshold value step value Sp.
HEX2BIN(Nr)	The binary of a hexadecimal number Nr.
HEX2DEC(Nr)	The decimal of a hexadecimal number Nr.
HEX2OCT(Nr)	The octal of a hexadecimal number Nr.
IMABS(Cn)	The absolute value (modulus) of a complex number Cn.
IMAGINARY(Cn)	The imaginary coefficient of a complex number Cn.

IMARGUMENT(Cn)	The argument theta, an angle expressed in radians of a complex number Cn.
IMCONJUGATE(Cn)	The complex conjugate of a complex number Cn.
IMCOS(Cn)	The cosine of a complex number Cn.
IMDIV(Cn1,Cn2)	The quotient of two complex numbers Cn1 and Cn2.
IMEXP(Cn)	The exponential of a complex number Cn.
IMLN(Cn)	The natural logarithm of a complex number Cn.
IMLOG10(Cn)	The base-10 logarithm of a complex number Cn.
IMLOG2(Cn)	The base-2 logarithm of a complex number Cn.
IMPOWER(Cn,Nr)	A complex number Cn raised to an integer power Nr.
IMPRODUCT(Cn1,Cn2)	The product of two complex numbers Cn1 and Cn2.
IMREAL(Cn)	The real coefficient of a complex number Cn.
IMSIN(Cn)	The sine of a complex number.
IMSQRT(Cn)	The square root of a complex number Cn in x+iy text format.
IMSUB(Cn1,Cn2)	The difference between two complex numbers Cn1 and Cn2 in x+iy text format.
IMSUM(Cn1,Cn2,...)	The sum of complex numbers in x+iy text format.

OCT2BIN(Nr)	The binary of an octal number Nr.
OCT2DEC(Nr)	The decimal of an octal number Nr.
OCT2HEX(Nr)	The hexadecimal of an octal number Nr.

External Functions

External functions are loaded with add-in programs.

Function	*Returns*
EUROCONVERT(Nr,Se,Tt)	The number of Euros in currency value Nr of an EU single currency member, the currency value of an EU single currency member of Nr Euros, or the currency value of an EU single currency member from the currency value Nr of another EU single currency member by using the Euro as an intermediary. Se is a three-letter string that represents the source currency code (DEM for Germany, FRF for France, EUR for Euro, etc.), while Tt is a similar three-letter target currency code, or cell reference, to which you want to convert.
SQL.REQUEST(Ed,Qt)	An array of query results or the number of rows affected by the query Qt of an external data source Ed (a string specifying data source name, user ID, and password).

Financial Functions

Financial functions evaluate loans, annuities, depreciation and cash flows over a period of time, using numeric arguments. Where an optional parameter [Tp] is given the function will calculate for either an ordinary annuity or an annuity due, depending on the value you specified for type Tp. Percentages should be entered either as a decimal (for example, 0.155) or with a percent sign (for example, 15.5%).

Function	*Returns*
ACCRINT(Id,Sd,Ed,Rt,Nr)	The accrued interest for a security that pays periodic interest, where Id is the security's issue date, Sd is the starting date, Ed the ending (settlement) date, Rt the annual coupon rate, and Nr the number of coupon payments per year.
ACCRINTM(Id,Md,Rt)	The accrued interest for a security that pays interest at maturity, where Id is the issue date, Md the maturity date, and Rt the annual coupon rate.
AMORDEGRC(Ct,Pd,Fp,Sg,Pd,Rt,Yb)	The depreciation for each accounting period by using a depreciation coefficient, where Ct is the cost of the asset, Pd the purchase date, Fp the date of the end of the first period, Sg the salvage value, Pd the period, Rt the rate of depreciation, and Yb the year basis to be used.

AMORLINC (Ct,Pd,Fp,Sg,Pd,Rt,Yb)

The depreciation for each accounting period, where Ct is the cost of the asset, Pd the purchase date, Fp the date of the end of the first period, Sg the salvage value, Pd the period, Rt the rate of depreciation, and Yb the year basis to be used.

COUPDAYBS(Sd,Md,Nr)

The number of days from the beginning of the coupon period to the settlement date, where Sd is the settlement date, Md the maturity date, and Nr the number of coupon payments per year.

COUPDAYS(Sd,Md,Nr)

The number of days in the coupon period that contains the settlement date Sd, where Md is the maturity date, and Nr the number of coupon payments per year.

COUPDAYSNC(Sd,Md,Nr)

The number of days from the settlement date to the next coupon date, where Sd is the settlement date, Md the maturity date, and Nr the number of coupon payments per year.

COUPNCD(Sd,Md,Nr)

The next coupon date after the settlement date, where Sd is the settlement date, Md the maturity date, and Nr the number of coupon payments per year.

COUPNUM(Sd,Md,Nr)

The number of coupons payable between the settlement date Sd and maturity date Md for Nr coupon payments per year.

COUPPCD(Sd,Md,Nr)

The previous coupon date before the settlement date Sd of maturity date Md and Nr number of coupon payments per year.

CUMIPMT(Rt,Pp,Pv,Sd,Ed,Tp)

The cumulative interest paid on a loan of present value Pv between a starting date Sd and an ending date Ed at interest rate Rt, for a total number of payment periods of Pp. Tp is the timing of the payment (0 at end of period or 1 at beginning).

CUMPRINC(Rt,Pp,Pv,Sd,Ed,Tp)

The cumulative principal paid on a loan of present value Pv between a starting date Sd and an ending date Ed at interest rate Rt, for a total number of payment periods of Pp. Tp is the timing of the payment (0 at end of period or 1 at beginning).

DB(Ct,Sg,Lf,Pd)

The depreciation allowance of an asset with an initial value of Ct, life Lf, a final salvage value Sg for a specified period Pd, using the declining balance method.

DDB(Ct,Sg,Lf,Pd)

The double-declining depreciation allowance of an asset, with original cost Ct, predicted salvage value Sg, life Lf, and period Pd.

DISC(Sd,Md,Pr,Rv)

The discount rate for a security, where Sd is the settlement date, Md the maturity date, Pr the security's price per $100 face value, and Rv the redemption value per $100 face value.

DOLLARDE(Fd,Fn)

The dollar price expressed as a decimal number of a dollar price given as a fraction Fd with an Fn fraction denominator.

DOLLARFR(Dd,Fn)

The dollar price expressed as a fraction to a dollar price given as a decimal number with an Fn fraction denominator.

DURATION(Sd,Md,Cr,Ay,Nr)

The annual duration of a security with periodic interest payments, where Sd is the settlement date, Md the maturity date, Cr the security's annual coupon rate, Ay the annual yield, and Nr the number of coupon payments per year.

EFFECT(Ni,Cy)

The effective annual interest rate given the annual nominal interest rate Ni, and the number of compounding periods per year Cy.

FV(Rt,Tm,Pt)

The future value of a series of equal payments, each of equal amount Pt, earning a periodic interest rate Rt, over a number of payment periods in term Tm.

FVSCHEDULE(Pr,Ir)

The future value of an initial principal Pr after applying a series of compound interest rates Ir.

INTRATE(Sd,Md,Ai,Ar)

The interest rate for a fully invested security, where Sd is the settlement date, Md the maturity date, Ai the amount invested, and Ar the amount to be received at maturity.

IPMT(Rt,Pr,Tm,Pv)

The interest payment for a given period Pr (between 1 and Tm) of a total term Tm of a loan with present value Pv at a constant interest rate Rt.

IRR(Rg,Gs)

The internal rate of return of range Rg of cash flows, based on the approximate percentage guess Gs.

ISPMT(Rt,Pr,Tm,Pv)

The interest paid during a specific period Pr (which must be between 1 and Tm) of a total term Tm of a loan with present value Pv at an interest rate Rt.

MDURATION(Sd,Md,Cr,Ay,Nr)

The Macauley modified duration for a security with an assumed par value of $100, where Sd is the settlement date, Md the maturity date, Cr the security's annual coupon rate, Ay the annual yield, and Nr the number of coupon payments per year.

MIRR(Rg,Fr,Rr)

The modified internal rate of return for a series of cash flows in a range Rg, with interest rates Fr, paid on money used in cash flows and Rr received on reinvested cash flows.

NOMINAL(Er,Np)

The annual nominal interest rate, where Er is the effective interest rate, and Np the number of compounding periods per year.

NPER(Rt,Pt,Pv,Fv)

The number of periods required for a series of equal payments Pt, with a present value Pv, to accumulate a future value Fv, at a periodic interest rate Rt.

NPV(Rt,Rg)

The net present value of the series of future cash flows in range Rg, discounted at a periodic interest rate Rt.

ODDFPRICE(Sd,Md,Id,Fd,Rt,Ay,Rv,Nr)

> The price per $100 face value of a security with an odd first period, where Sd is the settlement date, Md the maturity date, Id the security's issue date, Fd the first coupon date, Rt the interest rate, Ay the annual yield, Rv the redemption value per $100, and Nr the number of coupon payments per year.

ODDFYIELD(Sd,Md,Id,Fd,Rt,Sp,Rv,Nr)

> The yield of a security with an odd first period, where Sd is the settlement date, Md the maturity date, Id the security's issue date, Fd the first coupon date, Rt the interest rate, Sp the security's price, Rv the redemption value per $100 face value, and Nr the number of coupon payments per year.

ODDLPRICE(Sd,Md,Id,Fd,Rt,Ay,Rv,Nr)

> The price per $100 face value of a security with an odd last period, where Sd is the settlement date, Md the maturity date, Id the security's issue date, Fd the first coupon date, Rt the interest rate, Ay the annual yield, Rv the redemption value per $100 of face value, and Nr the number of coupon payments per year.

ODDLYIELD (Sd,Md,Id,Fd,Rt,Sp,Rv,Nr)

The yield of a security with an odd last period, where Sd is the settlement date, Md the maturity date, Id the security's issue date, Fd the first coupon date, Rt the interest rate, Sp the security price, Rv the redemption value per $100 of face value, and Nr the number of coupon payments per year.

PMT(Rt,Tm,Pv,Fv)

The payment on a loan with present value Pv, at interest rate Rt, for Tm number of payments and future value Fv.

PPMT(Rt,Pr,Tm,Pv,Fv)

The principal portion of the periodic payment on a loan of present value Pv, at interest rate Rt, for a number of payment periods Pr, leading to a future value Fv.

PRICE(Sd,Md,Rt,Ay,Rv,Nr)

The price per $100 face value of a security that pays periodic interest, where Sd is the settlement date, Md the maturity date, Rt the interest rate, Ay the security's annual yield, Rv the redemption value per $100 face value, and Nr the number of coupon payments per year.

PRICEDISC(Sd,Md,Dr,Rv)   The price per $100 face value of a discounted security, where Sd is the security's settlement date, Md the maturity date, Dr the discount rate, and Rv the redemption value.

PRICEMAT(Sd,Md,Id,Rt,Ay)   The price per $100 face value of a security that pays interest at maturity, where Sd is the security's settlement date, Md the maturity date, Id the issue date, Rt the interest rate, and Ay the security's annual yield.

PV(Rt,Tm,Pt)   The present value of a series of payments, each of amount Pt, discounted at a periodic interest rate Rt, over a number of payment periods in term Tm.

RATE(Tm,Pt,Pv,Fv)   The periodic interest rate necessary for a present value Pv to grow to a future value Fv, over the number of compounding periods in term Tm at Pt payments per period.

RECEIVED(Sd,Md,Ai,Dr)   The amount received at maturity for a fully invested security, where Sd is the Settlement date, Md the maturity date, Ai the amount invested, and Dr the security's discount rate.

SLN(Ct,Sg,Lf)	The straight line depreciation of an asset of cost Ct for one period, given its predicted salvage value Sg, and life Lf.
SYD(Ct,Sg,Lf,Pd)	The sum-of-years' digits depreciation of an asset of cost Ct, given its predicted salvage value Sg, life Lf, and period Pd.
TBILLEQ(Sd,Md,Dr)	The bond-equivalent yield for a Treasury bill, where Sd is the settlement date, Md the maturity date, and Dr the Treasury bill's discount rate.
TBILLPRICE(Sd,Md,Dr)	The price per $100 face value for a Treasury bill, where Sd is the settlement date, Md the maturity date, and Dr the Treasury bill's discount rate.
TBILLYIELD(Sd,Md,Pr)	The yield for a Treasury bill, where Sd is the settlement date, Md the maturity date, and Pr the Treasury bill's price per $100 face value.
VDB(Ct,Sg,Lf,S,E,*d*,*s*)	The depreciation of an asset of cost Ct, salvage value Sg, life Lf, over a period from start S to end E. Depreciation-factor *d* and switch *s*, are optional. If *s* is 1 it returns declining balance depreciation for life, else straight line is used after E.

XIRR(Cf,Pd)

The internal rate of return for a schedule of cash flows Cf that is not necessarily periodic, where Pd is a schedule of payment dates corresponding to the cash flow payments.

XNPV(Dr,Cf,Pd)

The net present value for a schedule of cash flows Cf that is not necessarily periodic, where Dr is the discount rate, and Pd the payment dates.

YIELD(Sd,Md,Rt,Pr,Rv,Nr)

The yield on a security that pays periodic interest, where Sd is the settlement date, Md the maturity date, Rt the interest rate, Pr the security's price per $100 face value, Rv the redemption value per $100 face value, and Nr the number of payments per year.

YIELDDISC(Sd,Md,Pr,Rv)

The annual yield for a discounted security; for example, a Treasury bill, where Sd is the settlement date, Md the maturity date, Pr the security's price per $100 face value, and Rv the redemption value per $100 face value.

YIELDMAT(Sd,Md,Id,Rt,Pr)

The annual yield of a security that pays interest at maturity date Md, where Sd is the settlement date, Id the issue date, Rt the interest rate, and Pr the security's price per $100 face value.

Information Functions

Information functions perform a variety of advanced tasks, such as looking up values in a table, returning information about cells, ranges or the Excel environment.

Function	*Returns*
CELL(At,Rg)	The code representing the attribute At of range Rg.
ERROR.TYPE(X)	The error value.
INFO(At)	System information based on the attribute At.
ISBLANK(X)	The value 1 (TRUE), if X is an empty cell.
ISERR(X)	1 (TRUE), if X is an error value except #N/A.
ISERROR(X)	1 (TRUE), if X is any error.
ISEVEN(X)	1 (TRUE), if the number is even.
ISLOGICAL(X)	1 (TRUE), if X is a logical value.
ISNA(X)	1 (TRUE), if X contains #N/A.
ISNONTEXT(X)	1 (TRUE), if X is not text.
ISNUMBER(X)	1 (TRUE), if X contains a numeric value.
ISODD(X)	1 (TRUE), if the number is odd.
ISREF(X)	1 (TRUE), if X is a reference.
ISTEXT(X)	1 (TRUE), if X is text.
N(X)	A value converted to a number.

NA()   The error value #N/A.

TYPE(X)   A number indicating the data
                            type value of X.

Logical Functions

Logical functions produce a value based on the result of a
conditional statement, using numeric arguments. The various
functions and what they return are as follows:

Function	*Returns*
AND(N1,N2,N3,..)	The logical value 1 (TRUE) if all its arguments are TRUE.
FALSE()	The logical value 0.
IF(Cr,X,Y)	The value X if Cr is TRUE and Y if Cr is FALSE.
IFERROR(Expres,Num)	The value Num if the Expres is in error.
NOT(N)	The reverse logic of its argument N.
OR(N1, N2, ..)	The logical value 1 (TRUE) if any argument is TRUE.
TRUE()	The logical value 1.

Lookup and Reference Functions

This group of functions return values specified by a range
reference or array reference.

Function	*Returns*
ADDRESS(Rn,Cn)	The cell address specified by row Rn and column Cn.
AREAS(Rf1,Rf2,..)	The number of areas in the list of references.

CHOOSE(K,V0,..,Vn)

The Kth value in the list V0,..,Vn.

COLUMN(Rf)

The column number of a reference.

COLUMNS(Rg)

The number of columns in the range Rg.

GETPIVOTDATA(Df,Pt,Fd1,Im,Fd2,Im2,...)

The data stored in a Pivot Table report. Df is the name (enclosed in quotation marks) for the data field that contains the data you want to retrieve, Pt is a reference to any cell, range of cells, or named range of cells in a Pivot Table report, while Fd1, Im1, Fd2, Im2 are 1 to 126 pairs of field names and item names that describe the data you want to retrieve.

HLOOKUP(X,Ar,Rn)

The value of indicated cell by performing a horizontal array lookup by comparing the value X to each cell in the top index row in array Ar, then moves down the column in which a match is found by the specified row number Rn.

HYPERLINK(Loc,Fn)

A shortcut that opens a document stored on your hard disc, network server, or on the Internet.

INDEX(Rg,Rn,Cn)

The value of the cell in range Rg at the intersection of row-offset Rn, and column-offset Cn.

INDIRECT(Rf)	The cell reference specified in reference Rf in A1-style.
LOOKUP(Lv,Vr,Rv)	The relative position of an item in an array that matches a specified value in a specified order.
MATCH(Lv,Ar,Mtc)	The relative position of an element in an array Ar that matches the specified value Mtc of a lookup value Lv.
OFFSET(Rf,Rn,C,Ht,Wh)	A reference of a specified height Ht and width Wh offset from another reference Rf by a specified number of rows Rn and columns Cn.
ROW(Rf)	The row number of a reference.
ROWS(Rg)	The number of rows in a range.
RTD(Pid,Sr,Tc)	Real-time data from a program that supports a registered COM automation add-in program of Pid, server name Sr (where it is to be found), and the data topic Tc to be retrieved.
TRANSPOSE(Ar)	The transpose of an array.
VLOOKUP(X,Ar,Cn)	The value of indicated cell by performing a vertical table lookup by comparing the value X to each cell in the first index column, in array Ar, then moves across the row in which a match is found by the specified column number Cn.

Math and Trigonometry Functions

These functions evaluate a result using numeric arguments. The various functions and what they return are as follows:

Function	*Returns*
ABS(X)	The absolute value of X.
ACOS(X)	The angle in radians, whose cosine is X (arc cos of X).
ACOSH(N)	The arc (inverse) hyperbolic cosine of number N.
AGGREGATE(N,Op,Ref1..)	Where N is a number form 1-19 specifying which function to use; 1 for AVERAGE, 2 for COUNT, etc., Op is a number from 1-7; 1 for ignoring hidden rows, 2 for ignoring error values, etc., Ref1 is the first numeric argument for functions that take multiple numeric arguments for which you want the aggregate value.
ASIN(X)	The angle in radians, whose sine is X (arc sin of X).
ASINH(N)	The arc (inverse) hyperbolic sine of number N.
ATAN(X)	The angle in radians, between $\pi/2$ and $-\pi/2$, whose tangent is X (arc tan of X - 2 quadrant).
ATAN2(X,Y)	The angle in radians, between π and $-\pi$, whose tangent is Y/X (arc tan of Y/X - 4 quadrant).

ATANH(N)	The arc (inverse) hyperbolic tangent of number N.
CEILING(N,Sig)	The rounded value of N to nearest integer or nearest multiple of significance Sig.
CEILING.PRECISE(N,Sig)	The rounded up value of N to nearest integer or nearest multiple of significance Sig. If N or Sig is zero, it returns zero.
COMBIN(N,Obj)	The number of combinations N for a given number of objects Obj.
COS(X)	The cosine of X (X in radians).
COSH(X)	The hyperbolic cosine of X.
COUNTIF(Rg,Cr)	The number of non-blank cells within a range Rg.
DEGREES(X)	The value in degrees of X radians.
EVEN(X)	The rounded value of X away from 0 to the nearest even integer.
EXP(X)	The value of e raised to the power of X.
FACT(X)	The factorial of X.
FACTDOUBLE(X)	The double factorial of X.
FLOOR(N, Sig)	A number N rounded down towards zero by nearest multiple of significance Sig.

FLOOR.PRECISE(N,Sig)	A number N rounded down to the nearest integer or nearest multiple of significance Sig, but if Sig is zero, it returns zero.
GCD(N1,N2,..)	The greatest common divisor of two or more integers.
INT(X)	The integer part of X.
ISO.CEILING(N,Sig)	The rounded up value of N to nearest integer or nearest multiple of significance Sig. If N or Sig is zero, it returns zero.
LCM(N1,N2,...)	The least common multiple of two or more integers.
LN(X)	The natural log (base e) of X.
LOG(X,N)	The log of X to a specified base N.
LOG10(X)	The log (base 10) of X.
MDETERM(Ar)	The matrix determinant of an array.
MINVERSE(Ar)	The matrix inverse of an array.
MMULT(Ar1,Ar2)	The matrix product of two arrays.
MOD(X,Y)	The remainder of X/Y.
MROUND(N,M)	A number N rounded to the desired multiple M.
MULTINOMINAL(N1,N2,...)	The ratio of the factorial of a sum of values to the product of the factorials.

ODD(X)	The rounded value of X away from 0 to the nearest odd integer.
PI()	The value of π (3.1415926).
POWER(X,N)	The value of X raised to the power of N.
PRODUCT(Ls)	The result of multiplying the values in list Ls.
QUOTIENT(Nm,Dm)	The integer portion of a division, where Nm is the numerator, and Dm the denominator.
RADIANS(X)	The value in rads of X degrees.
RAND()	A random number between 0-1.
RANDBETWEEN(Bm,Tp)	A random number between the numbers bottom (Bm) and top (Tp) you specify.
ROMAN(N,Fm)	The Roman format Fm (as text) of number N.
ROUND(X,N)	The value of X rounded to N places.
ROUNDDOWN(X,N)	The rounded value of X down to the nearest multiple of the power of 10 specified by N.
ROUNDUP(X,N)	The rounded value of X up to the nearest multiple of the power of 10 specified by N.

SERIESSUM(X,N,M,Cs)	The sum of a power series based on a formula, where X is the input value of the power series, N the initial power to raise X, M the step increment of N for each term of the series, and Cs the set of coefficients by which each successive power of X is multiplied.
SIGN(X)	The value of 1 if X is a positive, 0 if X is 0, and −1 if X is negative.
SIN(X)	The sine of angle X (X in rads).
SINH(X)	The hyperbolic sine of angle X (X in rads).
SQRT(X)	The square root of X.
SQRTPI	Returns the square root of (number * pi).
SUBTOTAL(Ls)	The subtotal in a list Ls or a database.
SUM(Rg)	The sum of values in range Rg.
SUMIF(Rg,Cr)	The sum in range Rg that meet a given criteria Cr.
SUMPRODUCT(Ar1,Ar2)	The sum of the products of array components.
SUMSQ(N1,N2)	The sum of the squares of the arguments.
SUMX2MY2(Ar1,Ar2)	The sum of the difference of squares of corresponding values in two arrays.

SUMX2PY2(Ar1,Ar2)	The sum of the sum of squares of corresponding values in two arrays.
SUMXMY2(Ar1,Ar2)	The sum of squares of differences of corresponding values in two arrays.
TAN(X)	The tangent of angle X (X in rads).
TANH(X)	The hyperbolic tangent of angle X (X in rads).
TRUNC(X,N)	The truncated value of X to N decimal places.

Statistical Functions

Statistical functions evaluate lists of values using numeric arguments or cell ranges. Old name is backward compatible. The various functions and what they return are as follows:

Function	*Returns*
AVEDEV(Ls)	The average of the absolute deviations of values in list Ls.
AVERAGE(Rg)	The average of values in range Rg - text entries are ignored.
AVERAGEA(Rg)	The average (arithmetic mean) of values in range Rg, including logical values and text - logical TRUE evaluates as 1, while FALSE evaluates as 0.
AVERAGEIF(Rg,Cr)	The average (arithmetic mean) of all the cells in a range Rg that meet the criteria Cr.

AVERAGEIFS(Rg,Cr1,Cr2)	The average (arithmetic mean) of all the cells in a range Rg that meet multiple criteria Cr1, Cr2, etc.
BETA.DIST(X,Al,Bt,A,B) old name BETADIST	The cumulative beta probability density function.
BETA.INV(Pb,Al,Bt,A,B) old name BETA.INV	The inverse of the cumulative beta probability function.
BINOM.DIST(Sc,Tr,Pb,Tp) old name BINOMDIST	The cumulative distribution function if Tp is TRUE, else the probability mass function, with Tr independent trials and Sc successes in trials and Pr probability of success per trial.
CHISQ.DIST.RT(X,Fr) old name CHIDIST	The chi-square distribution, evaluated at X and Fr degrees of freedom for the sample.
CHISQ.INV.RT(X,Fr) old name CHINV	The inverse of the one-tailed probability of the chi-squared distribution.
CHISQ.DIST (X,Fr,Cu)	The chi-square distribution, evaluated at X and Fr degrees of freedom with Cu determining the form of the function. If Cu is True it returns the Cumulative distribution; if False it returns the probability density.
CHISQ.INV(Pr,Fr)	The chi-square distribution with probability Pr, evaluated at Fr degrees of freedom.

CHISQ.TEST(Rg1,Rg2)
old name CHITEST

The chi-square test for independence on the data in range Rg1, or a chi-square test for goodness of fit on the data in ranges Rg1 and Rg2.

CONFIDENCE.NORM(Al,Sd,Sz)
old name CONFIDENCE

The confidence interval for a population mean.

CONFIDENCE.T(Al,Sd,Sz)

The confidence interval for a population mean, using a Student's t distribution.

COUNTBLANK(Rg)

The number of cells that are blank in a range Rg.

COUNTIF(Rg,Cr)

The number of cells within a range Rg that meet the criteria Cr.

COUNTIFS(Rg,Cr1,Cr2)

The number of cells within a range Rg that meet multiple criteria Cr1, Cr2, etc.

CORREL(Rg1,Rg2)

The correlation coefficient of values in ranges Rg1 and Rg2.

COUNT(Ls)

The number of values in a list.

COUNTA(Rg)

The number of non-blank values in a range Rg.

COVARIANCE.P(Rg1,Rg2)
old name COVAR

The sample covariance of the values in ranges Rg1 and Rg2.

COVARIANCE.S(Rg1,Rg2)	The sample covariance, the average of the products of deviations for each data point pair in two data sets Rg1 and Rg2.
CRITBINOM(Tr,Pb,Al)	The largest integer for which the cumulative binomial distribution is less than or equal to Al, with Tr Bernoulli trials and a probability of success for a single Bernoulli trial Pb.
DEVSQ(Ls)	The sum of squared devia-tions of the values in list Ls, from their mean.
EXPON.DIST(X,Lm,Ds) old name EXPONDIST	The exponential distribution.
F.Dist(X,Fr1,Fr2,Cu)	The F-distribution at value X with Fr1 and Fr2 degrees of freedom for the 1st and 2nd samples. Cu is a logical value. If TRUE it returns the cumulative distribution function; if FALSE the probability density function.
F.DIST.RT(X,Fr1,Fr2) old name FDIST	The F distribution at value X with Fr1 and Fr2 degrees of freedom for the first and second samples.
F.INV(Pb,Fr1,Fr2)	The inverse of the F probability distribution. The F distribution can be used in an F test that compares the degree of variability in two data sets.

F.INV.RT(Pb,Fr1,Fr2)
old name FINV

The inverse of the F probability distribution.

FISHER(X)

The Fisher transformation.

FISHERINV(Y)

The inverse of the Fisher transformation.

FORECAST(X,Yo,Xo)

The value along a linear trend.

FREQUENCY(Rg,Bin)

The frequency distribution as a vertical array Bin.

F.TEST(Rg1,Rg2)
old name FTEST

The associated probability of an F test on data in ranges Rg1 and Rg2. Used to determine if two samples have different variances.

GAMMA.DIST(X,Al,Bt,Cm)
old name GAMMADIST

The gamma distribution.

GAMMA.INV(Pb,Al,Bt)
old name GAMMAINV

The inverse of the gamma cumulative distribution.

GAMMALN(X)

The natural logarithm of the gamma function.

GAMMALN.PRECISE(X)

The natural logarithm of the gamma function. If x is non-numeric, it returns the #VALUE! error value. If x <= 0, it returns the #NUM! error value.

GEOMEAN(Ls)

Returns the geometric mean of the values in list Ls.

GROWTH(Yo,Xo,Xn,Ct)

The values along an exponential trend.

HARMEAN(Ls)	The harmonic mean of the values in list Ls.
HYPGEOM.DIST(Ns,Ssiz,Pp,Psiz) old name HYPGEOMDIST	The hypergeometric distribution probability of a given number of successes Ns, given the sample size Ssiz, population success Pp and population size Psiz.
INTERCEPT(Yo,Xo)	The intercept of the linear regression line.
KURT(Rg)	The kurtosis of the values in range Rg.
LARGE(Arr,K)	The largest value in a data set.
LINEST(Yo,Xo,Ct,St)	The parameters of a linear trend.
LOGEST(Yo,Xo,Ct,St)	The parameters of an exponential trend.
LOGNORM.INV(Pb,Mn,Sd) old name LOGINV	The inverse of the lognormal distribution with parameters mean Mn and standard deviation Sd.
LOGNORM.DIST(X,Mn,Sd) old name LOGNORMDIST	The cumulative lognormal distribution with parameters mean Mn and standard deviation Sd.
MAX(Rg)	The maximum value in a range.
MAXA(Rg)	The maximum value in a range. Does not ignore logical values or text.
MEDIAN(Ls)	The median value in list Ls.

MIN(Rg)

The minimum value in a range.

MINA(Rg)

The minimum value in a range. Does not ignore logical values or text.

MODE.SNGL(Ls)
old name MODE

The most common value in a data set.

MODE.MULT(N1,N2)

The vertical array of the most frequently occurring, or repetitive values in an array or range of data.

NEGBINOM.DIST(Nf,Ns,Pb)
old name NEGBINOMDIST

The negative binomial distribution that there will be a number of failures Nf before the number of successes Ns, when the constant probability of success is Pb.

NORM.DIST(X,Mn,Sd)
old name NORMDIST

The normal cumulative distribution function for X, with a distribution mean Mn and optional standard deviation Sd.

NORM.INV(Pb,Mn,Sd)
old name NORMINV

The inverse of the normal cumulative distribution.

NORM.S.DIST(X)
old name NORMSDIST

The standard normal cumulative distribution.

NORM.S.INV(Pb)
old name NORMSINV

The inverse of the standard normal cumulative distribution.

PEARSON(Ar1,Ar2)

The Pearson product moment correlation coefficient.

PERCENTILE.INC(Rg,K)
old name PERCENTILE

The Kth sample percentile among the values in range Rg.

PERCENTILE.EXC(Rg,K)

The Kth percentile of values in range Rg equal 0 to 1, exclusive.

PERCENTRANK.INC(Ar,X,Sg)
old name PERCENTRANK

The percentage rank of a value in a data set.

PERCENTRANK.EXC(Ar,X,Sg)

The rank value in a data set as a percentage (0 to 1), exclusive of the data set.

PERMUT(N,Nc)

The number of ordered sequences (permutations) of Nc chosen objects that can be selected from a total of N objects.

POISSON.DIST(X,Mn,Cm)
old name POISSON

The Poisson distribution (depending on cumulative factor Cm) of X observed events and Mn expected number of events.

PROB(Rgx,Pb,Ll,Ul)

The probability that values in Rgx range are within lower limit Ll and upper limit Ul of probability Pb.

QUARTILE.INC(Ar,Qrt)
old name QUARTILE

The quartile of a data set.

QUARTILE.EXC(Ar,Qrt)   The quartile of a data set, based on percentile values from 0 to 1, exclusive.

RANK.EQ(It,Rg,Od)
old name RANK   The relative size or position of a value It in a range Rg, relative to other values in the range, ranked in order Od.

RANK.AVG(N,Rg,Od)   The relative size or position of a number N in a list of numbers Rg. If more than one value has the same rank, the average rank is returned.

RSQ(Yo,Xo)   The square of the Pearson product moment correlation coefficient.

SKEW(Rg)   The skewness of the values in range Rg.

SLOPE(Yo,Xo)   The slope of the linear regression line.

SMALL(Ar,K)   The Kth smallest value in a data set.

STANDARDIZE(X,Mn,Sd)   The normalised value of X from a distribution characterised by mean Mn and standard deviation Sd.

STDEV.S(Rg)
old name STDEV   The population standard deviation of values in range Rg.

STDEVA(Rg)   An estimate of the standard deviation based on a sample, including logical values and text.

STDEV.P(Rg) old name SDEVP	The standard deviation based on the entire population.
STDEVPA(Rg)	The standard deviation based on the entire population, including logical values and text.
STEYX(Yo,Xo)	The standard error of the predicted y-value for each X in the regression.
T.DIST(X,Fr,Cu)	The Student's t-distribution used in the hypothetical testing of small sample data sets.
T.DIST.RT(X,Fr,Tr) old name TDIST	The Student's t-distribution, evaluated at X and Fr degrees of freedom for the sample, with test direction Tr.
T.DIST.2T	The two-tailed Student's t-distribution.
T.INV(Pb,Fr)	The left-tailed inverse of the Student's t-distribution.
T.INV.2T(Pb,Fr) old name TINV	The inverse of the Student's t-distribution.
TREND(Xo,Yo,Xn,Cn)	The values along a linear trend.
TRIMMEAN(Ar,Pb)	The mean of the interior of a data set.
T.TEST(Rg1,Rg2,Tl,Tp) old name TTEST	The probability associated with a Student's t-test.

VAR.S(Rg)
old name VAR   The sample variance of values in range Rg.

VARA(Rg)   An estimate of the variance based on a sample, including logical values and text.

VAR.P(Rg)
old name VARP   The variance of values in range Rg based on entire population.

VARPA(Rg)   The variance of values in range Rg based on entire population, including logical values and text.

WEIBULL.DIST(X,Al,Bt,Cm)
old name WEIBULL   The Weibull distribution.

Z.TEST(Arr,X,Sg)
old name ZTEST   The two-tailed P-value of a z-test.

Text Functions

Text functions operate on strings and produce numeric or string values dependent on the function.

Function	*Returns*
BAHTTEXT(N)	A text in Thai using the ß (baht) number format of the supplied number Nr.
CHAR(X)	The character that corresponds to the code number X.
CLEAN(Sg)	The specified string Sg having removed all non-printable characters from it.

CODE(Sg)

The code number for the first character in string Sg.

CONCATENATE(Sg1,Sg2)

One string made up of several strings.

DOLLAR(N,Dm)

A number in text form, using currency format.

EXACT(Sg1,Sg2)

The value 1 (TRUE) if strings Sg1 and Sg2 are exactly alike, otherwise 0 (FALSE).

FIND(Ss,Sg,Sn)

The position at which the first occurrence of search string Ss begins in string Sg, starting the search from search number Sn.

FIXED(N,Dm,Nc)

A number N formatted as text with a fixed number of decimals Dm. If Nc is 1 (TRUE) it prevents the inclusion of commas.

LEFT(Sg,N)

The first (leftmost) N characters in string Sg.

LEN(Sg)

The number of characters in string Sg.

LOWER(Sg)

A string Sg with all the letters converted to lowercase.

MID(Sg,Sn,N)

The N characters from string Sg beginning with the character at Sn.

PROPER(Sg)

A string with all words in string Sg changed to first letter in uppercase and the rest in lowercase.

REPLACE(O,S,N,Ns)	A string with N characters removed from original string O, starting at character S and then inserts new string Ns in the vacated place.
REPT(Sg,N)	A repeated string Sg, N times. Unlike the repeating character (\), the output is not limited by the column width.
RIGHT(Sg,N)	The last (rightmost) N characters in string Sg.
SEARCH(Sg1,O,S)	String Sg1 in original string O, starting at character S.
SUBSTITUTE(Sg,O,Ns,N)	A new string Ns substituted for old string O in a string Sg. N specifies which occurrence of the old text you want to replace.
T(X)	A value X converted into text.
TEXT(X,Fm)	A number X formatted into text.
TRIM(Sg)	A string Sg with no leading, trailing or consecutive spaces.
UPPER(Sg)	All letters in string Sg converted to uppercase.
VALUE(Sg)	The numeric value of string Sg.

Index